Masters of the
Soviet Cinema

Masters of the Soviet Cinema

Crippled Creative Biographies

Herbert Marshall

Routledge & Kegan Paul
London, Boston, Melbourne and Henley

First published in 1983
by Routledge & Kegan Paul plc
39 Store Street, London WC1E 7DD,
9 Park Street, Boston, Mass. 02108, USA,
464 St Kilda Road, Melbourne,
Victoria 3004, Australia, and
Broadway House, Newtown Road,
Henley-on-Thames, Oxon RG9 1EN
Set in 10/12pt Baskerville by
Input Typesetting Ltd, London
and printed in Great Britain by
St Edmundsbury Press
Bury St Edmunds, Suffolk

Library of Congress Cataloging in Publication Data

Marshall, Herbert, 1906–
Masters of the Soviet cinema.
Includes bibliographical references and index.
1. Moving-picture producers and directors—Soviet
Union—Biography.   2. Moving-pictures plays—History and
criticism.   3. Moving-pictures—Soviet Union.   I. Title.
PN1993.5.R9M338   1983   791.43'023'0922 [B]   83–3347

ISBN 0–7100–9287–3

Contents

Plates

Grateful acknowledgment is made to the National Film Archive Stills Library for permission to reproduce Plates 3, 4, 11–20, 22

Acknowledgments

First I wish to express deep gratitude to my wife, Fredda Brilliant, for her unfailing support in all my efforts, and in the case of this book for her conscientious editing of the original manuscript – no easy task.

I would also like to thank the editorial staff of Routledge & Kegan Paul plc for their painstaking care.

Finally thanks to Southern Illinois University at Carbondale, USA, for its continuing support to my Center for Soviet and Eastern European Studies, despite economic stringencies, which enables me to continue with my research and to write and produce books such as this one.

Herbert Marshall

Introduction

The theme

The initiative for this work came from a publisher, Mr Brian Southam (formerly an editor and director of Messrs Routledge & Kegan Paul Ltd), after having heard a series of broadcasts I had given for the BBC entitled *Herbert Marshall Remembers*. This in turn had been originally proposed by Dr Martin Esslin, then head of Radio 3, who had the broadcasts transcribed, edited and published in the BBC's organ the *Listener*.[1] Later they were translated and broadcast to the world in many languages, including Russian.

It took me some time to find a suitable short title for the book. My working title was *Soviet Personalities I Had Known – and Their Fate*, obviously too long. Then suddenly I found the apt title in a Soviet press interview with a man who knew all these personalities I was writing about, who was one of their circle and a leading film director himself. He is the only one of their generation still alive. His name is Sergei Yutkevich.

In his early days he had been a fellow student and close friend of Eisenstein, but during the Stalin period became his severe critic from the official 'socialist realist' Communist Party point of view. Only for one brief period, in the heady Khrushchev days, did he criticize the excesses and tyranny of Communist Party society, and he told how he and his students in the same State Institute of Cinematography (known by its Russian acronym, GIK, the Gosudartsvennyi Institute Kinematographii) suffered – he was expelled, his students imprisoned and one nearly executed, because of his 'formalist' teachings. The very sin he had been levelling against Eisenstein!

He declared, in a rare burst of honesty (never to be repeated) that everyone must now tell the truth about the many crippled biographies in the Stalin period. I quote:[2]

> We must tell our viewers what happened. Tell it honestly,
> sincerely, truthfully, passionately, without looking back. . . .
> How it was not long ago, when art, and indeed not only art,
> was subjected to the taste of one man [Stalin]. How many
> crippled creative biographies rise up in one's memory.

And that is exactly how I am trying to tell about what happened.
No doubt Yutkevich will be among those criticizing me, for now he
is an official Party spokesman, taking the hard Brezhnev line in the
area of cinematography.

The words he uses in the Russian could be translated either
'crippled creative biographies' or 'crippled artistic biographies' –
and that is what I mean too. None of the artists I am writing
about were crippled physically in limb or in their health through
incarceration in a Gulag prison camp, or by ill treatment, or torture
or privation or starvation. They were technically 'free', well-fed,
even pampered by the State with high salaries, privileges of living
space, cars, special private stores, extra bonuses for Honors
received, their own dachas, luxury rest-homes and sanatoriums and
special medical care. If they were ill, they went to the hospital for
the top echelon of Soviet society, Barvikha, and when they died
they had a great State funeral with eulogies from every side. Such
was external treatment in that so-called socialist society. Nevertheless most of them had heart attacks that coincided with the moments
of the most vicious Party attacks on them and their artistic work
and I know that Pudovkin, Dovzhenko and Eisenstein died of heart
failure. For despite all this apparent pampering they were crippled
mentally and, above all, creatively.

That is the tragedy of these great artists that most people are not
aware of.

Yet at a superficial glance they seemed lucky. For on top of all
the terrors they escaped and the well-paid positions they held, they
were loaded with honours and titles. They had Orders of Lenin or
Stalin, of the Red Star, were People's Artists of the Republic or of
the USSR, and even Members of the Supreme Soviet of the USSR,
with all the extra privileges of Soviet aristocrats. But all to no avail.

For they were crippled by the very fact that eventually their
artistic and creative development was stultified, nullified, vilified,
crucified by Stalin and the Communist Party.

But that is not all. The next crippling factor was the fact that they escaped the terror, but their nearest and dearest friends and fellow artists did not. Even worse – not only were those near and dear to them arrested without warning or trial, imprisoned, even executed, but their nearest relatives, wives and children were often arrested with them. And even if not – those left free had to go through the hell of social ostracism unparalled in any so-called civilized society. They would be dismissed from their jobs, expelled from their schools and universities, dispossessed of their living apartments, shunned by their former comrades and friends and had to be 'condemned' as 'relatives of enemies of the people.' But that is still not all!

Still more crippling was the fact that no one dared lift a hand or say a word to defend or help either those arrested as 'enemies of the people' or their relatives who were still not arrested. For whoever did so would themselves inevitably be arrested – with all the consequences.

Who dared do that? Only the very bravest. Right up to his own arrest Meyerhold tried to help others whose plight was worse than his own. Pasternak refused to sign an approval of the execution of Russia's leading soldiers. There were such heroes – as Solzhenitsyn and Medvedev have testified (in their books *Gulag Archipelago* and *Let History Judge*).

But by and large everyone kept silent, including the men I am writing about. Not only they, but also the very highest in the land. Even Zhemchuzhina Molotova, wife of Molotov, the Minister of Foreign Affairs and closest collaborator of Stalin, was imprisoned. (She was Jewish and when she met the first Israeli ambassador Mrs Golda Meir at an official gathering exclaimed (in Yiddish), 'I too am a Jewish child!' For that she was arrested.) The wife of the Soviet president, Kalinin, was in prison too. But the minister and president both went on co-signing Stalin's decrees of butchery – often with added invectives – each knowing their turn might come next, as Khrushchev revealed in his famous de-Stalinization speech.

Two of Eisenstein's closest friends and collaborators, Isaac Babel and Sergei Tretyakov, were arrested – nothing was said. Two of his leading pupils at the GIK (both women and my fellow students) were arrested, one the wife of a Red Army general and the other the wife of Boris Pilniak, the famous writer – but not a word was said. But Eisenstein's greatest wound was from the arrest and execution of Meyerhold, his second father, and the teacher and inspirer of hundreds of artists, including Eisenstein, Okhlopkov, Yutkevich, Piscator and Brecht. Over this loss Eisenstein wept bitter silent tears, as his memoirs reveal.[3]

One could go on. The list of innocent victims is endless and the silence about them horrendous – but that is still not all!

In 1935, at the First Congress of Soviet Writers, Isaac Babel had bravely declared that an artist had the right to remain silent. But Stalin's reply behind the scenes was that 'silence is treachery.' The Communist Party would not let anyone be silent. No, they had to extol even louder the dictator and the Party responsible for all these horrors. For, as Alexander Tvardovsky, the Soviet poet, wrote – after Stalin's death – 'Who, to his face, didn't glorify him?'!

In his poem, 'Beyond the Beyond', he wrote,[4]

When life from the living
Was cut off by Kremlin walls,
Like a spirit of terror he ruled us –
We knew no other names at all.

In city and village we speculated
How to praise him even more,
For nothing can be omitted or added –
Thus it was in this land of ours . . .

Thus he lived and ruled in this land of ours,
Holding the bit with stubborn hands,
And who, to his face, didn't glorify him,
Didn't laud him? Find such a man!

He wasn't a son of the East for nothing.
To the end those traits he preserved
By that stubborn, that ruthless
Justice and injustice he administered.

But which of us can serve as judges?
Decide who was right, who was guilty then?
For we are talking about human beings –
And aren't all gods created by men?

Did not we, singers of honourable themes,
In all simplicity proclaim aloud
To the world, songs and poems about himself,
Which he personally put into our mouths?

Did not we, in the hall of ritual,
Before even the words were out of his mouth,
Before even he commenced his latest speech,
Did not we already shout from the floor:
'Hurrah! He will be right once more!'?

But such poems are not reprinted any more. The truth must be told, as Yutkevich once proclaimed, but which he now covers up. This book is an element of the truth that is now gradually being concealed in official biographies. Now in their writings about these great artists in the Brezhnev era, all is sweetness and light.

Even Khrushchev's euphemistic expressions are no longer used, such as 'illegally repressed during the period of the cult of the personality'; nothing is now said about 'violations of revolutionary legality,' or 'aberrations from the Leninist norms of justice.' No longer, indeed, is the cover-up, entitled 'the cult of the personality of Stalin,' used at all. That has now switched to another Communist Party, to China and its Stalin, Mao Zedong.

Of course the irony is that these expressions were also falsifications, as if the cult hadn't been created and promulgated by the Communist Party and its Secret Police. There never was any such thing as 'revolutionary legality' or 'Leninist norms of justice.' Lenin clearly stated, 'The revolutionary dictatorship of the proletariat is rule won and maintained by the use of violence . . . *rule that is unrestricted by any laws.*' (My italics. HM.)

However even these poorly disguised falsified cover-ups are no longer used. Let me give an instance of the predicaments this leads to: a second volume of the official *History of the Civil War* now includes references to many of the early Bolshevik revolutionaries murdered by the Party. But nothing is said about how or where they died. Just their birth and death dates. The book passed all the echelons of censorship, including, as it was such an important work, the Central Committee. It received the final imprimatur for printing and publishing. Then suddenly at the very last minute printing was halted.

After such high-ranking censorship how could that have happened? It transpired that someone had noticed in the index of the major participants in the *History of the Civil War*, which included only births and deaths, that the final date (which corresponded to the height of the Party terror under the Secret Police Commissar

Yezhov) kept repeating itself so many times as to speak out too loudly, despite the total censoring out of other allusions to their tragic end.

Born 1898   Died 1938
Born 1889   Died 1938
Born 1875   Died 1938 and so on!

Another example of the crippling effect of Communist Party society can be seen when one reads contemporary Soviet biographies of so many who were imprisoned and murdered, and the author has to deal with the subject as if nothing abnormal had happened. And now once again in Soviet life is appearing, in the phraseology of the period, the cult of the personality – but the name changed to Brezhnev and no doubt will to his successor.

The contents and my credentials

The material in this book is a montage of memorabilia, culled from my own personal recollections, diaries, notes, unpublished autobiography, as well as letters, documents, press cuttings, articles and books in various languages, but mainly from Soviet sources.

The personalities in this case were film directors, whose early fame was mainly in the silent film era and the transitional period to sound film. They all reached their pinnacle of fame in the late 1920s or early 1930s, with the exception of Eisenstein, who came back to stardom, so to speak, in the late 1930s and early 1940s.

Finally, I knew every one of them personally, some more intimately than others. They behaved toward me with great friendliness and helpfulness. I know every one of their films, and their film scripts, whether permitted or banned. I knew the background of their cinema world, for it was mine too for seven years inside the Soviet Union and nearly five years outside, as a wartime employee of the Soviet Government in the Soviet Film Agency attached to the Soviet Embassy in London. During this latter period all Soviet films sent to London first came through my hands and I made English versions of most of the outstanding ones. Apart from this I was involved in the furthering of Soviet film showings in Great Britain, in my own Film Guild of London (1929–30) and the London Film Society and the Workers' Film Association, later member of a committee of the Association of Cinema Technicians, as well as serving as a member of the General Council of the Society for Cultural Relations with Foreign Countries in London, working closely with its Soviet counterpart in Moscow, known as VOKS.

The Soviet film directors I am writing about are acknowledged by the highest authorities to be amongst the greatest in the world. In an international film critics symposium (at the International Fair, Brussels 1957 and later) that chose the ten best films of all time, the films of three of these directors were chosen: Eisenstein's *Battleship Potemkin*; Dovzhenko's *Earth*; and Pudovkin's *Mother*. Out of these ten, *Potemkin* was chosen as the best film of all time. I have compiled a separate book about this film, a definitive history, in fact the biography of a film.[5] Here too I have attempted to tell the truth.

Vertov, for his part, is acknowledged to be the outstanding documentary film-maker and pioneer in the history of cinema. All of these men are now dead. All four died a 'natural' death, a rare phenomenon in their era and society. All of them, at one time or other, were damned and castigated and punished by the CPSU, accused of various Communist sins, such as 'formalism,' 'intellectualism,' 'objectivism,' 'cosmopolitanism,' and being 'under the influence of Western decadence, bourgeois modernism and capitalistic hang-overs.'

Their creative work was crippled by the CPSU in the Stalin period of their lives, as my essays will prove, but after their deaths they are now acclaimed as great 'Communist Party inspired' artists. Their various birthday or deathday commemorations are filled with paeans of praise, with hardly an intimation of the tragedy of their lives. Everything negative is censored out and their films and works once damned as anti-party and anti-socialist realist formalism, even counter-revolutionary, are now included under the great everspreading umbrella of 'socialist realism'!

Here then is an account of what really happened to them as far as I have been able to establish it. One cannot stress too much the difficulty of obtaining even simple information in the Soviet Union. For example, in any other civilized country one could write, say, to the courts or prison authorities about a certain prisoner, his sentence and his whereabouts, and get an answer. In the Soviet Union not only would there be no reply, but it might be considered anti-Soviet provocation or even espionage by the KGB. Similarly, I was told recently by the Lord Chancellor of England, the top lawman in

England, that when on some occasion he has written to his opposite number in the Soviet Union – Mr Rudenko, Prosecutor General of the USSR – about some Soviet or other citizen being prosecuted in the USSR, *he has never had a reply*. This despite the fact that they know each other personally, having both been prosecutors on the same side during the Nazi war crimes trials at Nuremberg.

Long-time experience with the Soviet bureaucratic apparatus clearly indicates that any attempt to get information at all, let alone any true information, is almost impossible if it deals with some 'sensitive' area. And any area can be designated 'sensitive' by them, to suit the given 'general line' of the moment. Now there is a general cover-up for the tragedies and terror of the Stalin era. My task is to uncover and prove the truth.

As my own personal recollections and experiences would be little proof on their own, I have documented every statement I could, mainly from sources within the Soviet Union, but also others from outside. I try to give chapter and verse wherever possible.

Furthermore, as we are dealing mainly with film directors it is necessary for the reader to have some understanding of what films are being dealt with and as, quite often, they have never been seen by present-day readers, I have tried to give a description of the films concerned, however brief, as well as the circumstances of their creation and reception in the USSR and abroad.

In retrospect what a tragic story is that of the artist in a Communist Party society, whether that of Stalin or Mao. Each time the Party finds its Zhdanov or Chiang Ching to terrorize art. But each artist in his own way tries to survive under the terror. Some are luckier than others. Eisenstein and his fellow film-makers less so, because they were film-makers, not poets or painters. A poem can be created and hidden in somebody's head (as with Akhmatova or Mandelstam's wife), a painting can be hidden in a cupboard, for they are one-man productions. But a film requires a vast technical apparatus and many stages of collective work before it comes into being. And in Eisenstein's day there were no small film or small cine cameras that could be smuggled in. So the film artist has to submit to the terror and bless it, while at the same time using whatever leeway he can within the officially allowed limits to express his true self. This is nothing new in the history of the struggle of artists against their masters, whether Shakespeare or Pushkin, Shostakovich or Pasternak.

The artist uses his tools in this struggle – metaphor, imagery, allegory, fable, *double entendre* and what Russians call *inoskazanie*. It is clear that in *Bezhin Meadow*, though the surface story is about collectivization and a peasant boy informing on his family and thereby getting killed, in Eisenstein's treatment it becomes the biblical allegory of Abraham sacrificing Isaac.

And in *Ivan the Terrible* the young patriotic emperor becomes a fratricidal-paranoic murderer – clearly representing Stalin the terrible.

So when Eisenstein is criticized for not having spoken out against the tyrant the question arises, what would I have done?

Open revolt would have meant an end to all film-making, perhaps to his life. And the choice Eisenstein made was to live and to try and go on making his films, and at least putting his theories on paper for the future socialism with a human face.

Pudovkin beautifully portrayed the comman man, the little man, in his films *The End of St Petersburg* and *Mother*. But then with the growth of Stalinization he was forced to give up his beloved theme and against his will had to work on portraying military satraps, imperial colonizers and tsarist tyrants, as positive characters of history.

Dovzhenko was accused of 'pantheism' and 'biologism', the unity of God and man and nature, of life and death, of past, present and future.

Dziga Vertov tried to show the universality of grief, for example, in his *Three Songs of Lenin* and then afterwards was eventually forced to make no more films on any theme, let alone a universal one.

This book is my attempt to show that these great artists, who were striving like all the great artists of the world to understand the universality of human endeavour, for that reason got into trouble, because in the Soviet Union the only universality allowed is that of the Communist Party and what it considers universal. And yet despite that, as Galileo said, '*E pur si muove*' ('Nevertheless it moves'), and the human condition is still striving to understand itself in the universe, despite all the traumas and fetters that are placed on it by political structures such as Communist Parties.

Herbert Marshall
Professor Emeritus

Vsevolod Pudovkin

How I met Vsevolod Pudovkin

Life is an unbroken, linked-up chain of events. But sometimes there is a key link in the chain – which, if grasped, changes the whole nature of the chain, its direction, its strain, its pulling power.

That happened to me three times in my life.

Once when I went to Russia.

The second time when I went to India.

The third time when I went to the United States.

My life, even life-style, and philosophy changed in each of those periods. Here I write about the link to Russia and to the key person who is really the principle cause of this particular book and all the events and people in it – and that is my first personality: Vsevolod Illarionovich Pudovkin.

And in order to explain how I met Pudovkin and changed my life, a few more links in the chain are necessary. One was my interest in cinema, in unusual films, which included, of course, in those days, German, Swedish, and Russian films. I began to go to the London Film Society's private showings of many banned films including Russian ones. Then I started my own avant-garde film society.

The next link in the chain was when I went, with my eventual bosom friend, Lionel Britton, to an international Avant-garde Film and Photo Festival held in Stuttgart, Germany in 1929. There for the first time, I met a Russian film director, Dziga Vertov, and saw his documentary films. That was the beginning of *cinéma vérité* – '*Kino Pravda*'. (This I will deal with in my chapter on Vertov.) That was another link.

I came back excited by what I had seen, overcome by the power of Russian montage. I introduced it into my avant-garde film society, the Film Guild of London, and at the next Annual Amateur

Film Festival our society won all the first eight prizes and I won two of them for my film and photo work!

At the Film Guild of London, our first showing was the film *Red Russia*, a documentary that for the first time gave some inkling of what had happened in that country.

Meanwhile, I had come across the bulletin of VOKS (The Society for Cultural Relations).[1] Through this bulletin, I learned that there was a university of cinema in Moscow, at that time the only one in the world, the GIK.[2] It had been founded by a decree of Lenin in 1919, and was headed by leading Russian film-makers. I immediately decided I wanted to study there, but how? Then the opportunity arose. The London Film Society announced that with the showing of the Russian film *Mother*, its director, Vsevolod Pudovkin, would be coming to give a lecture in London. There for the first time we saw Pudovkin's films *Mother* and *The End of St Petersburg*.

I remember that, at the end, some of the audience cheered the Bolshevik workman in the film who called for 'all power to the Soviets!' But even those who did not agree in the slightest with the film's politics or its message were quivering with emotion at its artistic impact. This impact helped to swing one in favor of the message.[3] It was a wonderful example of the power of art. But at its conclusion, the orchestra played 'God Save the King,' almost as a kind of insurance against what had happened! Later, there were questions in Parliament. There were phrenetic objections to showing such films. It was known that the Special Branch of Scotland Yard had taken a hand in checking on the possible showing of *Potemkin*, which had been banned by the British Board of Film Censors, alongside such classic German films as Pabst's *Joyless Street*.

Nowadays it is impossible to recreate the shattering impact those early Russian revolutionary films had on everybody. Afterwards, we were invited to Stewart's Restaurant in Regent Street where Pudovkin was to talk, 'with discussions to follow.'

Here is an extract from the talk Pudovkin gave:[4]

To find the necessary sequence of pieces and the necessary rhythm of their combination – in that lies the chief task of art of the director. That art we call montage. Only with the help of montage was I able to solve such a difficult task as work with the actors.

The point is, I consider the chief danger for a person, being filmed, is what is called 'character acting'. I want to work only with real material – that is my principle. I consider, that to show a stuck-on beard, grease-painted wrinkles and theatrical acting alongside real water, real trees and grass is impossible, this contradicts the very elementary conception of style.

What then should we do? It is very difficult to work with theatrical actors. . . . I tried to work with people who had never seen theatre or cinema, and with the help of montage I was able to achieve certain results. . . . For example in the film *Storm Over Asia* I needed a group of Mongols to look ecstatically at a valuable fox fur. I invited a Chinese conjurer and filmed the faces looking at his wonders. When I joined this piece together with the fur in the hands of the salesman, I got the effect I wanted. . . . All the time I am working on perfecting this method. Of course, in this way one can only shoot short pieces of separate faces, and the art of the director is to be able to make a whole living figure from these pieces, by means of montage.

Following the talk a discussion took place. Someone I didn't know spoke, followed by Ashley Dukes, Edmond Dulac, Anthony Asquith, Carl Freund, Victor Hilton, and myself; Ivor Montagu was chairman. Ashley Dukes attacked the film as Bolshevik propaganda and this, of course, in a sense was true. He could also draw on the experience of his wife, that wonderful classic ballet dancer, Madame Rambert, who was an immigrant from the Russian Revolution.

With my background of street corner heckling, I didn't hesitate to enter the forum. I defended the film and Pudovkin and attacked Ashley Dukes.

Pudovkin's talk was a revelation to me, as one who was just beginning to produce and study films.

By now we have had a tremendous amount of theorizing on the art of the cinema but it is important to realize that this was the first attempt in the world to produce a basic theory about what was hardly considered art.

After the meeting, I went up to him. He greeted me with great friendliness because of my open defense for him at that meeting.

I told him of my aims; that I was at the moment working with John Grierson, editing films for the Empire Marketing Film Board; that I had made two films that I think he would be interested in:

The Royal Borough of Kensington, about slum conditions in that part of London, and *Hunger Marchers*, about unemployment, depression, and the battle against all that. I asked him if it would be possible to go and study in Moscow. He said that he was a teacher at the Institute of Cinematography, that they had never had any foreigners before from the West, but he would inquire and if it was possible he would see if I could study there.

Months went by. Then came a letter from the Anglo-American Section of VOKS. It was signed by Pera Attasheva, the assistant and later the wife of Eisenstein, who knew English superbly.

That letter changed my life . . . it was, one might say, the missing link!

Pera was Moscow correspondent for the avant-garde journal *Close up* and might have read about me and the Film Guild in that same journal.

The letter said that 'on the recommendation of Professor V. Pudovkin, the State Institute of Cinematography, Leningradskoye Chaussee, Moscow, would accept Herbert Marshall as a student in the Director's Faculty.'

When eventually I did get there I had to pass an oral entrance exam, on the panel of which sat Pudovkin and a graduate, Stepanov, who knew English. They asked me personal and political questions and then I had to undergo a special exam to determine 'if the applicant has any special artistic ability sufficient for professional cinema work' and his degree of artistic development. Pudovkin confirmed that he had seen my two prize-winning films *Hunger Marchers* and *The Royal Borough of Kensington*. Then I had to write a film scenario on the spot, based on a theme I could choose. I submitted a script based on a short story of Maupassant, called 'Two Friends,' which has survived.

Pudovkin and Stepanov read it and explained it to the examining board. My candidature for studentship was now approved in principle, except that I had to take an intensive course in the Russian language and (though I didn't understand it at the time) pass the scrutiny of the Communist Party secretary of the Institute. We met. He was an Old Bolshevik, a former Red Cavalry Commander, and he looked it. He was bullet-headed, and full of scars (later when we became friends he showed me his whole body, smothered with scars of a dozen wounds from the Revolution and the Civil War). One thing in my favor was that he was a friend of Pudovkin.

He looked at me belligerently. He questioned me as if with his gun: 'Name? Profession? Social standing? Descent?' Stepanov was translating. He explained that this meant, was my father a proletarian or a white-collar worker? I answered, 'A worker.' Savitsky again shot a question. 'Your father – what does he actually do?' 'He's a bricklayer – when he can find a job!'

There was an instant change. Savitsky grinned with pleasure, gripped my hand till it was nearly smashed by his great tough fist. '*Khorosho. Pervoi kategorii!*' ('Fine. First category!') Stepanov explained, 'That means you're accepted as a student of the first category, which means better food rations, cheaper transport, accommodation, theaters, and stipend.'

I was soon to learn how important that was in those days.

Pudovkin's faithful protégé: Savitsky

The scarred and belligerent Party secretary, Savitsky, called me in for another meeting – and from then on we became great friends. I did not realize until later what power was and is wielded by a secretary of the Communist Party of the Soviet Union at any level. He is virtually the dictator of any organization under his authority, and he is the chief link in the chain of control by the Communist Party over the whole Soviet Union. He has (I learned much later) only one rival who can outvote him, in the ideological-political sphere particularly, and that is the secret police representative of the GPU,[5] now the KGB, in the same organization.

In every organization there is a *troika* (a trio): the Party secretary, the trade union representative and the GPU representative holding some nominal position; and both of the latter are in any case Party members, and subject to its discipline.

But in the early days of the establishment of Stalinism the Party man was still considered the most powerful, and only later did the GPU take over directly under Stalin – with results only too terrifying, as history has shown. So Savitsky only had to express his wish and it was law. And he was to be my patron – which I realized later helped ease the many problems a foreign student, hardly knowing the language, had to face in that still belligerent society.

And it was due to Pudovkin! Because Savitsky worshipped Pudovkin. It seemed when he was invalided out of the Red Army, loaded with wounds and honors, he had become a film fan. He was offered a Party secretaryship for his services, and insisted on it being in the film industry. Thus, he came to Mezhrabpom Film – which was a section of the International Workers Aid – a Communist organization to aid Communists and fellow travelers throughout the world.

Mezhrabpom was housed in the same building as the GIK, the former notorious Yar Restaurant, famous for its gypsy choir and the alleged orgies of Rasputin. So Pudovkin literally worked next door to where I was studying and we were often to meet in those early days. Here too, I met many of Pudovkin's associates, in particular his scriptwriter Nathan Zarkhi, and his type-actors, Chistyakov and Savitsky.

Zarkhi later gave lectures on 'Film scriptwriting' at the GIK which I was to attend. Chistyakov and Savitsky were great favorites of Pudovkin. A. Chistyakov was a former bookkeeper whom Pudovkin had chosen for 'typage,' i.e., just to play himself as a documentary type character, but then he learned the art of acting in Kuleshov's workshop and became the famous creator of the roles of the father in *Mother*, of the worker in *The End of St Petersburg* and leader of the Partisan Detachment in *Storm Over Asia*.

I gave Chistyakov lessons in English – as I coached Pudovkin too – but after a couple of years, I lost sight of him and never knew what happened to him. But Savitsky remained a constant pillar of support for me, particularly in the oncoming battles over a visa to remain in Russia, as the gradual ousting of foreigners took place under the growing influence of Stalinism.

Luckily for me, as I learned later, Savitsky considered Pudovkin not only his maestro but his dearest friend who had given him roles in his films as a 'documentary type'. Just playing his own rough-diamond self.

A photo of him in the role of a worker was published in the English edition of Pudovkin's book *Film Technique and Film Acting*. (See Plate 20)

He would invite me to his modest home, quite near the GIK on Leningradskoye Chaussee. He fed me at times when food was very scarce. We were on strict rations in the first year of the Five-Year Plan. But as a Party secretary, he had access to a special store from which to get goods that were in short supply. At that time, I thought he deserved it as a veteran of the Revolution and Civil War. He suffered considerable pain from time to time – though he didn't show it in the GIK. At home he would relax and in my presence felt free to talk about his battles and his scars. He had been a commander of the Red Cavalry in Transcaucasia.

To me, he was the ideal Bolshevik in my then romantic revolutionary days, before disenchantment with Stalinism set in. He would have sacrificed himself without the slightest hesitation if the Party had demanded it. He would proudly show me his old Red Army uniform as a commander, his chest filled with the honors he had won.[6] (See Plate 19)

He was also a member of the Society of Old Bolsheviks which then meant those who had been members of the Bolshevik section of the Russian Social Democratic Party before the Revolution until they too were 'liquidated' by Stalin.

Then, one day he was retired from the GIK as Party secretary, and Varlarmov was appointed. His state of health was not good. But this happened when I was away on film location and I never saw him again. Where he moved to I don't know. All I knew was that it was on Party orders and no one ever questioned that – except me. But I got no answer.

Then years later came the tragic revelation. My old faithful friend and comrade, Savitsky, loyalist of the loyal, faithful of the faithful, Old Bolshevik, Red Commander, Victor of the Revolution and the Civil War, holder of the Orders of the Red Star and Red Banner, Party agitator and Party secretary, had been arrested as 'an enemy of the people' in 1938 during Stalin's purges and had disappeared into the GPU's prisons and the Gulag and was never heard of again. There was no relative or friend after rehabilitation to find out what had happened to the lone Savitsky except Vsevolod Pudovkin. But it was years before I met Pudovkin again – when I would be able to ask him. What happened to Savitsky? Why?

The personality of Pudovkin

Pudovkin was always a dynamic figure, always on the move, always brimming over with enthusiasm. He was above all a sportsman, and though originally I was invited to see him at tennis or join him, I'm afraid I was never much interested in sport, and that avenue I never explored. But his friends and Ivor Montagu will attest to his love of sport and dancing.

The film director, S. A. Gerasimov, who knew him well, writes:[7]

He was a supreme dancer. He had no musical education, but he was able to enjoy music, and enjoyed every note with refined inspiration. He would sit at the piano and search for accords, enjoy the fact that he could bring out such concordance from the piano.

Meeting with someone he had never met before, he instinctively directed all the power of his charm in order more quickly to subjugate him, to make the other fellow like him; and that he could do so well! . . . Pudovkin could do so much. He had been educated as a chemist, and no doubt, that somehow formed and disciplined his artistic vision. He could sight-read from a text brilliantly, he read it without ever seeming to look at the lines on the page, he experienced it to the full, acting the whole text, at once finding the subtlest shading and intonation in the dialogue, reproducing the action from the author's description with such visualization, that whole scene came to life before you.

All who knew him well cannot remember him in a state of tiredness, fatigue, weak will, drowsiness, or lacking in morale.

His close friend, Ivor Montagu, writes: 'He had a big, athletic frame. He won the badge "Ready for Labor and Defence." Run a mile, swim a mile, ride a mile, parachute jump and the rest, all to certain standards.'[8] When he and Ivor were consulting with each other at the numerous Communist-controlled 'peace conferences' they attended, Ivor recounts how when they got into an argument (that Ivor puts down only to a difference in temperament, not in politics!),[9]

Suddenly Pudovkin put down his brief case. 'Let's run,' he said, without any other preliminary. We set off. . . . Finally we both sprinted and arrived in a perfect dead-heat to much handkerchief waving by Moussinac and others in the style of miners encouraging whippets. . . .

That was how I remembered him from the 1930s until our fateful meeting in 1949 in Paris, but then he was no longer his old self. He seemed tired, spiritually as well as physically, he was sombre where he had once been full of life, and he had the air of tragedy about his brow, such as later I sensed in other friends and contemporaries who had survived the Stalin era.

Pudovkin's biography

In Moscow I got to know Pudovkin's background. I give here a brief account of what I learned of his origin and training.

He was born in Penze, Russia, in 1893, from what was known in those days as *sluzhaschii*, i.e., white-collar families, not the highest class in the new proletarian state! In high school he was interested in natural science and went on to the physics-mathematics department at Moscow University. He was also keen on painting and music, which was revealed later in his film-making days, but he made no special study of them. In 1914, he was mobilized for the Tsarist army just before graduation. He served in the artillery and was wounded and captured. He spent three years in German prison camps, then escaped in the German revolutionary days of 1918. In prison he learned German and English. He met British prisoners there; he always showed a liking for England and the English. He returned to Moscow in 1918, worked at an evacuation center for displaced persons, and then in a chemical laboratory of an arms factory.

He became interested in the new 'art' of cinematography, and applied to join the first State School of Cinema (later my GIK), established by Lenin who declared then, 'For us the most important art is the cinema.' Pudovkin said that it was seeing D. W. Griffith's film, *Intolerance*, which excited his interest in the art of the film. The first director of the school was the veteran actor, Gardin. Pudovkin always wanted to be an actor, a predilection he followed through in most of his films, though not as consistently making an appearance as Hitchcock. (Here for the record are the roles he played throughout his life: A Red commander, farm laborer, Red Armyman, an adventurer, a Fascist, a worker, a police officer, a German officer, the star part in the film of *The Living Corpse* by Tolstoy, Fedya Protasov, a shop assistant, a longshoreman, the Holy Simpleton, and Count Menshikov.) Here at the film school he was a student participating as an actor, designer, and scriptwriter.

In 1921, he participated in one of the first really Soviet films, appropriately called *The Hammer and Sickle*, about the class war in the village during the first years of the struggle of the Russian Communist Party for total control. In this film he worked as assistant director, set designer, co-scriptwriter, and played the leading role of the farm laborer.

Then, in 1922, he entered the workshop of Lev Kuleshov. For him this was the turning point, for the genius of Kuleshov lay in being the first theoretician of cinema art experimenting with his theories in his workshop, where he worked out his theory of what we now know as 'montage,' 'the Kuleshov effect' and 'Kuleshov geography,' as well as the theory of the non-actor, the *naturschik* or *typage* as it was called in Russian. Pudovkin went on to participate, making various agitprop films (i.e., agitation and propaganda – a term which eventually entered the English language).

By 1925, he began to chafe under, what was to him, the constricting rules of Kuleshov. He said (perhaps with hindsight, many years later), 'I saw no possibility of my fitting in, with my organic demandingness and inner excitement, to the dry form which Kuleshov preaches. In me was a powerful instinctive striving for the living man.'[10]

He took part as an actor in a film produced at Mezhrabpom Film-Russ called *Bricklayers*, following which he was entrusted with producing his first independent film *Chess Fever* (1926), a two-reel comedy, using the principles of montage he had learned from Kuleshov. He edited shots of the chess expert Capablanca so arranged as to make him appear to play a part in the development of the story.

Pudovkin at the state film school

It is not realized now how difficult and spartan were the conditions under which Soviet films were made in the early 1920s. Here is an account of that very time by Kuleshov, about the very school that Pudovkin studied at and that I was to join eleven years later![11]

The first state film school GTK (later to be called GIK) was established in Moscow in 1919. From this point forward, my fate is inextricably linked to pedagogical work . . .

The organization of the school constituted a great many large and interesting tasks – a new, revolutionary cinema had to be born, which swept away all the traditions of salon cinematography with its ersatz-psychological dramas, with its sugary-sentimental 'kings' and 'queens' of the screen . . .

But however difficult it was during this period, we shall never forget the wonderful days of the Twenties.

An independent existence demanded from the 'Kuleshov

Collective,' as we were then known, a maximum concentration of will and strength. First, we had to have some means of sustaining ourselves. We were as poor as could be – only because Kuleshov had something left over from an 'old wardrobe' were some of us 'dressed-up,'.– one was wearing his leather jacket, another – his new rope-soled shoes, while Pudovkin, one remembers, went about in trousers consisting of two separate halves and held together by safety pins. Occasionally, the pins would come apart.

Kuleshov relates many adventures that he and his group went through to survive, to produce and to justify their film theories. Pudovkin displayed his daring as an actor in many ways in making *The Death Ray*. Kuleshov writes, 'Pudovkin leaped from a four-storey height, and unsuccessfully at that – smashed himself up and lay ill some weeks (the firemen used got careless and lowered their nets during his fall).'[12]

But then came a period without work which lasted close to two years. Because we worked as a collective with new methods, opposed to the old theatrical film methods of Khanzhonkov and Yermoliev[13], the film-makers of the old school began to slander us, while the management, under their influence, began to fear us. . . . We were each separately offered jobs in one or the other organizations but with the provision that we should not work together. The directors-distributors were, in particular, incredibly opposed to Khokhlova.[14]

   Finally, I, myself arranged jobs for some comrades, because I was regarded as a definite authority by the heads of the film studios. I arranged for Pudovkin to go to Mezhrabpom-Russ. He made a non-theatrical film there at first, and then began to work on *Mother*.[15]

We now reach the epoch of the 'films that shook the world' and the emergence of the great triptych.

Pudovkin's Great Triptych

Pudovkin's first feature films were *Mother*, *The End of St Petersburg* and *Storm Over Asia*. In retrospect, it is seen that Pudovkin's whole creative output falls into four parts. First, the training-experimental period under Gardin and Kuleshov; the first independent experimental productions *The Chess Player* and *Mechanism of the Brain*; the first trilogy of great feature films, *Mother*, *The End of St Petersburg* and *Storm Over Asia*. Then came the second and final experimental productions, *A Simple Case* and *Deserter*. After these, he could make no more experiments. Third there was the switch to patriotic-historical themes of four films, *Minin and Pozharsky*, *Marshal Suvorov*, *Admiral Nakhimov* and *Zhukovsky*, out of which only one can be considered successful and that was *Suvorov*. Finally, his swan song, *The Return of Vassily Bortnikov*, was an attempt to return to the lyrical-personal theme of *A Simple Case*.

Much has been written about the three acknowledged masterpieces of the trilogy; they are part of the poetic style of Soviet cinematography which lifted them out of the usual stereotypes, though the critic Shklovsky accused Pudovkin of creating films that were centaurs: prose plus poetry to an uncanny degree. Pudovkin's *Mother* and *The End of St Petersburg* supplied the other side of the medal to Eisenstein's *Potemkin* and *Ten Days that Shook the World*. Pudovkin concentrated on the individual out of the mass, Eisenstein on the mass out of individuals. As Moussinac said, 'Eisenstein's films resemble a cry, while Pudovkin's resemble a song.'

The school I call poetic included the four Soviet giants of the 1920s, Eisenstein, Pudovkin, Dovzhenko and Vertov, and their films were not only poetic in the use of metaphor and artistic images but also in their structure.

Eisenstein consciously designed *Potemkin* in the form of a five-act classic tragedy, which he himself analyses in his essays.[16]

Pudovkin and his scriptwriter Zarkhi consciously designed *Mother* in the form of a sonata.

Reels 1 and 2: *Allegro*: saloon, home, factory, strike, chase.

Reel 3: Funeral *adagio*: dead father, scene between mother and son.

Reels 4 and 5: *Allegro*: police, search, betrayal, arrest, trial, and prison.

Reels 6 and 7: A mounting furious *presto*: spring thaw, demonstration, prison revolt, ice-break, massacre, death of a son and mother.

Pudovkin, Golovnya, his cameraman, and Koslavsky, his scenic design artist, utilized and created the material background for the film *Mother*, which didn't fall into the extremes of photographic naturalism usual in presenting workers. In fact, there is a brilliant fusion of stylization with the realistic background in Pudovkin's first three films. This is the same principle that Meyerhold and Eisenstein used. He learned his almost graphic space *mise-en-scène* and *mise-en-cadre*[17] from Kuleshov.

Yutkevich notes the influence of V. Serov (1865–1911), the famous Russian artist, on Golovnya's and Pudovkin's shot compositions. Also, the influence of the theory of photogenetics of the film scenarist and critic Louis Delluc (1890–1924), which helped Pudovkin to choose the proper material cleansed of its naturalistic detailization and to choose images which generalized expressive forms.

In order to create an image of backwardness and neglect of the slums, Pudovkin and Golovnya did not create a complex and florid, decorative background. Simple mud and dirt filmed from above was a sufficiently expressive image to show the poverty of a factory district.

One of the most powerful episodes in the film *Mother* is the montage counterpoint of pieces of spring background and the melting of the snow and children's play, in contrast to the prison cell where Pavel (the son and revolutionary worker) is confined.

Inherent in these artistic compositions were extended metaphors; in *Mother*, spring, which in Russia is heralded by the ice breaking on the rivers, is cut parallel with the growing intensity of the workers' demonstration. This parallel metaphor is exemplified in *Storm Over Asia* by its Western title, in which the sweeping away of colonial oppression and rule is enveloped in a 'storm on the heath', which blows away everything in its path, including the intervening foreign soldiers of imperialism. However, this film is also in the category of what one can call 'the cinema of pseudo-fact,' for Pudovkin introduced British soldiers in *Storm Over Asia* and defended this fiction as poetic license.

It is significant that the purely fictional events like the British troops in Mongolia and other fictional parts in Eisenstein's *Potemkin* became accepted as documentary events because of the style of these early Soviet films. Certain shots from both Eisenstein's and Pudovkin's silent films have been used in documentaries and newsreel compilations, as if they were actual shots of the real revolution or civil war!

Storm Over Asia was justified as being a fictional feature film anyway, but that was not the way it was originally presented.

It was revolutionary truth, 'socialist realism' as it was eventually labelled.

The Soviet critic Karaganov in the first major biography of Pudovkin[18] says that the theory of intellectual cinema, in its time, was severely criticized as absolute formalism and completely foreign to Soviet cinematography, but that it does deserve a more historical, a more serious attitude, and he apologizes both for the attacks and for the denigration of Eisenstein's theory! But so much damage had already been done to the artists as well as to their ideas.

Incidentally, he does not make any serious analysis. When the film *Storm Over Asia* was shown on the Soviet screen, there were conflicting opinions both about its treatment and its evaluation. It was particularly attacked by RAPP,[19] which was then the official dogmatic line presented by the leading members of the Party. Having thus shown that the film did not have great triumph in the Soviet Union, Karaganov goes on to say, 'Triumph also is achieved in foreign countries. It brought great honor to Soviet cinema. It was a bright page in the participation of our revolutionary cinema in the class struggle of the late twenties and early 1930s.'[20]

Indeed *Storm Over Asia* had such a reception in Berlin that Pudovkin himself could not believe the Berlin public could reach such an emotional climax toward the end of the film, for when the *Storm Over Asia* was blowing through the film there was a roar from the audience. People jumped on to the chairs, shouted, whistled, screamed, waved their hands, and did almost unimaginable things as a reaction to the power of his film.

Karaganov goes on to quote what the Berlin Press said: 'The new film of Pudovkin, *Storm Over Asia*, is a masterpiece, profound, moving, and a shattering event. *Storm Over Asia* is an event in the history of cinematography.'[21] The Berlin newspaper *Preussische Zeitung* called the film one of the greatest epics in the history of cinema.

I could go on quoting the extravagant praises the film received, but Karaganov cannot quote parallel reactions from the Soviet Press! He shows how the film was received in Holland and then banned, and also the extraordinary reception in England, where questions were raised in Parliament as to why such a film was allowed to be shown. In reply the Home Secretary, Joynson-Hicks, said that at the time he hadn't been in London so that it didn't come to his attention, and then Mr Kenworthy, a Labour Party

MP asked how Joynson-Hicks could not be in London when England was threatened with such danger![22] Here again, Karaganov had to follow the Party line and say that 'the English offered great sums of money for *Storm Over Asia* but it wasn't sold to them because it seemed they wanted to buy the negative in order to destroy it.'[23] This was absolute nonsense, of course. Anyway, as a result of all this, it is clear that the film had a colossal success abroad which it did not have at home. This applies to all of the great films of the 1920s, now lauded as the highest achievements of the Communist Party.

The next phase, in the 1930s, marked the beginning of Pudovkin's difficulties, as with all the great artists of the Soviet Union.

Under Stalin, the Party was beginning to take tighter control, freedom was decreasing, travel abroad lessening, censorship becoming tighter and more centralized and artistic choice subordinated to Party choice, various styles becoming 'streamlined' into social realism. This meant that scripts had now to be written for preliminary censorship in the form of the so-called 'cast-iron scenario' in which every shot was described and illustrated, and all titles and dialogue put down in precise detail. This meant that the brilliant improvisations of Eisenstein in *Potemkin*, like the classic Odessa Steps sequence, could never have been made. Nor the wonderful 'intellectual montage' that Pudovkin took from Eisenstein to create the idea of freedom in prison, war, and stock-exchange contrast or the ice-breaking river of the Russian spring on the natural background of the First of May workers' demonstration, which is developed beyond its natural function and transformed into a cinematic metaphor: 'Here is the new Spring of Revolution. Here is the workers' surging river of ice sweeping away everything in its path!'

But the Party was suspicious of metaphors – its critics attacked Eisenstein, Dovzhenko and Pudovkin for their 'poetic styles,' in *Ten Days that Shook the World*, *Zvenigora* and *Earth* and in Pudovkin's next picture, *A Simple Case*.

Pudovkin's next three films, *A Simple Case*, *Deserter*, and *Minin and Pozharsky* 'marked a period of comparative failure. The first was the worst: *A Simple Case* . . . the relationships in the story . . . were incomprehensible to the audience.'[24]

Let us see what Pudovkin was trying to do. The original title of the film was *Life Is Very Good*, which is a reflection of Mayakovsky's classic poem 'Very Good' – in praise of the aftermath of the Revolution which is 'Very Good.'[25]

Here Pudovkin was trying to create a psychological study of the successful revolutionary returning to build a new society in civilian life – from destruction to creation. He also wanted to experiment with it as his first sound film and for developing his theory of what he called '*die zeit-loup*' i.e. close-up in time and (although he wouldn't admit it in so many words) to attempt what Eisenstein postulated as the highest form of cinema, 'intellectual montage.'

I had been with Pudovkin as a student-observer during the shooting of this film, as well as during the editing. Then came a special showing at the GIK. It ran silent. I remember we were all disappointed. As I have said, Pudovkin was not only my patron, but a friend who would call me in from time to time to get an outsider's opinion of his editing. I had the temerity to give him some advice on *Deserter* which I discovered later he adopted. So now in relation to *A Simple Case* he showed me an experimental sequence he had edited, which he wanted to include in the film. I realized that it was an example of Eisenstein's intellectual montage (that he had been lecturing us about at the same period) and supported its inclusion in the film.

Let me give an outline of the story and its experimental sequences. The scriptwriter Rzheshevsky[26] had based the idea for *Life Is Very Good* on an essay by the Soviet journalist Mikhail Koltsov, but it also reminded another Pudovkin biographer, Yezhuitov, of Cecil B. de Mille's film *Why Change Your Wife?* In both films a husband leaves his wife for another woman and then, after the failure of the new relationship, realizes the superiority of his first wife and returns to her. The tragedy of the comparison really is that de Mille didn't have to worry whether or not his film had a clear social message, or that it had to promulgate the political idea of the wife because of her class standing being superior to the girlfriend. But Soviet artists had to. So Pudovkin's girlfriend was shown as 'a girl with a fox-fur on her shoulders, with a vulgar hair-do; another variation of the petty bourgeois "vamp".'[27]

Pudovkin of course chose Rzheshevsky's so-called 'emotional scenario' instead of the usual 'cast-iron' shot-by-shot script, in order to be able to experiment, just as Eisenstein had chosen the same writer's script for his ill-fated *Bezhin Meadow*. Both men wanted greater freedom from the censorship of their studio and Party controllers.

This story in effect is the simplest triangular drama which the Communist Party critics have so attacked for being 'bourgeois'. Now Pudovkin tried to make it 'class-conscious,' by making two points of the triangle – the man and wife – working-class comrades-in-arms of the Revolution, while the third point – the other woman – is a petty bourgeois 'vamp' type with no relation to the class struggle or the Revolution.

Briefly, the story is of a Red Army commander, Langavoi, who is attracted by a petty bourgeois girl and divorces his wife, Mashenka. His comrades upbraid him for his behavior and he finally realizes his mistake and returns to Mashenka.

During the action there is a flashback to the Civil War expressed in this much-criticized 'intellectual montage' sequence. The following is a detailed description of that sequence from my own notes taken during the showing in 1931.

Part II: A flag is waving slowly. Soldiers sleep in the trenches. A small group are on the look-out. Then comes the attack. Barrage. Shots. Explosions. Man at machine gun, wounded. A girl takes his place. The whole scene becomes a synthesis of destruction, the rhythm of the negative. Exploding shell, bomb, gun, tank, earth, men. Blaring light, flashing darkness. The man-conserved energy of nature is man dispersed centrifugally, while the flag slowly waves. Rhythm of destruction.

Part III: Spring, the exploding significances now are reversed into the rhythm of creation, not explosions but implosions, concentrating whirlpools of energy, peripheral diagrams all now receding to a central point – from all the borders of the film frame the black is sucked into a pinpoint of light – everything centrifugal is now centripetal – in line, plane, mass, color. Then in this fantastic concentration of energy, beings form tiny shapes, more implosions to form more tiny shapes, which start to move and consort and crack and their outer surface begins to crack like shells; and from each one slowly emerges a waving prong of white, that probes about in the darkness until it finds its way along the line of least resistance – upwards. More and more, these waving lines surge in a parallel and vertical direction, until they reach through the dark to the surface, to the light. . . .

By now one realizes they are shoots from seeds, literally shooting upward. New life is pushing up from the earth. The fertility of the earth is giving birth in front of one's eyes and then the young shoots grow and grow into young corn, moving, flowing, surging, a sea of growing corn – which ripens to rich full-eared corn. And then all the growths surge into plants and shrubs and bushes and trees to bud and flower and blossom and it is *Spring!*

Now, as I see it, here was a brilliant instance of intellectual montage, in which Pudovkin tried essentially to show the dynamic nature of reality and what eventually merged as spring and all that it implies to the human being. He showed what went into creating that spring, what energy, what forces, what power.

So we have the Red Army man at the front surrounded by destruction, explosions, and death, growing more abstract.

Here, brilliantly, Pudovkin shows the forces of explosion which are centrifugal, exploding out, destroying; then the forces of creation, which are centripetal, which throw in energy in order to give birth to a new life. Antithesis and synthesis.

That is the secret of this sequence of intellectual montage which was so difficult to understand.

Pudovkin spent ten months revising his film. Finally it was completed and, of course, had to be shown not only to the Chief Censors, but to the Chiefs of the Chief Censors, which included Stalin and Voroshilov. It is said they greeted it with some applause but more irritation, and thereafter Pudovkin was in trouble.[28]

So with this film and this sequence in particular Pudovkin, like Eisenstein, came up against the philistines who always wanted everything concrete. Terrified of the abstract, they always wanted things prosaic, they were always terrified of the poetic. Even in 1955, after Stalin's death, his legacy was continuing: Groshev, then Director of the GIK, wrote in his preface to Pudovkin's essays:[29]

A certain amount of abstractionism was inherent in the period of the creation of Soviet cinematography by many masters of cinema and was undoubtedly linked with their incorrect conception of the peculiarities of film art, as a form of perception of reality. Directors found themselves at that time under the influence of the anti-realistic theory of the so-called intellectual cinema, and strove to transmit to the screen this or that idea not through typified individual characters, *but by means of symbols, metaphors, abstract abstractions* [*sic!*].

A tribute to the idea of intellectual cinema was even given by Pudovkin in the film *A Simple Case*. But that error was quickly realized and fully criticized by Pudovkin himself.

Then in 1969 the same type of Party hack editors of the official Soviet History of Cinema[30] described this 'intellectual' sequence as

the monumental pathos of the prologue coming out of scenes of the Civil War, isolated montage pieces illustrating a certain natural cataclysm of nature (sic). . . . Here Pudovkin's experiments included the '*zeit-loup*' and 'poem to nature', an independent poetic picture of the rotation of nature. . . . To the average spectator it was incomprehensible and to cinematographers as an overpowering formalistic piece in the style of the French 'avant-garde'.

Here the hangover of Stalinist criticism is evident but almost parallel stern critics of those terrifying times now change their tune in these post-Stalin days. For instance, Professor Weissfeld, a leading Soviet film critic who was one of those who participated in the Stalinist attacks on the great directors we are writing about, now says this:[31]

The film *A Simple Case* was considered a Pudovkin failure. True, it lacks organic unity. The vacillations of the director and the contradictoriness of the critics of the scenario and the first editing of the film reduced its final editing to a certain 'patchiness'. Yet, nevertheless, even today, after forty years, one senses in it the temperament of an innovator.

The reticence of intonation, chastity, purity – that is what distinguishes this film story.

So this once bitterly condemned 'formalism' and Pudovkin's experiment in furthering Eisenstein's intellectual cinema – all this which Weissfeld and his fellow Party critics vilified in the Stalin period – is now 'valuable'. Then Rzheshevsky's story was made the villain of the piece and its author was sent to a Gulag prison camp and Koltsov was executed – now their story is 'chaste and pure'! Out of the mouths of the very critics who originally condemned them, as they condemned Eisenstein! Now Pudovkin is an innovator, not a 'formalist'!

What happened to *A Simple Case* was the beginning of Pudovkin's artistic suicide, for with it began the increasing intrusion of control by non-artistic organs into the artistic process.

In dealing with Pudovkin (as also with Eisenstein), one comes up against these two categories, the cast-iron film script and the emotional scenario, that need interpretation. To an outsider, this sometimes seems a lot of fuss about nothing, as it concerns only the style in which a film script or scenario is written. In the case of our Western terminology and practice we deal first of all with a film *treatment*, not the scenario or the final shooting script.

The thesis regarding the cast-iron film script was that it should be a complete description, in verbal form, of what the final picture would be on the screen. That is, it clearly shows exactly what story or plot characters will be used and developed within the action and the dialogue. It should show how it would actually be edited in the final version.

Some directors like Hitchcock or Eisenstein eventually drew a picture of every shot alongside the filming directions to make sure they got exactly what they wanted from their cameramen. On the other hand, in their early films, particularly those in the 1920s, those of Chaplin, Eisenstein, and others were shot from a mere outline, improvised on the spot. That is how the great classic *Potemkin* was made.

This improvisation and treatment, based on a mere sketch or sheer improvisation on the spot, considerably altering a given scenario, is something that is not palatable to those who want to control strictly what the artist produces, and especially not to the Communist Party.

It was probably in the revolt against this that the writer, Alexander Rzheshevsky, as well as Pudovkin and Eisenstein at one time, promulgated what was called the 'emotional scenario.' We will show examples of these, but it can be clearly seen that such a scenario is really not a scenario but a treatment, a springboard for the fantasy, imagination and skill of the director, who will eventually make it into a film. In effect, it is what the spectator should perceive and apprehend upon seeing the finished film on the screen. So that if Rzheshevsky writes, 'a wonderful man is walking by,' it is up to the director to find ways and means of filming his actor so he will come out 'a wonderful man' and that is how the audience will eventually perceive him. Pudovkin said, 'Rzheshevsky . . . determines the emotional content and the sense of the film without determining the visual contours.'[32]

But, of course, this type of script was much too vague for the censorship of the Soviet film industry and that is the reason why, in the end, the emotional scenario was damned, as well as the films that were made from it, in particular Pudovkin's *A Simple Case* and Eisenstein's *Bezhin Meadow*, both of which became tragic failures.

However, contemporary newspaper reports said that the film *A Simple Case* 'having been suppressed by Soviet censorship, Pudovkin, because of so-called "petit bourgeois idealism" which supposedly pervaded the film, had been deprived of his worker's card and banned from the Communist Party.'[33] This was printed in the then sympathetic journal *Experimental Film*.

The rumors about his fleeing to Berlin and hoping to get to America were, of course, highly exaggerated, but the criticism of 'petit bourgeois idealism' supposedly pervading the film was, of course, made. But Pudovkin's reply is very instructive. He wrote:[34]

> This whole business is utterly false and absurd. You know how such things take place in Russia. The State has given the cinema an educational role, in the broadest sense of the term. It is not possible for any person to film anything he pleases. Each script, before entering production, is submitted to the various departments which pass judgement upon its cultural, artistic, and ideological values. If any details are found amiss, the writer is called in, and, together with the head of the department in question, he corrects his work.
>
> As for my own picture, it was not suppressed by censorship. Quite to the contrary, it was approved for public showing. And, as in the case of almost all important Russian pictures, it was openly discussed in the different circles competent to judge it. This criticism, because of the extremely varied public opinion in USSR, brought up several suggested changes in certain parts of my film; which is a great point in favor of the general feeling of artistic and social responsibility on the part of the spectators as well as the technicians.
>
> My so-called flight from Moscow has an equally simple explanation. I am employed by the Mezhrabpom (the Workers'

International Relief [WIR]), which has its headquarters in Berlin. My position required frequent commuting between the city and Moscow. In that manner, I played in *The Living Corpse*, which my old friend Otsep was making in Berlin.

Conferences have been underway for several months to arrange for my going to Hollywood and directing a picture, employing the technical sound and dialogue equipment used in the California studios, equipment which far surpasses that available even in the best studios in Europe.

Already, in 1931, we see that the interference in a Soviet artistic work is reaching its climax, interference first allegedly from below but prompted from above, and then from 'the different circles competent to judge it,' i.e., the Communist Party, its Central Committee and, finally, Stalin. But, of course, there was by then a diminishing of the alleged 'extremely varied public opinion in USSR' which 'brought up several suggested changes in certain parts of the film.'

The changes were laid down by Stalin, just as they were later on concerning a scenario by the same author, Rzheshevsky, for Eisenstein's tragically aborted *Bezhin Meadow*.

Incidentally, although Pudovkin wrote about his plans for the visit to the USA which he hoped to make, *he was never allowed to go*. After Eisenstein's other aborted Soviet film *Que Viva Mexico* (see p. 203) and his protracted stay abroad, against Stalin's wishes, no other leading film artist of the Soviet Union went abroad, nor any theater or musical or opera-dance group, until after the Second World War, and then only specially trusted people, carefully guarded the whole time.

Deserter

Pudovkin's next film was to be a Mezhrabpom co-production with Prometheus Film of Berlin, and in March 1931 he visited Hamburg to prepare the production of this film based on the life and struggle of Hamburg's dock workers. The script was then called *S.S. Pyatiletka (Five-Year Plan)*. Pudovkin wasn't aware that this was his last trip abroad for nearly fifteen years. The rise of Nazism and its final success in January 1933 inevitably brought to an end the German-Russian co-production, and at the same time heightened the conflict in the script. Its hero, the Communist Karl Renn (played by the leading actor of the Moscow Art Theater, Boris Livanov), 'given the choice of living a safe, protected life in the Soviet Union, sees himself as a deserter of his comrades and prefers to return to fight in Germany.'[35]

The irony of history is that those German Communists who stayed in the Soviet Union, as a lesser risk than fighting Hitler on their own ground, actually ran the greater risk to their life and liberty. Most of them were eventually arrested, condemned without trial, executed, sent to the Gulag, or handed over to Hitler.

Meanwhile, oblivious to all this, of course, Pudovkin went on with the second stage of his experiment in sound film and counterpoint in *Deserter*, for which he would eventually be severely criticized. He wrote a pattern of natural sounds into his first film sound track, using the noises of shipyards and docks, even getting the great ships in Leningrad Docks to play their deep-sounding hooters in rhythm and counterpoint, and finally the triumphant revolutionary music in counterpoint to the shooting down of the workers' demonstration. Here is how he analyses his treatment:[36]

> Instead of the music following realistically the ups and downs of the demonstration, the surge forward, the clash with the police, then the retreat of the workers beaten down by the police force, it was composed in one 'single-purposed unity'. A march of the workers striding on confident of victory until its triumphant musical climax, in juxtaposition to the inevitable defeat on the image. Despite this apparent defeat the revolutionary workers are morally victorious.

I remember how, when I was shown the rough-cut of the film, this episode was almost in the middle of the film and I involuntarily said it had to be a final climax at the end, as a result of which, to my utter astonishment, Pudovkin re-edited the film and ended with this climax!

In *Deserter*, there is a brilliant use of slow motion which turned a realistic shot into an artistic image: an unemployed worker commits suicide in despair by hurling himself into the river. His leap from the stone parapet into the swirling waters is taken in semi-slow motion, and so instead of falling down, the man appears to be sucked down into the water, which envelops him in a great fan of oncoming enclosing waves, until it seems he is sucked under by some terrifying blind force.

In his first major films, Pudovkin is still dealing with an individual against the background of social and military revolutionary action, but as the English critic Robson points out,[37]

> He is far more concerned with social movements than with the inner workings of the peasant's mind – he is mainly concerned with the individual's reactions to the objective events that envelop him – the mother and son and abortive revolution, the peasant and the successful revolution, a Mongolian trapper versus imperialism. The subjective aspect of the character is not delved into, but the very title of *Deserter* is a subjective attitude, here the 'hero' is virtually the whole film, filled with pangs of conscience for having deserted his revolutionary comrades. As Robson perceptively points out, 'in Pudovkin's films the individual is the anvil, in Eisenstein's he is the hammer.'

I should like to give one more example of editing in *Deserter*, which shows that two rhythmical lines – sound and image – can be united in different ways.

When I spoke of the editing of the simplest aspects of dialogue, it turned out that in sound, reality as it were was fixed objectively, but in the image there was a representation of the subjective attitude of the viewer to that reality.

One can also do the opposite: fix objectively the actuality of the image, but in the sound give a subjective evaluation of that actuality, in relation to each viewer.

In the last part of *Deserter* is shown a demonstration of workers in Berlin and its dispersal by the police. How was that done?[38]

What Pudovkin did was this: in the visual image he showed the demonstration, gathering, marching, confronting the police, clashing, beaten and finally dispersed. The banner waves in front at the start, it falls, is fought for, and then as the workers retreat, it retreats with them. But the counterpoint in sound, the subjective point of view he talks about, was represented by a single uninterrupted piece of music, a militant proletarian march, stern and assured of victory, increasing in power with measured tread from the very beginning to the very end, a continuous rising climax, so that though the visual conclusion was failure and retreat, the aural conclusion was triumphant victory.

In other words, Pudovkin tries to indicate what to him was the profounder reality, the eventual victory of the proletariat, expressed by the music in counterpoint with the image.

The Very Happiest (1938)

When Pudovkin started to make the film called *The Very Happiest* he was working with his scriptwriter Zarkhi. This was the period of what was then known as the theory of non-conflict. And here is another extraordinary phenomenon of Communist Party life, that in the very era Stalin declared was the era of growing class conflict (even inside the so-called socialist and communist society), Party theoreticians at the same time were developing the idea that in a socialist society, among its socialist members, there *cannot* be any basic conflict! We see here a reflection of what Mao Zedong theorized later about antagonistic and non-antagonistic conflicts. When one realizes that the whole basis of drama is conflict, the idea of removing conflict and still creating drama is an absurd contradiction put forward by the Party theoreticians of those days.

The second contradiction, of course, was the fact that the Party demanded films, as Yutkevich expressed it, with simple narration, narrative and plot. Pudovkin himself said, 'For us, cinema work is the most important, and the most significant task for the present time is the creating of entertaining mass films.'

Even Karaganov has to point out the contradiction of the theoretical ideas of Pudovkin in experiment and the practice demanded by the Party.

It is significant that during the period of Stalin's consolidation of terror, between 1933 and 1938 when the first great purges took place, neither Eisenstein nor Pudovkin completed any films – Pudovkin made none for five years, Eisenstein for seven years. Five years in the life of a film director is a long time.

Another factor was the great tragedy involving Pudovkin's closest friend and colleague, Nathan Zarkhi, the scriptwriter, with whom he had made all of his great silent masterpieces. He and Zarkhi were driving one day from the outskirts to Moscow in a new Czech Tatra car, a very powerful car. It seems Pudovkin was driving and through his error there was a terrible accident, in which he was quite seriously injured, but his friend Zarkhi was killed.

I remember when I talked about it with him some time afterwards, he still broke down in tears, at what he felt was his own guilt in killing his dearest friend. This alone made it impossible for him to work for quite a while, quite apart from the growing Stalinism around him. Then he tried to make up for it, at least, by completing the film he had started with Zarkhi, called *The Very Happiest*. It also had titles such as *Victory* and in America, *Mother and Son*.

Victory is the name of a plane that can fly round the stratosphere. It is piloted by Klim Samoilov. His brother, also a pilot, wants to come along as a crew member but is refused. The plane disappears during the flight. Klim's mother comforts his pregnant widow and urges her other son Alexander to fly the second experimental plane over the same dangerous route. Of course he does so and finds and rescues his brother, still alive on a deserted island. In their flights they had broken many speed and distance records and return in triumph to their homeland.

Here was the simple narrative and plot the Party demanded and the only conflict was between man and nature.

Zarkhi had intended the figure of the mother in Soviet society to parallel his figure of the mother from Tsarist society, but he never finalized the script before he died.

Pudovkin never really recovered from this tragedy, although he attempted to finish the film he and Zarkhi had started. But his heart was not in it. His colleague Doller and other scriptwriters eventually completed the film. But it was a failure.

Pudovkin, experiments and the poetic cinema

There has recently come to the Soviet Publishers List a important book entitled *Vsevolod Pudovkin*, by Dr. A. V. Karaganov, whose doctorate is in art, a leading critic and historian of theater and cinema (henceforth referred to as Karaganov). Here we have the first serious and sincere attempt to encompass the life and work and significance of Pudovkin. Again, however, we have an example of the limitations that the Communist Party puts on its theoreticians. However the sincere writer does his best to express the truth, despite the pressures of Party control and censorship, and a good deal of it emerges in the latest book on Pudovkin.

It brings out quite clearly the distinction between the epoch preceding Stalin and the Stalinists. Karaganov says it was primarily[39]

the freedom for discovery, for experimenting, revealing and testing. Moreover, the process of renewing the language and style of cinema brought to their creative work new qualities: when the revolution came on to the screen as a subject of representation, it also called for revolution in the art of the screen itself.

They all pay tribute, then and now, to the great experimental work of Lev Kuleshov, who for those very experiments was eventually labeled a total formalist and unable finally to create any films. It is tragic, as the writer shows, that in later years of the Stalinist period, Pudovkin would even criticize not only Kuleshov, but his own experiments from the point of view *then*, i.e., Party attacks on formalism. The author criticizes Pudovkin for attacking Kuleshov in the 1930s as if he had done that in the 1920s! Here again is the same problem of attempting to rewrite history.

Another of the basic problems in Communist Party society is the problem of Party control over artistic works. In the 1920s, already the pro-Communist artists were calling on the Party to take greater and greater command over production of works of art![40]

The most important fact [is] that the decision on ideology from above, on the part of the State, in its essence correct, has placed before cinema workers the task of creating new methods in a purely formal sense. The dictatorship of ideas, the dictatorship of thinking gives birth to new forms!

When you see this, you realize what a tragic trap the Communist Party prepares for its artists, for having once proposed that the Party dictate its ideas and thinking, so that the artist can create forms, it then gets to the point where the Party now dictates not only ideas and content, but what forms shall this content be clothed in. Stalin gave them his slogan to conform to: *nationalist in form, socialist in content.*

The 1920s were the era of the greatest polemics, but following this, a group of cinema directors including Eisenstein, Pudovkin,

Romm, Kozintsev, Trauberg, Yutkevich and Popov issued a document entitled 'A Party Discussion on Cinema Affairs'[41] in which they placed before the Party Conference the question of increasing and organizing the production of films, and further requested that a special organ be created which would carry out Party politics in cinema.

Such an organ was created: the Committee for Cinematography under the Soviet of Peoples' Commissars of the USSR. The first chairman of the committee (1929) was the leading Party statesman, Y. A. Rudzytak,[42] and Pudovkin was elected on to the committee.

In retrospect, it can be seen that these directors dug their own graves. They themselves asked for the Party to take complete control of their artistic work, the result of which was eventually suicide.

Elsewhere, I have pointed out the fact that Pudovkin insisted *experiment* was a necessary part of the evolution of art, and, of course, of the cinema. Karaganov writes about Eisenstein and Pudovkin, that in creating their great films they were also researchers, *experimenters*, explorers, and testers.[43] He quotes specifically from Pudovkin's article 'The Creation of Cinema Regisseur' saying, 'progress, the movement forth of cinema art, is impossible without experiment.' But Karaganov goes on to say that[44]

> There is very little experimental work in the West. [!] Commercially, themes have long ago been clarified and re-digested. The success of a film is determined primarily by the amount of money it can collect and the entertainment value which the petty bourgeois spectators will pay for. But with us the uninterrupted growth of actual tasks demands newer and newer researchers in the sphere of methods of presentation. In these conditions, to experiment is necessary in different directions.

Of course, this is sheer hypocrisy, since all the problems of Eisenstein, Pudovkin, Dovzhenko and Vertov arose when they began to experiment after their first successful films. Then experiment was considered wasting time on 'formalism' instead of on themes and subject matter that the Party wanted. They were damned and frustrated in every direction, and in direct contradiction to his own statements Karaganov eventually goes on to prove the opposite! It was Stalin personally who 'dissuaded' Eisenstein from making his proposed film on Marx's *Das Kapital*!

Karaganov goes on to say that Pudovkin's evaluation of the necessity for experiment was more historically correct than that of later critics of Soviet cinematography, that even where Pudovkin used the term *one-sided formalism*, in 1927 this wasn't a dirty word, not a swear word, but a formula of analysis. Pudovkin pointed out that in the middle of the 1920s there was a synthesis of theme, aim and method and points out with gratitude the researches of the Kuleshov school for methods which were technically speaking formalistic, but inevitable and necessary. In the course of his experiments, Pudovkin wanted also to further develop the theory of Eisenstein's intellectual cinema and intellectual montage.

But a resolution of Sovkino in 1929 insisted on the thesis of 'experiments understood by the millions'. Another Soviet film critic, Bleiman, says,[45]

This is internally contradictory and also a stereotyped judgement. . . . One must not be afraid, one must not work only to play for safety. Our cinematography needs daring. No genuine revolutionary film will be understood by the millions, unless it confirms its stylistic tradition.

But despite Bleiman's correct criticism of this Sovkino thesis, in a short time 'experiment' became a dirty word unless it was 'understood by the millions,' in the opinion of the Party and its wise leader Stalin. But it was clear that, following the golden era of the silent film and the arrival of sound, experiment was essential, as well as the switch from the revolution of the masses to individualization within those same masses – the transition from the epic to the lyric. This Pudovkin tried to do with his films *Deserter* and *A Simple Case*, for which he was castigated. He tried to carry forward in his own way the intellectual cinema of Eisenstein, particularly in the wonderful episode of 'Spring' in *A Simple Case*.

This was the only example of intellectual montage I found in Soviet Cinema following the 'Gods' sequence in *October*, so often quoted by Eisenstein and others. Only during and after Khrushchev's era did new examples of poetic intellectual montage emerge – particularly in Paradjanov's *The Color of Pomegranates*.

The era of experimentation ended in the middle of the 1930s and gradually the very physical area for experimentation in cinema was reduced to nothing, when an average of one hundred feature films a year was reduced to ten feature films a year. So the era of the so-called poetic film gave way to the so-called prosaic film.

Karaganov now regrets that the particular art of Eisenstein, Pudovkin, and Dovzhenko, known as poetic cinema, was attacked not only in the 1920s but also in the 1930s and even some twenty years later! He says research into poetic cinema for many years was replaced by polemics attacking the creators of these films for new retreats from realism.

He picks on the first monograph on Pudovkin, published in 1951–2, whose author, A. Maryamov, is still a secretary of the Union of Soviet Cinematographers. He said that unfortunately Maryamov's work was a generalization, not only of the knowledge gained since then in the history of cinema, but also of critical one-sided evaluations which were considered to be still valid even in 1953.

Maryamov attacks *The End of St Petersburg* because Pudovkin 'abstracted phenomena, deprived them of personalization which inevitably led to formalism.' And now, twenty years after Maryamov, Karaganov says, 'well, of course, these were not poetic formalistic films, they are the poetic language of epic and the concrete expression of its peculiarity.'[46]

Then we come to a fantastic statement; having now tried to negate all the attacks on these great geniuses for thirty to forty years, which made their lives a misery and ruined their art, he goes on to say,[47]

> The history of Soviet cinema convinces us that these cinema epics of the revolution *were the first mighty flights of socialist realism* in the art of the screen, even though then such terminology was not in full use. [!]

Such is the arrogance of the Soviet critic of today, and he goes on to say, 'otherwise we would have to limit socialist realism in cinema within the frames of the narrative domestic psychological film.'[48] He says that even then,[49]

> [the] best film of all times and all people, Eisenstein's *Potemkin*, would have been outside these frames and could have only been forced into the category of socialist realism with great reservations. Or we would have tried to find in Pudovkin's trilogy elements of psychological, domestic cinematography or,

what is even worse, to place these great discoveries of Pudovkin, the area of creating epic characters and developing poetic language, under the category of formalism.

And, of course, here Karaganov has a problem; he tries to do this new and false categorizing because the new wave of Soviet cinematography headed by those geniuses Sergo Paradjanov and Andrei Tarkovsky, is a repetition on a higher scale of the poetic school of Eisenstein, Pudovkin, Dovzhenko, and Vertov. Karaganov in particular, quotes the film of Ilyenko and Frach, *White Bird on a Black Background* and the film of Alov and Naumov based on Bulgakov's play *Flight* saying, 'in the case of these films we meet with a variation of poetic language and style and a rejection of the simple narrative, substituting instead many-meaning poetic *double entendres*.' And this new wave of poetic cinema meets its climax in Sergo Paradjanov's masterpiece *The Color of Pomegranates* which is the acme of total intellectual cinema – and in its day was also banned, from 1970 onwards.[50]

Patriotic films

Now begins the era when the great artists of the 1920s began producing Stalinist-guided films, in which they no longer were sole producer-directors, as in the golden silent pre-Stalin days. Now they had to have a more Party-trusted comrade as a co-director: Eisenstein had Vasiliev and Pavlenko, and Pudovkin had Doller. But more significant than all this was the change of theme; as Pudovkin put it, 'From now on the subject of my films will be the power of the Russian State,'[51] almost exactly echoing the theme of the personally chosen bodyguards, the *Opprichniki*, in *Ivan the Terrible*, and their chorus and oath, '*Radi Russkovo Gosudarstva Velikovo*' ('For the sake of the Great Russian State').[52] The image of the Revolution, the rank and file worker becoming politically literate and the key participant in its victory, now gives way to the very opposite, the great leaders, Stalin's own proposed subjects, the great Russian generals and admirals and Tsars. The very characters who in all previous Leninist-Marxist literature had been castigated as tyrants, imperialist colonizers, suppressors of popular revolts, Ivan the Terrible, Marshal Suvorov, and Admiral Nakhimov, are now heroes. We see a total reversal of the major objective of all these artists' previous films.

Minin and Pozharsky

The problem is that the Soviet critic, like Karaganov, has always to criticize around the subject without hitting the nail on the head. For example, the name of Stalin is mentioned incidentally only once in his whole biography of Pudovkin. But never does he point out that Pudovkin's problems were mainly due to the dictatorship of Stalin. He quotes the justification Pudovkin makes when dealing with military themes: 'The task of the Soviet artist, every day, every hour, every minute, is to prepare himself and others in the country as a whole for the forthcoming decisive battle for the victory of Communism.' Though we see the contradiction, that the boosting of Russian chauvinistic patriotism not internationalism is now the basis for the victory of world Communism!

The production qualities of these films were also affected by the fact that Pudovkin had to switch from themes he knew and loved as in his trilogy. His accustomed use of real 'types,' documentary background, location shooting, real places and things, now were to be replaced by theatre actors, studio sets, theatrical props and painted backgrounds. In his essay 'How I Became a Film Director,' he said,[53]

> Completely foreign to me, and somewhat frightening, was the necessity to construct in advance. . . . All this took me away from the living, completely unexpectedness of reality (which I was so used to) into the sphere of stylized work mainly in the studio. Thus my first experience bears, I think, the marks of my inability to handle historical material.

The story of Minin and Pozharsky is set in the seventeenth century during the so-called Time of Troubles, when the Poles occupied Moscow. With no one in authority, pretenders to the throne of Ivan IV are quarrelling and two Russians arise as leaders: Prince Pozharsky, an aristocrat who tries to form a volunteer army to fight the invaders, and a merchant, Kuzma Minin, who does the same thing in Novgorod. They join forces and liberate Russia in October 1611.

The Communist Party wanted Pudovkin to stress that Minin was 'a man of the people,' a hero out of the masses.

But Pudovkin writes:[54]

Minin and Pozharsky was, as our people like to call it, a 'wide canvas' epic, but in the very width of its coverage of events the living characters of the heroes drowned and dissipated. They became chess figures and pawns, with names and places in the plot but having no faces. What took place was the exact opposite of *The End of St Petersburg* where the individual face of the hero and his fate and his particularly personal character was transformed into a generalization of reality . . . however much I tried to 'guy' the viewer with 'real' mud on the streets and roads or carefully copied armor, a sense of real life did not exist. The generalizations of the study remained cold and froze the blood of the human images.

So this film turned out to be in an operatic, academic style, not only in its decor but in its performance and the playing by the actors. The characters were one-sided and presented as schematic historical conceptions. History in this film by Pudovkin, Doller, and Shklovsky was only construed as a sequence of exploits and victories confirming the glory of Russia. Their leading characters were shown only as military warriors caught up in a stream of courtiers and serfs.

What is infuriating, however, is to read the Soviet critique of the one-sidedness of past film productions. Not laying it all on the shoulders of the Communist Party and particularly of Stalin, but on the poor producers and directors who were forced to make these films!

Karaganov says,[55]

In a sense, Pudovkin, Doller, and Shklovsky shared the mistakes and weaknesses of the authors of many historical biographical films and plays of the 1930s and 1940s. Those films and plays in which the themes and motives struggle for patriotic unification of the people, for the independence, power and greatness of Russia, were worked out in complete isolation from the themes of the struggle of oppressed peoples against their oppressors.

He points out the fact that all these heroes were courtiers or aristocrats who owned serfs. The majority of those mobilized into the army were serfs. Karaganov says that there was a falsification in the presentation of serfdom and slavery, then common to Russia, and particularly of its landowning class and aristocrats. He writes that 'episodes in the film showed that only some of these aristocrats were really democratic in the treatment of their serfs.'[56] In fact, this was not only in Pudovkin's film but in many of the historical biographical films and plays of the period. It seemed to be a typical thing for 'democratic' treatment of serfs in Tsarist society, according to the Communist Party of the Soviet Union!

What emerged on the screen was a unity of the nation on a non-class basis, contradicting the Party's own tenets of Marxism and Communism. So we see that now Pudovkin's treatment of *Minin and Pozharsky* is clearly categorized by a modern Soviet critic as a falsification of history.

Marshal Suvorov

So what happens after *Minin and Pozharsky*? Pudovkin is asked to do a film on another military figure, Marshal Suvorov. Despite the fact that Pudovkin had made it clear that he didn't really like historical themes, that *Minin and Pozharsky* was a failure, nevertheless the Party, in other words Stalin, demanded that he make another film with a Tsarist hero.

Karaganov says,[57]

Pudovkin refused. Though he was interested in history and though he understood the significance of the images of the great warriors of Russia for the patriotic education of the Russian people he didn't want to concentrate now on historical themes. Above all, he was interested in contemporary themes.

But it made no difference, in the end; he had to make the film, although there is an attempt to show that he chose it voluntarily when we know that at first he categorically refused.

The film tells only part of the story of Marshal Suvorov, one of the greatest military leaders in history. It shows his conflict with the Tsar Paul I, a cruel, stupid autocrat. At one time he is exiled by the Tsar, and he is only brought back when Russia was in danger from Napoleon. In his exile he dictates his classic book on military strategy called *The Science of Victory*.

One outstanding sequence reveals the Tsar's cruel despotism. On parade, angered by some minor infringement of his Prussian-style rules, Tsar Paul orders a whole regiment, 'To Siberia, forward march!'

The film deals with Suvorov's victory over the Poles and his classic campaign over the Alps to Italy. All his victories are made through unorthodox tactics.

But this time the film is not weighted down with historical military detail but gives full expression to the extraordinary character of Suvorov, his eccentricities as well as his genius as a military tactician.

His own eccentric behaviour shocks the courtiers but makes him beloved by his soldiers. He is summoned to see the Tsar, and enters the royal quarters where all the Tsarist generals are gathered in full dress uniform. Suvorov passes through them, slithers on the polished parquet floor, loses his hat and the little cane he always carries, even during his campaigns. Everyone wonders what sort of clown this is. But no sooner is he alone in the royal presence than his real character is visible, upright, leaning proudly on his cane, looking piercingly straight into the eyes of the Emperor. His behavior in the anteroom was only to mock the lackey-courtiers and 'floor polishing generals.'

There is no time to go into a deep analysis of what happened in the treatment of Suvorov in relation to truth, except to say that Suvorov was undoubtedly an incredibly interesting character and a man who had his own conflicts with the Tsar, which in the end came down to the problem of aristocracy and serfdom. But that, of course, could not be dealt with in the film Stalin wanted. In fact, Suvorov's battle was against the Prussian military ideals of the Tsar; his own ideas of the treatment of the individual soldier were more democratic.

Again, a conflict took place between the producers, Pudovkin and Doller, and the president of the Committee for Cinema Affairs, I. Bolshakov, who ordered corrections and amendments to be made in the scenario. Protests were made by the producers to the director of Mosfilm about these distortions. Karaganov goes on to say that there was no place in the film for the drama of a general, a Russian, who was fighting in the wrong war, in a war which became another shameful step in the history of turning Russia into 'a prison of the peoples'.

The Polish campaigns of Suvorov were shown only from a military point of view and the triumph of patriotism, as it was officially considered, was shown from the point of view of the autocracy. That was Stalin's angle. Interestingly enough Karaganov goes on to quote Lenin's point of view on this very Russian Tsarist campaign against Poland. Lenin supports Hertzen in his defense of Poland against Russia. Lenin wrote, 'When the whole crowd of Russian liberals retreated from Hertzen for his defense of Poland, when the whole of "educated society" turned away from *The Bell*[58] Hertzen was not troubled.[59]

'He continued to stand up for the liberation of Poland and to lash out against the oppressors, the butchers, the hangmen of Alexander II. Hertzen rescued the honor of Russian democracy.' Lenin quotes Hertzen's letter to Turgenev, 'We saved the honor of our Russian name, and because of that suffer from the slavish majority.'[60]

But inevitably Karaganov puts the blame on the producers of the film (not on the Party's directions) for ignoring Lenin and Hertzen! He says,[61]

> The creators of the film *Suvorov* and their consultants obviously never thought about such dimensions of patriotism and the national honor of the Russians, which Lenin and Hertzen used. Passion about military glory and patriotism of soldierly feats were separated by them completely from the social problems of serf-owning, Tsarist Russia. The theme of the liberation from serfdom and the confirmation of human individuality is dealt with only as the theme of liberation from the Prussian military doctrines of the Emperor Paul and from the limitations of court etiquette. Therefore, social class problems as in Minin and Pozharsky, were outside the bounds of this film's 'dramaturgy.'

So in effect, the present-day critic really devastingly condemns his own Party and Stalin for falsification of history and in forcing the artist to artistically incarnate those falsifications.

Nevertheless *Suvorov* was a success for Pudovkin and won a Stalin Prize First Class. (It was released in Britain by the Anglo-American Film Corporation during the war, with subtitles by myself.)

Pudovkin and the Second World War

Such a loyal Party member as Pudovkin at once felt himself mobilized from the first day of the war and participated in making war
films. For no. 6 in a series called *Military Film Albums* he shot a
short film with his co-director Doller, a two-reel novelette called *A
Feast at Zhirmunka*. It dealt with collective farmers in an area occupied by the Nazis and how they reacted, showing their growing
hatred of the invader. Karaganov said this film was one of the first
Soviet works of art to create the 'science of hatred.' At that time
the Soviet journalist Ilya Ehrenburg and the poet Constantine
Simonov also wrote exhortations and poems of hate about the
Germans.

Then, in 1941, the Moscow Film Studios were evacuated to Alma
Ata. Here Pudovkin began to work on his next full-length film *The
Murderer Takes to the Road*,[62] based on a short play by Bertolt Brecht.
It is interesting to note the basic theme and its relationship to
internal Soviet life – perhaps one of the hidden reasons it was
eventually banned. Karaganov explains:[63]

> The permeating theme of the film was set forth by its literary
> sources: fear, cultivated by Fascism, fear, internally deforming
> man, destroying in him all normal behavior, making him a
> coward, a villain, a traitor. Total fear. It leads a perfectly
> reasonable German citizen to begin to fear his own under-age
> schoolboy son: where has he gone? Will he inform on them?
> And what did they say in his presence? Shouldn't they forbid
> him to leave the house? But that may give cause for fresh
> suspicions and informing. They will have to cajole him. . . .
> Parents 'bribing' their very own son, isn't that a paradox, isn't
> that a phantasmagoria! However, on the screen – it is not a fairy
> tale, not a nightmare, but indeed normal everyday actuality . . .
> and in another episode people are afraid of everything. A careless
> word, which can be interpreted topsy-turvy, a family account
> book where prices of goods are listed, old, 'pre-Hitler', simple
> human points of view.

On reading these words of the Soviet critic, one has only to
substitute Soviet Communism for German Fascism, pre-Stalin for
pre-Hitler and the exact description fits – the cap fits. This is exactly
what happened under the Stalinist terror, as is documented by

so many, particularly in Yevtushenko's and Aseyev's poems, each entitled 'Fear.'[64]

The fear of one's own family informing was so real because the Party and the Young Communist League and the NKVD (now the KGB) encouraged such informing as 'patriotic Party-minded behavior.' Indeed such a family informer was the very hero of Eisenstein's film *Bezhin Meadow*, which I write about elsewhere.

Apart from its theme, it suffered because it was by Bert Brecht who had been banned in the Soviet Union since the 1930s, and it was not produced until after Stalin's death.

Is it any wonder that this full-length film of Pudovkin was banned and eventually all mention of it dropped from the official histories of Soviet cinema?

The Russian People

Now Pudovkin was commissioned to make a film version of Simonov's successful play, *The Russian People*, and his polit-commissar this time was the same D. Vasiliev who made sure that Eisenstein didn't depart from the Party-approved script of *Alexander Nevsky*. But despite the political control, or more probably because of it, 'Pudovkin's film is a failure' said the Party censor chief, A. S. Scherbakov, to Simonov. 'Nevertheless we released it for distribution, but changed the title, so it shouldn't compromise the fine play *The Russian People*. . . . There were no broad sweeps, no distances, no mass scenes, no Russian countryside – one did not feel any scale.'[65]

In 1943, the Committee for Cinema Affairs decided to make a film about the defense of Moscow and the battles of 1941. Simonov was to write the script, and he asked that Pudovkin again be his director. But the cinema committee was dead against it, in view of the failure of his other script *The Russian People* at the hands of Pudovkin. Simonov's influence eventually prevailed. His pro-Stalinism did not die with Khrushchev, he was responsible for many attacks on fellow artists which led to arrests, imprisonments, and deaths. But he was a good writer. Pudovkin decided to use Simonov's front-line diaries as the basis of his film; but then the film was stopped. Later, Simonov was criticized by the pro-Stalinists for these very diaries published as a book. Even in victory, Stalin and the Party wanted not the truth about the war, as in Simonov's day-to-day diaries from the very front lines, but again war as 'social realism', i.e., as seen through the rose-colored glasses of Stalin and his henchmen. Simonov, after Pudovkin's death said, 'Pudovkin loved this script very much, he very much wanted to make this film and was hurt very badly when it became impossible to carry out his plan.'[66] Instead, it was proposed to Pudovkin that he make a film about the great Tsarist naval hero, Admiral Nakhimov. Again he fought against it, as he had done over every one of his patriotic heroes. In a letter to the highest authorities, he pleaded and argued about the importance and necessity of the Simonov film; because of his deep attachment to *The Road to Smolensk*, he 'couldn't reconcile himself to the impossibility of creating it on the screen.'[67] He went on, however, in his true Party subservient way, 'if, however, it would be said that this film, in the way it had been conceived, actually was not needed by the contemporary spectator – then he would go on to work on *Nakhimov*.'[68] Suffice it to say that it was not needed by Stalin and his henchmen – nor, therefore, by the 'contemporary Soviet spectator,' who had not the slightest say on the fate of films decided for him.

Admiral Nakhimov

It seems that Pudovkin, continuing his polemic with Eisenstein, wanted the style of his *Nakhimov* to be the opposite of *Ivan the Terrible*. He pointed out that 'in Ivan events and facts of history are shown in generalizations, the film is purged of domestic everyday naturalistic details. Each character is the bearer of one definite idea, in him is clearly expressed one definite trait of character. *Admiral Nakhimov* is being made wholly "from the position of revealing the very subtlest, detailed traits of his character".'[69] But then Pudovkin goes on to contradict this, saying, 'whose whole being and thought strives to one feeling, a man possessed with a mighty love for his country, to the Russian people, and who is a genius – if one can be allowed to phrase it – in his patriotism.' [sic]

> If the dramaturgy of *Ivan the Terrible* reminds one of a chess problem, and actions of certain characters of moves in solving that problem, then *Nakhimov* is the opposite, bearing within itself all the characteristic traits of the everyday drama of the descriptive style.[70]

However, despite all of Pudovkin's good intentions, it paved the way to hell. He became one of a whole pleiad of artists who in one bunch were attacked by the full weight of Stalinist censorship headed by Zhdanov and his famous 1946 decree. Here is the actual material of the period, issued by the Party, the explication of Stalin and Zhdanov's attacks on film directors Zhukov, Eisenstein, Pudovkin, Kozintsev and Trauberg. At the same time they were lauding sycophantic films about Stalin as being a 'new stage of Soviet cinematography'. The contemporary Soviet handouts wrote:

An outstanding example of this harmony of form and content is the film *The Oath* which was enthusiastically received by the whole country. The way writer Peter Pavlenko and director Michael Chiurelli were to show with tremendous emotion and power how, after the death of the great Lenin, the great Stalin fulfills, in life, *The Oath* which he pronounced at the unforgettable funeral days of 1924.

Parallel with this grand success throughout the world [sic] was carried the news that the Central Committee of the Communist Party of the Soviet Union in their decree of 4 September 1949 subjected to a ruthless criticism the films, *The Great Life*, 2nd part, director Leonid Zhukov; *Ivan the Terrible*, 2nd part, director Sergei Eisenstein; *Admiral Nakhimov*, director Vsevolod Pudovkin; and *The Simple People*, directors Gregory Kozintsev and Leonid Trauberg.

Why does the Central Committee criticize such famous directors? For their ignorance, and for their untrue representations of events which they are portraying in productions. The theme of the great hero and patriot Nakhimov is replaced by insignificant details.

In his own obsequious words this is what Pudovkin said about this infamous decree:[71]

The Central Committee of the VKP(b) in its decree pointed out that the film *Admiral Nakhimov* was a failure and erroneous. The essence of the errors consisted in the fact that in preparing the film script we had approached the study of the historical material with inadmissible carelessness and superficiality, material which should have formed the basis of an artistic story about the great Russian naval commander, P. S. Nakhimov, and we created a film distorting historical truth.

As a result Pudovkin had to remake this big feature film, including scenes which the Party demanded of the naval strategy and the great military and naval victories of Russian arms. He had not only to remake the film almost entirely, but also to apologize abjectly.

But even though Pudovkin concentrated, slavishly following orders, on the strategy and military victories of the Russian admiral Nakhimov, and produced a film the Party approved of, it was a failure.

So these films that Pudovkin and others were *forced* to make are condemned by the honest critics of Soviet cinema today.

It is interesting that Karaganov actually quotes Leo Tolstoy, who wrote about the very same period, which included Admiral Nakhimov and the Crimean War, and says that 'when we compare Tolstoy with Soviet scriptwriters and Soviet film-makers, we have a falsification of reality.'

'Tolstoy as a witness was more dialectical, more realistic than the creators of the film of Nakhimov.'[72]

A Soviet commentator wrote:[73]

His production of the film *Admiral Nakhimov* in its first version was harshly condemned in the decree of the Central Committee . . . but, in its second version received the Stalin Prize of the first degree – witnessing indeed how responsively and carefully the regisseur-Communist responded to the Party criticism, what great and profound lessons he drew from it.

This eulogy is unsigned but sums up the tragedy of the artist under the Communist Party, particularly in Stalin's day – for Pudovkin was indeed more responsive to its commands than any of his peers, and came to an even more catastrophic artistic bankruptcy thereby.

Zhukovsky

Then Pudovkin was asked to produce a film about Zhukovsky (1847–1921), 'the father of Russian aviation'. This was at the beginning of the era of what is called in Russia 'the priority of Russian over foreign inventions and developments.' This is an era in which the Russians invented everything, from the split pea to the tank, radio and the airplane, and this is what *Zhukovsky* dealt with.

This film, Karaganov says, became really an illustration of a popular lecture on the history of aerodynamics. It was conceived as a 'symbiosis of fictional and popular scientific films'. Zhukovsky was an aviation inventor, a theoretician investigating the mathematics of aerodynamics and flight. Of course the Party, at that time, demanded that the film should show the superiority of Russian invention and that their theorizing was better and more advanced than any foreigner's. It was, incidentally, the period of Lysenko in agriculture,[74] and the Party and its Secret Police removed his scientific opponents under the pretext that they were servile to foreign ideas. Hence as Karaganov says,[75]

According to the *nomenklatura* of biographical plays and films of that period it was simply laid down that the outstanding man of learning always had conservative opponents not only above him but in his own milieu. And so they appear. They make pronouncements suiting their scientific title and their function in the plot, carry out underhand activities against new inventions, but it is all so according to the stereotype, so expected and so uninteresting. . . . So this scene was written and produced in *Zhukovsky* with a personage literally repeating a boring spectacle.

Apart from this, Pudovkin, who was, of course, trained as a scientist and had made two scientific films, wanted to present to the public the scientific theories of Zhukovsky in a cinematic form. 'But as soon as this popular lecture on the history of aerodynamics gives way to ideological or moral conflicts, the film begins to slide into a schematic straight line and the characters turn into movie stereotypes.'[76]

Thus is introduced a character called Rybakov who is a test pilot skeptical of all his Russian theory. Eventually, instead of testing the glider of his teacher, he is inveigled abroad and 'betrays his friends and teacher, betrays the science he serves and emigrates to study in a French aviation school, flies, achieves glamorous records and crashes to death during one of his tests, thus demonstrating that aviation without aerodynamics cannot live'[77] – by which he means, of course, Russian aerodynamics.

Suffice it to say that this rather pitiful attempt at another form of Russian chauvinism, so typical of the Stalinist Party era, was also a failure. Pudovkin, once again obeying the Party line as a soldier, loses another battle.

The Return of Vasily Bortnikov

With the death of *Ivan the Terrible* a great blight was lifted from the Holy Simpleton's soul, though I doubt if he even consciously thought that way. Undoubtedly Pudovkin felt it, and proved it by choosing as his next film, which turned out to be his last, the subject that the Party had forbidden him for the last twenty years of his life. He came back to the simple fundamental human triangle, but from a completely new angle, and therein lies the interest.

The conflict in the triangle he had filmed before (in *A Simple Case*) was the choice of one man between two women. According to Party-instilled dogma, it had to be the choice between two class representatives, one from the progressive class and one from the reactionary class. Character was determined by class. The good character naturally came from the good class (the working class). This class point of view, so hammered by the Communist Party, was one that completely distorts the human perspective. However, here, by his own choice, Pudovkin shows that fundamentally he too disagreed with his Party's 'Marxist' teachings. He now chooses a drama of the triangle in which the conflict is not the so-called eternal class conflict, but an eternal human conflict.

The choice in this case, of a woman between two men, is not one of the choice between the good and the bad, one from the good class and one from the bad class. Now they are theoretically of the same class and now equally good. Now the real tragedy is, how can one choose between the good and the good?

Special Soviet problems arise not just from the system but from the clumsy nature of the vast area of the Soviet Union, when during the war communications between the front line and the rear were so bad, so protracted, so cut off. In many other armies, a soldier on leave would be able to go home and visit his family, but this hardly ever happened in Soviet society, unless he was mortally wounded. Distances were so vast and the breakdown and problems of transport so great and the discipline so rigid that it would have been impossible for a man from the front lines of Western Russia to go to the East, thousands and thousands of miles away, in less than a week or two or even three weeks. His whole leave would have been spent going one way even if he got it! This was eventually the story of *A Ballad of a Soldier* by Chukhrai, made in the more liberal days of Khrushchev.

When the soldier-hero is given special leave to visit his mother he has forty-eight hours to get to her, forty-eight hours with her and forty-eight hours back to the front line. The endless distances of Russia are shown but he takes ninety-six hours to get to his village, where there are only women, a few old men, and children. As he meets his mother, he has only just time to say hello and goodbye and leave immediately to catch a train back!

This basically is the story of *The Return of Vasily Bortnikov*: the problem of a soldier who had been away for so many years, cut off from his family, where communications were so poor, with letters hardly received by either party, so that in the end he is missing and presumed to be killed.

The film script of *The Return of Vasily Bortnikov* was an adaptation of the novel *Zhatvy (Harvest)* by B. Nikolayev and E. Gabrilovich, the latter an experienced film scriptwriter. Just at this time, near the end of Stalin's life, there were some beginnings and stirrings of more liberal thinking.

With the opening of the film one sees that Pudovkin, freed of the false theatricalization of the Tsarist military films, now returns to his own pure cinematography. Here is a passage from his script:[78]

Wet earth. Puddles. Over a distant bridge thunders a train. In the twilight dusk walks Vasily, in his great army overcoat with a suitcase in his hand, a rucksack on his back, unshaven. Again and again he appears passing across the screen, in order once more to disappear and then appear again from the frame of the shot. Already in that heavy, importunate, dragged-out approach to his home, these shots give some kind of hazy sensation of ill omen and alarm. No, Vasily does not fly on the wings of love to his own home, spurred on by many wartime years of longing for his wife, he goes home with great difficulty. After many years of the unknown into the unknown.

Karaganov points out that not a word is said about this specifically, and yet it is all said on the screen. Once more the screen spoke for Pudovkin cinematographically, without theatrical supports, easing his communion with his audience, in a way that had never emerged in his historical films.

Pudovkin creates what one could call a psychological landscape; both in the angle of shooting, rhythm and editing of the movement of the man on this wet uncomfortable earth.

Then comes the meeting of Avdutia with her husband, not with gladness but with tears. Vasily had been presumed dead. Eventually Avdutia married Stephan. Now, all three of them are going to meet. Already, this meeting presages 'classic drama,' a triangular drama once more, with a jealous, insulted husband, there might even be a fight, bloodshed. Vasily, as has been seen, is a hot-headed, stubborn man angry in his grief and already his fist, in close up, clenches. But unlike a counter-blow, you see a close-up of the face of Stephan, with obviously recent war wounds still healing. So here we have a drama of three good people placed in an extremely difficult situation. The war had thrown Vasily into a long hospital convalescence of unconsciousness, a coma, rewarded with funeral ceremonies that brought Stephan into the house of the widowed Avdutia. Such a war prevented the classic development of the drama.

Now Pudovkin is not carried away by sound or dialogue, he is at his most restrained. Vasily asks Avdutia to sit down, he also asks Stephan. Then begins the important part of the conversation, but he cannot begin and finally says, 'Well now, tell me how is life? How is the collective farm?' That gives a way out and Stephan is at once grabbing the opportunity to talk about the problems of the collective farm. How the chairman of the farm had been replaced time and time again. How the collective farm had become impoverished.

Here again one can see immediately a difference of treatment as compared to Stalin's day. Then Pudovkin would never have dared suggest that a collective farm would become impoverished; all farms had become rich farms! A little bit more of the truth could now be told, even about that sensitive area, collective farms, for which so many millions of innocent people had been sacrificed and of which we have written elsewhere.

Now comes the minute when Vasily says, 'Now, what shall we do, Stephan Nikitich?'

Stephan says, 'Well, she must choose.'

Vasily says, 'Well, I shan't ask her.'

He is about to rise when Avdutia lets fall the cup and it smashes.

The smashing of the cup underlines, as it were, the words said by Vasily. He would not ask her to decide. Here we are returning to the psychological use of props, typical of Pudovkin at his best: the glass of steaming tea in *The End of St Petersburg* which tells the policeman that her husband isn't home, the use in *Mother* of the clock and kitchen sink, and the mother now over the kitchen sink again, with that homely gesture of drying the dishes.

'Here is his home, here I am his wife and he is not guilty of anything,' Avdutia says. So she decided to return to Vasily.

Here was the old Pudovkin. But both the scriptwriters and critics eventually admitted that the rest of the film was a failure, because it attempted to put in the Party line, to deal with the technological and administrative functions of the collective farm, the District Party Committee and the motor tractor stations of the period.

He goes on to say that 'the shortcomings are due to the fact that the artist only sees and shows the superficiality of life.'[79]

'The fear of leaving out the content of labor of the collective farm, or more accurately, its technology, interfered with the genuine revelation of characters.'[80]

Of course, this is the very thing that we have criticized throughout these essays. Even Eisenstein had to complain bitterly about how his treatment of the old and the new (about the state farm) was constricted by interdictions from above to purely technological concerns with the harvest, fertilizers, the sowing campaign, etc.[81]

The film continues to show the difficulties of the real return of Vasily Bortnikov, not only to his wife, but to his former life and to the problems of the collective farms – his spiritual return. In the end, Pudovkin uses his metaphorical style whereby the oncoming spring parallels the awakening of spring in the heart of Vasily.

It is significant that in finishing this chapter on *The Return of Vasily Bortnikov*, Karaganov has to come out and openly defend criticisms of the Soviet Union not only from the right but now from the left! He calls this 'bourgeois slander on socialism.' He uses this film as an example of how the truth of human relations is being suppressed. The fact that such truth had been suppressed for twenty-five years is, of course, dismissed.

We have seen the success of the human side of Pudovkin's films, which was based on the fact that now the class struggle no longer has any point, but genuine human relations that do eternally persist.

Such are the zigzags of the Party 'general line' – for just at the end of the war alliance that defeated Hitler, Pudovkin was able to write what was real:[82]

> I repeat: The world-wide comprehension of the film is a goal that must be identified with the all-embracing goal, imperatively required today, of a direct exchange of ideas of general human significance . . . a task which I feel all responsible film artists must face; to find and develop new film forms which will answer the universal desire for unity that has arisen among all the people of the world. Alongside the sound film . . . a new kind of film is waiting to be born . . . and [it is time] to begin work on this new film for all the world.

This is what the Soviet people wanted after the war, as is confirmed by the summer of 1944, by a Party member like the writer Vsevolod Vyshnevsky who made a speech at VOKS, the Society for Cultural Relations with Foreign Countries, in which he drew this glowing picture of 'cultural coexistence' after the war:

> When the war is over, life will become very pleasant. A great literature will be produced as a result of our experiences. There will be much coming and going, and a lot of contacts with the West. Everybody will be allowed to read whatever he likes.
> There will be exchanges of students, and foreign travel for Soviet citizens will be made easy.

But then Stalin started the cold war openly again and all these brave human words of universal co-operation were suppressed and all Soviet artists were now urged and commanded to make anti-foreign films and pro-Russian chauvinistic propaganda, and still no one is allowed to read what he likes or go where he likes. Nothing is 'made easy' for Soviet citizens.

My final meeting with Pudovkin

Our next and final meeting came after twelve years, at what I now realize was the height of the cold war. It was at the famous World Peace Conference in Paris in 1949.

When I learned that Pudovkin would be attending the Paris meeting of this conference I did all I could to meet him. It was not easy. Soviet citizens abroad are always protected by KGB guards, official and unofficial, and at the height of the Stalin tyranny even more so. Furthermore by then I had long quarrelled with the Communist Party of Great Britain and they wouldn't give me even an observer's card for the conference, which of course was a Communist Party front affair. However, I was anxious to meet Pudovkin and find out from him whatever I could about what had happened in the thirteen years since we had last met. Eventually I got in through some other foreign communists whom I had known, in particular the French Communist poet, Louis Aragon, and Elsa Triolet (the sister of Lily Brik). At the conference my wife, Fredda, and I met Paul Robeson, Pablo Picasso and Howard Fast.

I could not get to Pudovkin at the Soviet Embassy, but finally during an interval in the meeting I was able to make my way to the platform where he was sitting as the most important Soviet delegate. Luckily I was able to get a photograph of that meeting.

Pudovkin was as friendly as ever, but when I put to him bluntly two questions, he quivered, but nevertheless gave only the official Party answer.

One was: 'What had happened to Soviet cinematography since the days we had first met? It was a clear decline and fall, not only qualitatively but quantitatively. Instead of a hundred feature films a year, you were now only planning to produce *ten*! How could this be the basis for any artistic development, and what chance was there for our graduates from the GIK to make feature films?'

All he could say was that 'Stalin had given wise instructions that we should only make major films, epic films. Few in number, high in quality.'

I replied, 'That's like saying that a mountain range should only have its Everest or Mont Blanc and no other mountains, not even foothills!'

I even quoted Marx to him – quality emerged from quantity. But Pudovkin insisted that he was carrying out the general line of the Party. In doing so, he helped to condemn to oblivion all the talented students he and Eisenstein had so painstakingly trained at their own film institute! Freilich also writes that[83]

In 1948 the limitation of the production of full length films began ... and reached its critical point in 1951 with only nine feature films in that year, and that was a threatening figure. Independent of the quality of these nine pictures, it was considered that all of them would be masterpieces, for all the nine films were produced by experienced masters and were on the most important themes, and discussed with the best intentions at every stage of their work. Of course, none of these turned out to be masterpieces, because masterpieces cannot be planned. Who in their time ever imagined that the producer of *Strike* would create *Potemkin* in a year's time? And that this production would become, eventually, the best film of all times, and all peoples?

Then S. Drobashenko, writing about the period of limited film production, said:[84]

> this practically meant the path to feature films was closed for youth; on the other hand, the masters of the older generation met other complications. A demand for masterpieces in the apparatus of the Ministry of Cinematography gave birth to an atmosphere of double insurance, the pettiness of tutelage. Very few films were released, but then every picture had to go through numerous specially organized meetings, discussions about the actor's tests, about the artist's decor, about the costumes, and special instructions were given to the director, who *had* to carry them out. And very few films were released without having to be re-made. The films that suffered very much in this way included Dovzhenko's *Michurin*, the second half of *Ivan the Terrible*, *Light Over Russia*, *The Star*, and many others of that period, which eventually didn't appear on the screen at all.

After the war, when the USA was producing 430 feature films a year, India 500, Japan 200, the Soviet Union was making an average of ten a year! Only after Stalin's death did they start soaring to over 100 a year.

Quite apart from its obvious effect in the, as is now admitted, few and poverty-stricken films of the Stalin era, I learned also about the resulting personal tragedies of my Eisenstein co-students, whom I met in one group in Tbilisi in 1960, in the 'liberal' Khrushchev days.

It turned out that most of them could not make one film for at least ten years after graduating as feature film directors from Eisenstein's group, and under the conditions of Soviet rigidity could not switch to another profession! They had to stay in the film studio they had been allotted to, where they continued as assistant directors, dubbers, or short-film makers. In any case, they were kept on the payroll at their minimum monthly salary even if they did nothing creative whatsoever.[85] These were the chosen students of Eisenstein whom he had declared were his 'hope for the future' – who knows what talent was lost? By the time of Stalin's death, they were already too old to create anything outstanding, and the conditions of employment prevented them switching to another profession and the restrictions limiting them to one town where they could live meant they couldn't move elsewhere.

It was a most dramatic exposure, and most of us were in tears at the lost years, the lost hopes, the lost ideals. Several had been in concentration camps where two had been killed as 'enemies of the people.' One Russian-Jewish ex-student told me that during the purges he expected the knock on the door in the early hours from the GPU just because he had been one of my close friends in the GIK! He waited with his things ready in a small bag for nearly a year before his fears subsided. For some reason or other, he was left out, but he was a wreck.

So much for Pudovkin's 'Approval of Stalin's wise decree' on limiting film production.

Then I asked him a second, personal question, concerning Savitsky, who had been our Party secretary in the GIK, a friend and idolater of Pudovkin, who had used him in his films as an actor, and who had disappeared in the 'purges', as I have recounted.

Here I touched him to the quick. He almost broke down, then recovered himself. He was carrying out Party orders with a soldier's meticulousness. He here literally clammed up and only said, 'It was a mistake! A big mistake!!' (*'Eto byla oshibka! Bolshaya oshibka!!'*) That was all; he would say nothing else.

All these 'mistakes' are now documented for posterity in Solzhenitsyn's monumental *Gulag Archipelago* and that other honest Soviet writer, Medvedev, in his *Let History Judge*. All these tragedies are dismissed as 'individual shortcomings and mistakes'!

All this was one colossal mistake. Pudovkin would not and could not say any more.

And on that we parted.

He then proceeded to carry out his duty as a 'soldier' of the Party at the Paris Peace Conference, together with his fellow 'soldier' comrade, Ivor Montagu, who writes in his personal memoir that at these peace conferences, between them 'there was no difference in substance, but a hell of a row on form!'[86]

Pudovkin, to the end of his life, continued to carry out his Party obligations.

The official eulogy on his sixtieth birthday said,

The faithful servant of the Party ended up with two Orders of Lenin, two Orders of the Red Banner of Labor, and three medals as Laureate of the Stalin Prize. He was Chairman of the Moscow District Committee for the Defense of Peace, Member of the Soviet Committee for the Defense of Peace, a delegate to most of the congresses dedicated to that Bolshevik purpose, an active member of VOKS.

Eisenstein, in his *Ivan the Terrible*, pinpointed Vsevolod Pudovkin as the 'Holy Simpleton,' as indeed in perspective he was; and yet, above all he was totally sincere in his simplicity. It was indeed sacred to him. He, of all the directors, actors, and artists I knew, seemed to remain totally dedicated to the very end, without revealing any doubts fundamentally as to the rightness of what the Party had done.

That is now for history to decide. Without him, I should never have gotten to Russia, or received a higher education. For me, he was a man who kept his word, a beautiful human being who changed my life.

It was no other than George Bernard Shaw who also encouraged me to go to Russia and on a postcard he wrote to me in his own hand during those very first few months I was in the Soviet Union. He said 'The Soviet Union is the most interesting country in the world for a young man to finish his education.'

When I proudly showed this GBS postcard to Pudovkin he inscribed in my copy of his book (which I still treasure), 'In memory of our meeting in the most interesting country in the world! W. Pudovkin 12/VIII/1930.'

Dziga Vertov

Now I am going to deal with perhaps one of the most unique film directors in the history of cinematography – Dziga Vertov – although that wasn't his real name. Not only did I know him for several years, but he was the first Russian film director I ever met and one who definitely influenced my whole life along with Pudovkin.

I happened to meet him together with my friend Lionel Britton, writer and linguist, who luckily knew Russian. This was at the International Avant-Garde Film and Photo Conference in Stuttgart, Germany. Here we met film-men like the Hungarian photographer Moholy-Nagy (from the Bauhaus) and Marc Allegret and Man Ray from France, Hans Richter, the German film-maker and Dziga Vertov from Russia. Britton and I were the first to bring to the English-speaking world news about this unique film director.[1] I quote from my diary contemporary notes on his lecture, so as to give a feeling for the time.

> Vertov gave a lecture followed by a showing of his film *Lenin's Truth* (from a series of his cinema journal *Kinopravda* (Cinema Truth). I quote: 'Pudovkin said the material of the film artist is not actors, plays, scenery, but pieces of film. Nevertheless Pudovkin used such in the making of his films, but Vertov uses only records of reality – no actors, no scenario, no scenery, nothing theatrical, only LIFE, and these fragments of life he puts together – mounts – montage – in various rhythmic ways, using all the possibilities of montage, of cutting, e.g.:
>
> 1 of single frames
> 2 of sections of single frames
> 3 of juxtaposition of frames and sections.
>
> His actual method of creation is this: he has several *Kinoki*[2]

or Kino-Eyemen in Moscow and wherever he travels in Russia, using several cameras: Debrie L., Kinamo, and Sept. All the shots taken are sent to his center in Moscow. Here he has a film library, indexed by numbers, and each roll is hung so it may be easily used. Here is where Vertov's real work begins: he takes these pieces of film, and puts them together according to a certain idea or pattern or theme. He told me that he could remember every number of every shot that was in his library. So, for instance, if he was mounting 'stillness' and 'movement' he would know that Nos. 500, 29 and 2711 were 'stillness' and 3, 2109, and 961 were 'movement' and he would take them and then, for example, put them together like this:

No.	Frame	
500	32	
3	8	
29	32	
2109	8	
2711	32	
961	8	etc.

Each film has a theme – expressed in his titles, for instance:

Lenin's truth
The sixth part of the world
The man with a movie camera
The eleventh year (of the Revolution)
Kino-eye: Birth, Marriage, Divorce, Death

Looking at the first, he has made several films with the title *Pravda – Truth*, i.e., *Soviet Truth*, *Lenin's Truth*, etc. This is the fundamental principle of Vertov's work – only Truth, only Life, only Reality.

The impact of Vertov's films was total when Britton translated the Russian subtitles for me. Here is a sequence from *Lenin's Truth* on the death of Lenin, which I noted, with its conflicting, alternating subtitles:

'Lenin is dead!'
'Lenin lives!'
'Lenin is dead!'
'Lenin lives!'
Lenin is lying in his coffin – dead.

'Lenin' and then a subtitle:
'Silent'
Crowds of people pass his tomb in mourning.
'Silent'
Then Lenin again.
Then people moving.
'Silent'
Lenin again.
'Silent'
Then a mighty rushing waterfall.
'Silent'
Then the waterfall superimposed with the figure of Lenin.
Then Lenin alive – speaking to the people.
'Lenin – silent'
'Lenin – still alive!'

The impact at the time was terrific. It is difficult to imagine its power some fifty years later. Or to remember it was a silent film. It seemed to be filled with the roar of rushing waters and the shuffling of millions of feet and unbearable silence.

Vertov's theory and practice has now become common – it was first adopted by Pudovkin and Eisenstein, as Vertov wryly comments; then in Europe and the USA. I brought it to England and used it no doubt in a manner that would be considered very primitive and naive now – in my first films *Hunger Marchers* and *The Royal Borough of Kensington*. They were also among the first films of 'social significance' in English film history and certainly the first left-wing documentaries about the working class. I still have a letter from the English correspondent of the German magazine *Film für Alle*, Charles Steinhouse, who in 1930 wrote *inter alia*, 'By jove, you have caused a controversy in England with your Vertov's montage.'

Vertov was virtually the prime pioneer of Soviet cinematography since the early days of the Revolution, a dedicated and faithful follower of the Communist Party of the Soviet Union, yet almost from the beginning he found himself in conflict with the powers that be, a conflict which we shall look into. His theories and practice were gradually banned under Stalin until he was reduced to impotent silence. Only with destalinization under Khrushchev did this non-person emerge and books about him were published. Now safely dead he is acclaimed as one of the great creators of 'socialist realism,' and his films declared 'masterpieces of Soviet cinema.'[3]

The biography of Dziga Vertov

Vertov wrote many articles in his time and made many manifestos and polemical statements, but no book about him or by him was published in his lifetime (as with Eisenstein). Let us look at those that eventually caught up with another Soviet crippled biography.

Not until 1962 did the first Soviet book about Vertov appear, by N. P. Abramov, along with a collection of Vertov's articles, diaries and notes edited by S. Drobashenko.

It is noteworthy that Abramov's book doesn't print his real name. The author says, 'Dziga Vertov (Dennis Arkadevich Vertov) was born in 1896 in Bialystok in the family of a librarian.' He doesn't say that his real name was Kaufman, that his cameraman Mikhail Kaufman was his brother. Nothing is said about the fact that he was Jewish; he is treated throughout as if he were purely a Russian, yet the author of the book is an Abramov! Nor does he indicate the problems Vertov had to cope with in Russian society because he was a Jew. He studied first at a school of music and then at the Psycho-Neurological Institute and finally at Moscow University.

There were two other students who joined the Psycho-Neurological Institute who later became famous Soviet personalities. One was Mikhail Koltsov who became a top journalist and the other was Abram Matveyevich Room who became a leading film director. When I learned these facts, it seemed somehow strange that these three people, who were all Jewish, should study at this medical Institute yet none of them took up that profession.[4]

Then I came across an extraordinary account by Victor Shklovsky of the life and work of Abram Room that gives a clue to the real reason for these three men choosing that Institute. He says,[5]

> Abram Matveyevich Room was born in Vilna . . . in Vilna lived mainly Jews. Room finished the Gymnasium (High School) there and went to Peter (St Petersburg) to study in the Psycho-Neurological Institute. Its students wore a cap with a badge of two snakes and a cup, but besides that had no other rights at all. Room entered this Institute because he wished to become a

medical man, and the Psycho-Neurological Institute accepted students without any standard percentage limitations.

This means limitation of Jewish students. This limitation of Jews to a certain percentage was standard in Russian institutions. Since the late Stalin days the same kind of percentage (abolished by the Revolution) has been introduced into Soviet institutions. The late Mikhail Romm, also a Russian Jewish film director, said that out of his class of twenty students in the directors' course at the GIK he was allowed one Jewish student. Unable to get accepted in any other Russian educational institution this explains why such outstanding personalities as Room, Vertov and Koltsov graduated from that Institute. Room kept his Jewish name, the others took on Russian names instead of Kaufman and Friedland.

Abram Room became one of the leading Soviet film directors, producing *Bed and Sofa* and *The Ghost That Never Returns*. Luckily he survived all the purges and as I write was celebrating his eightieth birthday. He was one of my teachers at the GIK.

Koltsov went even higher. In 1918 he joined the Communist Party, was adopted on to a special cinema committee to supervise the takeover of Russian cinematography by the Party. It was in that position he invited Vertov to work on Soviet newsreels. But then Koltsov went on to become a leading journalist for the Party and Stalin. He was sent as Stalin's special emissary to Spain during the Civil War and wrote for *Pravda*. But his *Spanish Diary* was not published as a book until 1957, when the foreword simply said, 'Koltsov wrote three books of his *Spanish Diary*. But he never managed to finish his work: the creative and social activity of the writer was cut short in December 1938.'[6]

This is a present-day Soviet euphemism for a bullet in the back of his neck from his own Party's secret police, the NKVD (KGB). The tragic end of yet another Russian Jew faithful to the Party. At the same time many Spanish refugees that Koltsov wrote about with such 'flaming Bolshevik enthusiasm' were being imprisoned in the Gulag.

However he was unerring in choosing Dziga Vertov to work in cinematography, because it seemed that Vertov, even in childhood, had a bent in that direction. In his autobiography he writes,[7]

In my boyhood years I began to be interested in different means of the documentary recording of the world of sound by montage, by means of stenographic writing, gramophone recording etc. In my 'laboratory of sound' I created a special documentary composition. A musical literary work, a montage. I was interested particularly in the recording possibilities of the cinema camera. The possibility of recording on film pieces of actual life, a chronicle of passing and unrepeatable events.

No doubt the literary experiments of the Futurists on what we now call poetry concrete, on the representational aspects of sound in verse, influenced him. Particularly Mayakovsky, who was his friend and whose influence he acknowledged.

Already in 1918 Vertov declared the cinema camera to be an absolutely universal means of recording reality on film, and he strove, in his own words, 'to create a new form of art. The art of life itself. Unacted newsreels, documentary cinematography.' He began to work at Koltsov's invitation in the Soviet Newsreel Studio producing *The Film Weekly*. But of course his material was still simple newsreel chronicles. There was no attempt at montage or film editing in the modern sense at all. But what pushed Vertov to the creation of the documentary film, as such, was the attempt to express new revolutionary content. He wasn't satisfied with what the newsreel gave him. He wanted it to express more truthfully and more passionately what was, to him, the true meaning of the Revolution. And it was then he proposed a series of film journals on a fixed theme, under the general title of *Kinopravda*, which means 'Cinema Truth', or what has now become famous as '*Cinéma-Vérité*'.

So Vertov was the first to edit a newsreel film into a documentary film on a fixed theme. Its form and theme changed with each issue, whereas the newsreel had the same format each week, odd unconnected episodes just strung together by subtitles like the front page of a newspaper. *Pravda* was of course the name of the Communist Party's leading newspaper. Vertov's *Kinopravda* was differentiated from the newsreel by its method of editing, its method of filming, character and means and use of subtitles. Vertov's films took the place of the major newsreels which were mainly foreign, issued by Pathé, Gaumont and L'Eclair. All of course belonged to foreign companies and disappeared when the Bolsheviks took over, as did also the import of film-stock, cinema equipment and finally foreign feature films. Then came the blockade of the Civil War, with the first Soviet newsreels copying the foreign ones, purely of an informational type. The film editor E. Svilova (later Vertov's wife) wrote in 1924, 'I can say without hesitation, nobody paid any attention at all to newsreel films. As far as I know, not a single director had any idea that one could edit newsreels and that newsreels represent life.'[8]

The Moscow Cinema Committee on which Koltsov sat was in charge of these Soviet newsreels and Vertov was in charge of preparing subtitles for them and directing the filming of cameramen on the various fronts of the Civil War. Then he began to travel all over the country, visiting the fronts in the so-called 'agit-train' of the CEC (the Central Executive Commiteee), and very soon he was promoted to be the compiler and editor of the weekly newsreel. They ran from 1 June 1918 to 20 May 1919. Over forty-nine numbers of this journal are preserved in the Moscow Central Cinema and Photo Archives. They contain over 200 subjects, of which half deal with Moscow and the rest are mainly about the front lines and the rear during the Civil War. Camera work of course was not of high quality, mainly long shots, filmed from one static set-up. They had to use old-fashioned and worn-out cameras, there was an acute lack of film-stock and processing was very crude. But the newsreel section did attract good cameramen, two from the feature film studios, A. Litsky and G. Giber, and talented newcomers like Eduard Tisse (later Eisenstein's crack cameraman), A. Lemberg and E. Yermolov. Then other film directors joined Vertov's newsreel unit including Lev Kuleshov, N. Tikhonov, M. Schneider, V. Garbin, G. Boltansky and P. Yermolov. In 1918 Vertov edited his first newsreel documentary called *The First Anniversary of the Revolution*. Then in 1920 came *The Battle of Tsaritsyn* (later *Stalingrad* and *Volgograd*). In 1921 *The Agit-Train of CEC* was dedicated to the work of the agit-train in the Civil War and then there was *The History of the Civil War*, which was in thirty parts and was the first serious attempt to deal extensively with such a subject in cinema.

Vertov's own pioneering ideas and practice had the support of no other than Vladimir Ilyich Lenin, who declared, 'The production of new films permeated with Communist ideas reflecting Soviet reality should begin with the newsreel . . . they should be of the publicist type along the lines carried out by our best Soviet newspapers.'[9]

In other words, it was the form then known in the theaters as 'the living newspaper', now Lenin proposed that it should be 'the film of the living newspaper'.

Eisenstein too gives credit to the fact that[10]

> In the early twenties the newsreel documentary films were the leaders in our cinema art. Many feature films of artistic cinema that were then being born undoubtedly bore the imprint of the creations of documentary cinematography, the sharpness of perception and facts, and the sharpness of sight and quick-wittedness in assembling what was visible. The rounding-off of life and actuality and still much more was done by the documentary film to the style of Soviet cinematography.

But though Lenin indicated what he wanted, it was not then an accepted principle and Vertov had to fight every inch of the way to create a new form of documentary film and not just the everyday newsreel. He took part in the polemics of the day, issued many manifestos – as did others on the Left Front of art – and they were inevitably assertive, aggressive and sweeping. Here is an extract:[11]

> I am the Cinema I. I am the mechanical I. I am the machine showing the world as it is, which only I am able to see. From today, forever, I free myself from human immovability. I am in continuous movement. I approach and retreat from things, I crawl under them. I climb on them. I move alongside of the galloping heads of horses. I cut at full speed into the crowd. I run in front of attacking soldiers. I throw myself on my back. I pace myself together with the aeroplane. I fall and I fly, together with falling and flying bodies.

Now that of course is trite today, but in 1923 it was really revolutionary.

Like Eisenstein in those days Vertov attacked 'the theatrical film' in which everything was created and shot inside a studio. He declared, 'Today the cinema does not need psychological or detective dramas. Today it does not need theatrical productions and foreign feature films.'[12]

Indeed in those days foreign films dominated the Russian screens. It didn't completely exclude them until the Stalin era, except for a very few chosen for their slant, negative aspects of western democracies, accordingly re-edited with ideologically 'correct' subtitles.

Vertov countered with his theory of 'life caught unawares.' His central idea was that of shooting 'life as it is,' catching it 'unawares,' filming the unprepared, unorganized, elemental events of everyday life, filmed so that the cameraman and his camera are not noticed by those being filmed. In this way he believed he would capture real life, as compared to life created artificially in a film studio.

Thus was born the first genuine Soviet documentary film, *Kino-Eye* (1924), in which Vertov tried to show the birth of all that was new in the Soviet Union after the Revolution and its struggle with the old. In order to 'catch life unawares' M. Kaufman, the cameraman, went everywhere, into the market-place, doss-houses, even a psychiatric hospital. It still had no compositional unity, but was a collection of shots on certain themes, which Eisenstein would have called 'a montage of attractions.' Leaving aside the editing potential of *Kino-Eye*, Vertov manipulated the camera in every conceivable way, with optical tricks, downward and backward motion, speeded-up motion, double exposures etc. (Remember in those days of silent film all these tricks had to be done in the camera. There was no optical printer.) Meanwhile he was still battling with manifestos against 'decadent bourgeois forms of art':[13]

> Down with the actor! Down with make-up! Down with film scripts! etc. . . . Cinema drama is the opium of the people. Cinema drama and religion is a deadly weapon in the hands of the Capitalists. Down with the bourgeois fairy-tale scenario. Long live life as it is!

In his theoretical works Vertov clearly laid down his principles of 'montage,' which was not just film editing, the cutting and joining of separately filmed scenes or shots. He was aware, like Eisenstein and Pudovkin, that montage was the composition of the whole film 'beginning with the first observation and ending with the finished film.' He wrote:[14]

> The Kino-Eyeman gives to montage a completely new significance and understanding: montage as *the organization of the visible world*. The Kino-Eyeman differentiates:
>
> 1 *Montage during the time of observation*: the orientation of the unarmed eye in any place, at any time.
> 2 *Montage after observation*: an intellectual organization of the visible according to these or those characteristic indications (signs).

3 *Montage at the time of filming*: orientation of the armed eye of the movie camera in the place investigated in Point 1. Adaptation to certain changing conditions of filming.

4 *Montage after shooting*: The preliminary organization of what has been filmed according to the basic indications. The indication of insufficient montage pieces.

5 *Judgment by the eye (searching for montage pieces)*: instantaneous orientation in any visible circumstances for catching the necessary linking shots. Exceptional attentiveness. Military rules for judgment by the eye: speed, attack.

6 *Definitive montage*: alongside major themes, the expression of tiny hidden themes. The re-organization of all the material into the best sequences. Highlighting the pivot of the film material. The linking up of analogous moments and, finally, the numbered calculation of the montage groups.

In filming in conditions that do not allow preliminary observation – say, in trailing (shadowing) with a movie camera, in filming unawares – the first two points drop out, bringing forward the third and fifth points.

In filming short sequences and in hurried shooting, the linking up of several points is permissible.

In all other cases whether filming one or several themes, all the points are to be carried out. Montage does not cease, beginning with the first observation and ending with the finished film.

The Cinema of Fact

Vertov propagated what he called 'the cinema of fact,' 'fact caught unawares.' He said,[15]

The studio facts (put forward as a proposal) after five years of stubborn experimental work, the method of the Kino-Eye has now completely conquered the sphere of the unacted film. (See 'First Reconnaissance of Kino-Eye', 'Lenin – Kino Pravda', 'Forward March, Soviets!', and 'The Sixth Part of the World'.) Now – as has been shown by the experience of the first years – the so-called artistic film (play film, film with actors), has taken over completely only one *external aspect* of the Kino-Eye which was sufficient to produce a great deal of noise (*Strike* and *Battleship Potemkin*)[16] in that area of cinema.

Vertov went on to attack the acted fictional film, as was his wont, and was happy that a leading critic, A. Fevralski, had supported him in *Pravda*, the Party newspaper (15 July 1926), saying that there should be *one center* for all non-acted films and for the workers of *Kino-Eye* and their productions.

Of course, in retrospect, they were only putting themselves more completely under the total control of the Communist Party and Stalin, who wanted everything in controllable units. Eventually various groups of differing styles in all the arts were forced together into one centralized organization and finally forced to work along one theoretical style, socialist realism.

But, alas, who knew it then?

Meanwhile Vertov goes on to declare,[17]

Our point of view: that alongside the United Film Studios of Grimaces [sic] (which will unite every kind of theatrical film production, from Sabinsky to Eisenstein) a Cinema Studio of Fact must be set up, combining all forms of Kino-Eye productions, from current newsreel releases to scientific films, from thematic Kino Pravdas to film marathons of revolutionary pathos.

Not FEKS[18] and not the Studio of Attractions of Eisenstein.[19] Not the Studio of Kissing and Cooing. Even film directors of this type have not yet died out. And certainly not the Studio of Death.[20] But simply the Studio of Facts.

The filming of facts. The sorting of facts. The distribution of facts. The agitation of facts. The propaganda of facts. The fists of facts.[21] The lightning of facts. The thunder of facts. The hurricane of facts. And separate tiny little facts.

Against cinema conjuring tricks. Against cinema mystification. For the genuine cinematification[22] of the workers and peasants of the USSR!

This of course was the program of the Futurists at the time, and Vertov was a member of this group alongside Sergei Tretyakov and Vladimir Mayakovsky. Tretyakov propagated 'the literature of facts' and Mayakovsky 'the poetry of facts.' They both produced works based on documentary facts. Here is an appropriate extract from Mayakovsky's epic poem of facts of the October Revolution, called 'Very Good':

Time
    is an unusually lengthy
                thing –
'Once upon a time' –
            but folk-poems passed by.
Neither legends,
        nor epics,
            nor epopees sing.
Stanzas now
      like telegrams fly!
Bend down
      and drink
           through lips parched and cracked
from the river
      known as – 'Fact'.
Telegraph wires
        those times strum and stir,
Heart
    and truth
        into one they combine.
In our fighters
      or in our land
           they were,
Or else
    in this heart
        of mine.

Not only facts about the Soviet Union and the Revolution but Mayakovsky's very personal life were all interwoven into his poetry. Facts were raised to the highest degree of literature, as they were by Vertov in cinema. But Vertov attacked the alleged documentary feature films, like Eisenstein's *Strike* and *Battleship Potemkin*, for filming only the external aspects of the fact and not the real facts. This is a point I am making both in this book and in my compilation *Battleship Potemkin*,[23] where such acted feature fictional films were shown as having been presented as if they were factual.

Indeed, in the early 1920s Lenin was often quoted as saying 'A true analysis of phenomena must be obtained by the comparing of a fact not with an idea but with another fact.'

But an iron contradiction now arises with the development of the Party's socialist realism and the increasing use of the modern form of the Potemkin Village syndrome. For now what is a fact or what is an idea has to be determined by the Communist Party and none other. So truth now is not obtained by comparing a fact with a fact but a pseudo-comparison of a fact with an idea. That is, the phenomenon as it is and phenomenon as it will be, or as the Party thinks it should be – that is so-called socialist realism. This means that the cinema or the prose or the poetry of *fact* is not what the Party wants. It doesn't want the fact as decided upon by artists or historians, but as decided upon by the Party. This could be a part-fact or a non-fact, as is proven by the whole behavior of the Party in dealing with the history and biographies of those it condemned as 'enemies of the people,' incarcerating them in the Gulag or executing them. Thereafter the Party deliberately wiped out all vestiges of their factual existence. They became non-persons, non-facts. This has all been thoroughly documented by Solzhenitsyn and others, but now it can be seen that this policy of deliberate falsification in all the arts inevitably meant the suppression of true documentary factual cinema and of its most staunch advocate Dziga Vertov. Only after the death of Stalin, in the Khrushchev era, was there a resurgence of truthfulness in Soviet cinema.

But how far, in fact, were any of these Soviet cinema artists *factual* in their films? We will find 'staged' facts in all their documentary films. Even Vertov, that staunch protagonist of reality 'caught unawares,' staged events in his films. Just a minor example – in one of his Kino Pravda (cinema truth) journals dealing with public reactions to a trial of counter-revolutionaries, one of the passengers in a tramcar in Moscow is shown jumping off the tram to buy the latest newspaper to follow the course of the trial. We found that the 'ordinary citizen' was played by no other than Vertov himself.

I can give my own evidence regarding the documentary truth of a film I helped to make with Joris Ivens, that Dziga Vertov of Holland. We were shooting a documentary about youth in industry in the first Five-Year Plan, in Magnitogorsk, where the giant iron and steel mills were being erected. We discovered that the bulk of the heavy labour was done by ex-kulak prisoners from the Magnito-gorsk Gulag, that the first blast furnace was built by American

engineers, teaching the Russians, the second by Americans and
Russians and the third by the Russians under American supervision.
In the final film nothing was shown of any of these factual events.
(The film was *A Song of Heroes*, directed and edited by Joris Ivens,
assisted by Herbert Marshall, Mezhrabpom Studio Productions,
1932.)

A famous case is the censoring by Stalin of Eisenstein's film *Ten
Days That Shook the World*, cutting out all the major protagonists
of the Revolution except Stalin, Kaganovich, Ordjonikidze. This
happened again in the case of Vertov's last great film and swansong
The Three Songs of Lenin, unlike Eisenstein's, a factual documentary.
Here too all close-ups and mid-shots of Trotsky, Zinoviev,
Kamenev, Radek and all the others murdered by the Party were
cut out. In the first Soviet book about this film (in the series,
Masterpieces of Soviet Cinema, Moscow, Izd. Isk. 1972) there are
many stills from the funeral of Lenin but around his bier we only see
Stalin, Kalinin, Voroshilov, etc., but not the key historic personages.

This extraordinary and wholesale absence of facts permeates the
total Soviet presentation of history and of course the 'factual documentaries' of Dziga Vertov.

Forward March, Soviet!

Vertov now came to creating his first full-length documentary film.
Though he had previously attacked the writing of a film scenario
as a hangover of the old discarded ways of working, in *Forward
March, Soviet!* he wrote what amounted to the first documentary film
scenario. His initial plan was to concentrate on Moscow, showing
the city in three phases of development:

1 Yesterday: Moscow Soviet (i.e. the Moscow City Council)
in the years of ruin.
2 Today: Moscow Soviet today – general evolution of
work in all spheres.
3 Tomorrow: Moscow Soviet in the future – general
achievements.

He then planned to shoot the whole film starting with dawn,
contemporary Moscow, then flashing back to Moscow of the past,
then forward again to reconstructed Moscow at evening and night,
thus putting past, present and future in one general outline of

twenty-four hours in the life of a city. This was two years before Walter Ruttman created his famous *Berlin – Symphony of a Great City* on the same morn to midnight principle, but only with contemporary Berlin. Vertov's idea was not only pioneering but more original.

Then Vertov finally decided to use the same pattern to make a film of the whole Soviet Union, calling it *One Sixth of the World*.

Vertov's originality is evident throughout the film. In one scene, dozens of Mosoviet buses come to the central square to greet Moscow. Each bus speaks through a loudspeaker, and the other buses reply with their horns. The buses then turn to the spectators and speak: 'Greetings . . . in the name of the Soviet . . . we fight . . . on the economic front!' This was three years before Dovzhenko's horses spoke in the famous scene from his silent film *Arsenal* (see p. 118).

After the sequence of the massed buses comes the subtitle, 'The square is silent . . . only the heart-beats of the machines. . . .' And the beating hearts of the machines are edited into a musical rhythm, a symphony of machines. And one remembers the parallel episode in *Battleship Potemkin* with the beating heart of the battleship and the pulsating rhythm of its engines.

Though the film *Forward March, Soviet!* was enthusiastically received by the Soviet press, the Moscow Soviet who had commissioned it rejected the film and the Soviet film distributors refused to exhibit it. It seems that the reason was Vertov's making two films, one continuing from the other, from Moscow as the subject of *Forward March, Soviet!* to the whole Soviet Union in *One Sixth of the World*. The first was created by the brilliant editing of newsreel and film archive material, whilst the second was almost wholly filmed by Vertov's Kino-Eyemen according to his scripted instructions, and in the end *One Sixth* was more emotional, more lyrical. One critic writes of this film, 'Separate episodes of the film were edited in consecutive alternating emotionally poetic subtitles and shots, giving the impression of poetic speech, close to the poetry of Mayakovsky.'[24] Actually *One Sixth* was originally supposed to have been an advertising film about Soviet production for export and sale abroad, and for showing at international trade fairs, for instance. It was to show the trade and economy of the whole vast territory of the USSR. But again Vertov made it a poem on his fatherland, with imagery structured like a poem of Mayakovsky or Walt Whitman, his favourite poets.

Even leading critics like Victor Shklovsky did not understand what Vertov was doing. They had expected a typical documentary newsreel-type film and instead found a poem filled with metaphors. Shklovsky wrote of the film, 'A man disappearing on wide skis into the snowy distance, becomes no longer a man, but a symbol of time going by. Things lose their substance and begin to appear as productions of the Symbolists.'[25] Vertov, the protagonist of facts, was also a poet who transformed facts into metaphors and symbols – poetry. And that too was dangerous, for eventually the whole poetic school of cinema was damned by the Party, as is evidenced throughout this book.

The Vertov triptych

It is quite significant that the four great film directors I am dealing with each created triptychs, which applies not only to the fact that there were three pictures in their triptych, but also in their religious connotation – though now the triptych is not by a devout Van Eyck for the Roman Catholic Church, nor by a devout Rublev for the Russian Orthodox Church, but by a devout Vertov, Pudovkin, Eisenstein or Dovzhenko for his Communist Party 'Church.' And each of their pictures was intended to be a paean of praise to the new order, to the 'new man,' to the new saviour – the Communist Party.

Each of these triptychs can be seen to have the imprint of their creator. Eisenstein's characters are not full-blooded realistic characters, but abstract and symbolic. He portrays the mass rather than the individual. Pudovkin, on the other hand, portrayed characters near to life and saw the individual reflecting the mass. Dovzhenko saw the symbolic in the individual. Vertov, at first, saw the documentary of the particular in facts, whether man or machine or things, which eventually he raised to the level of symbols. He, above all, was the conscious wielder of the movie camera as a weapon, a tool – indeed, the most mobile and universal tool, and he even made a film in honour of that instrument, *The Man with the Movie Camera*.

This is the first film of the triptych – virtually the deification of the man with the movie camera – the Kino-Eyeman – as the wielder of this incredible new weapon of art, which was about to be used to build the new society and spread its gospel round the world.

The second picture in the triptych was *Enthusiasm* or *A Symphony of the Don Basin*, which was the deification of industry and the industrial worker.

The third, *The Three Songs of Lenin*, was of course the deification of Lenin, contributing to the cult of the personality of Lenin as a great symbol presented to the whole world as its new savior.

Let us examine these three pictures composing the triptych.

In *The Man with a Movie Camera*, Vertov wanted to show the camera recording the tiniest details of domestic and everyday activity. The camera should be present during the birth of a human being and follow him to the grave. It should film man and woman at the moment of their registration for marriage in the civil registration marriage bureau and be alongside them when they divorce. The camera should accompany the bride and bridegroom from the bureau to the church. It should look into the hairdressers and the factory, float in the air over the streets and huge factories and blast furnaces. Then suddenly stop at the policeman's signal as he regulates street traffic. In all directions go automobiles, trams and carts.[26]

It is interesting to note, in the original idea Vertov described in 1925, that he talks about the couple going from civil registration to church, whereas nowadays they are expected, as a duty, to go to the memorial to the Unknown Soldier.

The film actually begins in a cinema theatre with the public entering and taking their places. The projectionist loads the projector, switches on and the screen lights up with the title PART ONE. The screen in the cinema merges with the screen on which the film is being shown. It is the morning of a great city. Throughout the film runs the theme of The Man with a Movie Camera. He is 'played' by Vertov's brother, Mikhail Kaufman. He is shown 'catching life unawares', on a moving crane, in a huge factory workshop, on a high factory chimney stack. He films beneath a train, bathes in the sea and comes out of a bar. At the same time the theme of the Kino-Eyeman is linked with the risks he runs, including lying down under or near passing vehicles. Beginning with the theme of morning, it has parallel shots of a woman sleeping and flowers. Then the woman awakening is cut together with shots of lilacs blossoming.

She washes herself and the streets are washed with falling showers. The woman wipes her face and her eyelids open and close and parallel window blinds open and close.

Vertov follows through the idea which was the basic idea of his theory, that the camera lens is like a human eye. So to illustrate this, a sprig of lilac is shown out of focus as the woman sees it when she wipes her eyes wet with water. In the next shot we see a moving lens on the camera and the sprig of lilac brought into sharp focus.

There is no plot as such, rather a series of episodes and cross-cutting in order to show the versatility of this key instrument of modern art.

The cameraman analyses technical methods and tricks that can be used. First, of course, there is the material he chooses to film and from what set-up or angle. Second is the cameraman himself, who goes through the whole film. The third is the editing, the montage, which is shown by the camera, giving examples of how, by editing, the editor can change, deform and transform the images of life that are being shown. Finally comes the cinema theater itself, where the spectators in that very cinema can see themselves as the 'heroes of the film,' on the very screen they are looking at!

Vertov uses every conceivable kind of manipulation of images of the external world. Streets are shown in a frozen frame and suddenly come to life teeming with people and traffic. Objects are shown in a way that they lose their normal outline and proportions. The Bolshoi Theater is suddenly split in two parts, which collapse into each other, as if blown up by a bomb. Pieces of film are edited so they become shorter and shorter until they are single frames alternating. Apparently unrelated shots are edited only according to compositional or rhythmic similarities. For example, the hands of a woman doing physical exercises are rhymed with a machine doing a similar movement. A beautician is covering the face of a woman with cream, the film cuts to another woman greasing a machine. Vertov sometimes divides the screen into two, three, four or more parts.

The experience of all this experimental work Vertov used to an extraordinarily telling degree in his next two great films, *The Three Songs of Lenin* and *Enthusiasm* or *A Symphony of the Don Basin*, proving that *The Man with a Movie Camera* was a necessary part of his evolution as an artist. Yet Abramov, writing in the post-Stalin Khrushchev period, in 1962, still applies to Vertov and *The Man with a Movie Camera* the Zhdanov-Stalinist accusations of 'formalism.' He quotes a criticism written at the beginning of the Stalinist purges, in 1936, as if it were still valid. He writes,[27]

> Affedorov-Davydov gives an interesting analysis of the methods in the film *The Man with a Movie Camera*: 'It was not accidental that this very film received the greatest recognition abroad by the aesthetes of the European avant-garde cinema. In it they welcomed Vertov's complete retreat from a realistic reflection of reality to an empty and fruitless play with form and the philosophy of rejection of an objective perception of the world. It is interesting that Dziga Vertov, even after he had created that wonderful realistic film *The Three Songs of Lenin*, which for a long time determined the evolution of documentary cinema, still did not understand the whole reactionary, anti-realistic essence of *The Man with a Movie Camera*.'

Here is what Vertov himself wrote at the same time, in reply to such critics, but it was not published until 1958:[28]

> In our Michurinsky garden we cultivated different fruits, different films. Why then shouldn't we have made a film about the language of cinema?
> The first film without words, not demanding a translation into any other language, an international film? . . . We considered that we were obliged not only to make films for wide distribution, but from time to time, films that create films. . . . If in *The Man with a Movie Camera*, content is supplanted by the means, that is obviously because one of the tasks of the film was to acquaint the public with the means, not to hide them as is usual in other films. If one of the aims of the film was familiarizing the grammar of cinema, it would have been strange if this grammar had been hidden. . . . Was that experience necessary? It was absolutely necessary for those times. In essence it was a daring, bold attempt to master all the approaches to filming actuality.
> . . .

And now comes the judgment of our allegedly post-Stalinist author, Abramov:[29]

Today one can with complete objectivity [sic] say that this film, just like other pseudo-innovative films of foreign 'cinema-avant-gardists', did not have the slightest influence on the development of the expressive means of the cinema. All these films remain barren, having only the character of a quickly passing and scandalous sensation, not able in any way to enrich the living and developing art. On the other hand *the wonderful experimental work* [My italics. HM.] of Dziga Vertov, subordinated above all to the expression of the Communist ideology, bore wonderful fruits long outliving their creator. One can only regret that Dziga Vertov is famous abroad more as the author of the formalistic films *Kino-Eye* and *The Man with the Movie Camera* than as the creator of genuine innovative films, *One Sixth of the World*, *Enthusiasm* and *The Three Songs of Lenin*.

However, in another place, in the same book, Abramov inadvertently admits that

The films of Dziga Vertov reflected a complex and contradictory process of his creative evolution, finding its extremest expression in the formalistic style of *The Man with the Movie Camera*, and the realistic talented film, *Enthusiasm*, which unfortunately was underrated by his contemporaries.

And here, of course, he doesn't mean Vertov's contemporaries abroad, they valued these films, as we show. No, they were 'underrated' by his Soviet contemporaries, following the instructions of the Communist Party of the Soviet Union headed by Zhdanov and Stalin, and their shadows still persist.

Enthusiasm or *A Symphony of the Don Basin*

The last film which Vertov produced in the Ukraine studios was *Enthusiasm*, its theme the industrial transformation of the Ukraine into a socialist state, concentrating on the iron and steel foundries and the coal mines in the Don Basin. This work coincided with the beginning of the sound film period, and so Vertov tried now to put into practice his theories about sound and the Radio-Eye. He didn't make just another technical recording of synchronized sound alongside the silent image. He saw sound as a new artistic dimension. Already, of course, Vertov had suggested sound by visual means in his silent films, in particular 'the hearts of the machines are beating' section of *Forward March, Soviet!* and in the counterpoint of titles and images in the 'Kinopravda' of *The Three Songs of Lenin*, and in *One Sixth of the World*, where the visual sequence was read as a continuation of the title phrases. For of course, title phrases and subtitles were obvious substitutes for spoken speech. Indeed, in the silent days, many people could be heard reading the titles aloud as they watched the film.

No doubt Eisenstein and Dovzhenko were influenced by these experiments of Vertov in the images of 'sounding' harps and 'tinkling' chandeliers in *October* and the falling concertina in *Arsenal*.

Vertov, having always been in conflict with the fictional, theatrical school of the silent film, clashed with it again when he came to sound film. One of his critics at the time, Ippolit Sokolov, wrote in an article called 'On the Possibilities of Sound Cinema':[30]

> Agitational and scientific films will be produced not in the lap
> of nature, not in the noise of the streets, but within the
> soundproof walls of the film studio, where no outside sound can
> penetrate. The sound movie camera will least of all film 'life
> caught unawares'. The unorganized and accidental sounds of
> our streets and buildings would become a genuine cacophony,
> a literally caterwauling concert.

Vertov passionately opposed this theory. For him the result of any falsifying of the genuine sounds of the world would have been caterwauling![31]

> The beginning of the work on *Enthusiasm* was preceded by the
> caterwauling theory of Ippolit Sokolov negating the very
> possibility of filming documentary sounds by ourselves or by
> foreign producers. It would have negated our work on
> *Enthusiasm*, which was a negation of this negation!

Indeed the film *Enthusiasm* seemed to explode from the screen, for suddenly into the dying bourgeois world blares a strident march of the Komsomol (Young Communist League). The world of religion explodes. Crowns and crosses fly into the air. The red flag and the red star fly on to the tops of church cupolas (by reverse filming). A church is transformed into a club for young factory workers. Icons are split in two (by double exposure). Overthrown belfries and clouds swirl by with such speed that they give the impression

of time itself surging ahead. Youth club sequences, as areas of new
life, are accompanied by the militant march. (Vertov wrote a special
musical scenario for the composer N. Timofeyev, showing exactly
the continuity of the shots and their rhythmic organization.) In the
clubs we see radio amateurs, young Pioneer girls sculpting a bust
of Lenin and Young Communists reading and studying.

The next major movement, 'Alarm,' is built on two contrasting
themes: first, 'to overtake and surpass capitalist countries,' and
second, 'the Don Basin has a breakdown!' The breakdown is caused
by lack of coal for the blast furnaces. (The Don Basin is the major
coal-producing area in the Ukraine.) At a factory meeting they
decided to send a special group of Young Communists to help the
Don Basin region dig more coal. They end the meeting singing the
Internationale, which overlaps with the delegation meeting the first
of the volunteers. Commenting, Abramov says something very
interesting:[32]

> In general one must say that the workers are sharply etched and
> portrayed superbly in this film. One must say that the human
> being in this film is presented with rare expressiveness, with a
> feeling of pride in his labor. When one sees this film now, it
> seems completely incomprehensible why Vertov's
> contemporaries missed what was the most important thing in
> it, the love for the worker and his talented presentation of him,
> noticing only the world of the machine and 'industrial noises'.

Of course the Soviet critic can't dot the 'i's and cross the 't's, for
it was the Communist Party to whom this was 'incomprehensible'!

The film ends with shots of a celebration and a demonstration
edited parallel with work in progress in the huge metallurgical
plant. Here Vertov created a daring counterpoint of sound. Shots
of those working in the factories and blast furnaces are accompanied
by the sound of the demonstration with its choral singing, its slogans
and shouts of welcome, while the shots of the streets, filled with
demonstrators, have a sound track of the industrial noises.

Writing in the days of the thaw, in 1957, Abramov attempts to
answer this condemnation of Vertov and his films:[33]

> Why did this film – that was so notable for its fruitful innovation,
> its deep patriotism and its daring artistic form and produced
> from the point of view of socialist realism [sic] – deserve

condemnation, particularly for the cacophony of sound coming from the screen?

Abramov contrasts this with its reception abroad. He quotes a letter from Vertov (in the archives of Svilova Vertov, his wife) from London in 1931 relating how, for the first time after many years, he 'really heard the phonogram of his *A Symphony of the Don Basin* on a good projection apparatus, which in the Soviet Union and even abroad did not exist in 1930.' (Here Abramov is exaggerating, because just before he had said how the Party refused to import foreign apparatus which already existed.) Dovzhenko also writes how he saw his films as they really were for the first time on western cinema screens.

It was on 17 November 1931 in a private viewing theater that Charlie Chaplin was shown the film *Enthusiasm*. I heard about it first hand from my friend Lionel Britton who was present and actually wrote this letter from Chaplin to Vertov, which the former signed:[34]

Never had I known that these mechanical sounds could be arranged to seem so beautiful. I regard it as one of the most exuberating symphonies I have ever heard. Mr Dziga Vertov is a musician. The professors should learn from him not quarrel with him. Congratulations. Charles Chaplin, London. 17/11/1931. United Artists Private Theatre, Wardour St. London W.1.

How was Chaplin to know that the 'professors' were simply carrying out Communist Party orders? Once again genuine appreciation of a great Soviet artist comes from abroad.

Abramov ends his chapter on *Enthusiasm* by saying,[35]

The criticism of this film, in so many ways unjust, deeply grieved Vertov. In his archives are notes where he writes with bitterness about the fate of this production.

'Was it necessary to speak about its shortcomings?'

'Of course it was necessary! But how was it necessary to speak? From my point of view one should have spoken of the shortcomings of a film that suffered in battle, tattered, battered, covered in wounds. Nevertheless a film that did not retreat before what seemed to be unsurpassable obstacles.'

Following the 'failure' of the film Vertov was forced to leave the

Ukrainian Film Studios, VUFKU, and some time later came to the Mezhrabpom Film Studios in Moscow, where he began his next film, *The Three Songs of Lenin.*

Historically one can note here that once again a genius was hounded from the Ukrainian film studios, just like the native Ukrainian, Dovzhenko, and in the Brezhnev period that other genius, the 'honorary Ukrainian' Sergo Paradjanov.[36]

The Three Songs of Lenin

It is ironic that in this Lenin film there was not a single thing that the Communist Party could object to. It was praised by the entire Soviet and foreign press, yet, nevertheless, it was the last film Dziga Vertov was able to make. In effect it is part of the Communist Party phenomenon, 'the cult of the personality,' for here Lenin is not only the leader of the Russian Revolution but the savior of the enslaved of the world and leader of the world revolution.

The three songs divide the film into three movements (the triptych again!) which are interrelated in subject and in the rhythmical organization of the filmed 'documents.' The opening line of the first song heard is, 'In a Black Prison was my Face,' referring to the yashmak or black veil which Muslim women had to wear; for this section deals with Soviet women of the East still under strict Muslim rules, even in the early years of the Revolution. The first song is accompanied by visual memories of the house in Gorkakh where Lenin died, the camera tracking past the window of his room and coming to rest gently on the famous bench on which he sat during his last days in the garden.

Inevitably there are certain exaggerations: the film starts off with this song as a 'document' about 'the folk songs of Lenin, which are sung the whole world over. For in the countries of Europe and America, in Africa and beyond the Arctic Circle, they sing songs of Lenin, about the friend and rescuer of the enslaved human being.'

The second song, 'We Loved Him,' tells about the funeral of Lenin, of the national sorrow, of the path the country took under the leadership of Lenin.

The third song, 'In the Great Brick City,' is dedicated to fulfilling Lenin's testament – building socialism, with Lenin living on in the work and feats of the Soviet people.

One brilliant image was the use of Lenin's simple white garden bench, shown at all seasons of the year, and when Lenin died, in the midst of that cruel winter, the seat is covered with snow. (See plate 3.)

Vertov acknowledges that the influence of Mayakovsky's poetry was most powerful in this film. A leading Soviet composer, Shura A. Shaporin, was specially commissioned by Vertov to write the music for the film, utilizing not only the various folksongs that he had collected from throughout the Soviet Union, but also natural sounds and noises of demonstrations, public speakers and the ordinary folk. A brilliant example of this occurs during the two minutes' silence for Lenin, when, following the artillery salute, the bells of the Spassky clock of the Kremlin and the howling of factory hooters merge with the music of Shaporin. Then rifles fire the final funeral salute and everything freezes: even an aeroplane in the sky suddenly freezes, a train stops, the people in Red Square are dead still, a sad woman stops in the middle of a snowy field, the machines and lathes in factories, the cranes stop still, different peoples, different nationalities all stay still, in the desert, the cities, the villages, and then the red flag on the house where he died slowly dissolves into the snow-covered empty bench in his garden.

Then it comes to the final song about overcoming the death of Lenin, with a counterpoint showing how, despite everything, the Soviet people are carrying out Lenin's will. Despite the backwardness and the things that still have to be done, there is a title: 'Through disorder . . . but they still go on. Through hunger . . . but they still go on. Through fire and flame . . . they still go on . . . led by Vladimir Ilyich Lenin.'[37]

But just see what the biographer-critic of the 1960s now concludes:[38]

The Three Songs of Lenin was the peak of Vertov's creative work. All the finest aspects of his directorial talents and skill were expressed in this most powerful and valuable representation. *It became the outstanding production of socialist realism in the documentary film* (my italics. HM.) and a classic of Soviet Cinema art.

Once attacked bitterly by the Party as 'formalism' and then ignored, Vertov's work is now 'socialist realism' and a 'Soviet classic'!

The whole world praised this film – all the leading newspapers of England, Italy, France, Spain, and the USA, and outstanding foreigners including Louis Aragon", William Bullitt the American Ambassador, Henri Barbusse, Harold Lloyd, André Malraux, Romain Rolland, Cecil B. de Mille and H. G. Wells.

I can sum up by quoting what H. G. Wells said:

> I had the happiness to see *The Three Songs of Lenin*. . . . It is one of the greatest and most beautiful films I have ever seen in my life. I congratulate Dziga Vertov and all those who worked on that film.

But after that masterpiece the Communist Party of the Soviet Union never let Dziga Vertov make another film – although he lived another twenty years.

In hindsight now one can see that Stalin and his sycophants would not have been pleased by the concentration of the cult of the personality on Lenin and not Stalin. This was made evident three years later when a number of shots linking Stalin with Lenin were inserted and an additional 700 feet at the end showing how Stalin was continuing Lenin's work. Stalin didn't forget that kind of omission.

Vertov as a pioneer of cinematography

In the preceding pages I have tried to give the reader some idea of the kind of films Vertov made, knowing that probably most or all of them have never been seen. To conclude my comments on his skill and artistry I give here some examples of his pioneering originality.

1 The use of subtitles in a Mayakovsky style, with staccato rhythmic effect, as in *Lenin's Truth* (see page 72). Mayakovsky printed his lines in meaningful accentuated segments, to show how the poems should be read aloud. This method Vertov adopted by using titles as shots, using different type-faces and sizes, which later was taken over by Eisenstein and Pudovkin with such effect in their classic silent films.[39]

2 Vertov actually included in one of his *Kino-Pravda* issues the first film shot by Eisenstein – 'Glumov's diary', used in his staging of Ostrovsky's *Even a Wise Man Stumbles* at his Prolet-Cult Theatre. And this, of course, was the 'acted fictional theatrical' material that Vertov was always attacking – but here it was presented as a piece of documentary everyday reality!

3 Vertov was the first Soviet documentary film-maker to include

synchronized speech, in his film *The Three Songs of Lenin*: unrehearsed utterances of a woman cement-worker and a woman collective farmer about their work.

4 Vertov was the first to use an animated diagram in a documentary film – to reveal the path of the illness of Lenin. On the screen is a calendar, then a clock, then changing cyphers, and a changing graph to show the temperature and pulse of the dying Lenin. Suddenly there is a black screen. On the blackness appears a title: 'Refractory sclerosis, the result of unbearable mental and physical work, brought on the catastrophe of 24th January 1924' – the day of Lenin's death.

5 Though technically a black and white film, Vertov used colour as a significant component in *The Three Songs of Lenin*. He had the film tinted blue, orange, yellow, red, and black and white and used the tint according to the mood of the editing. Yellow: the victorious years of the Revolution, the first steps at reconstruction. Blue: the first victories of the Civil War, the first achievements in factories, in towns and villages. Red: Lenin, and the victory of Lenin's ideas. Yellow again: famine on the Volga, destruction, fight against interventionists and then the black-white gamma: the sickness and death of Lenin and the national grief. The finale is Red: a symbol of Lenin in practice.

6 In the documentary film Vertov was the first to use every conceivable possible use of the movie camera, splitting the screen, superimposing many shots and titles, particularly in *The Man with a Movie Camera*. And this film too was a pioneering event; it was the first in the world about the very nature of cinematography, the movie-cameraman and his instrument, the film editor and his montage, and the overall directorial creativity.

7 Vertov also saw ahead to the invention of television and its universal appeal.

Here is a note I made in 1929 when we first met:

He has some remarkable ideas as to the future of cinema,
forseeing the time, which he believes not far distant, when films
will be presented not only in colour and relief and with the odors
proper to what is shown, but also telepathically. A film *thought*,
for example, by Vertov himself, would appear simultaneously
upon all the screens of the world, probably by that time installed
in private apartments rather than public cinemas. The forecasts

of this genius (I am chary of the word but in this case its full meaning is applicable) seems fantastic until we take the trouble of considering them carefully, when the possibility of their realization becomes undeniable.

So far I have tried to give as objective a picture as I can of Vertov's life and work and ideas; now let me give the other side of the coin, the subjective aspect revealed by the artist himself in his diaries, which luckily have survived and parts of which were published following the death of Stalin.

Extracts from Dziga Vertov's Diaries[40]

Vertov's diaries, like Dovzhenko's, are self-revelatory and open, unlike those of Eisenstein who, as far as we know, left no record of his innermost feelings.

Here is evidence of Vertov's state of mind, his honesty, his principles facing the totally unprincipled Communist Party, yet apparently unaware or unwilling to accept the fact that it was the Polit Bureau and finally Stalin that stopped dead his creative film work and condemned him to a living death.

Here in chronological order are some extracts I have translated. Let the man himself speak to the world from his silent Soviet grave.

Already in 1926, he experiences the first frost from the Party hierarchy:

12 April 1926[41]
Soviet cinematography is experiencing now unforgettable epoch-making days.

It has happened that the work of Kino-Eye has given birth to many current tendencies and groupings in Soviet and partly in foreign cinematography. It has broken all barriers, has emerged from prison underground and through the barbed-wire barriers of the higher administration, the simple administration and of distribution, has broken through the structure of the managers of cinema theaters and burst onto the screen.

Everything was against success.

It is New Year's Eve. There is 25 degrees of frost. But a 100% frost in lack of faith from the Army of film distributors. 100% frost on the part of those who stand high-up on the administrative ladder.

16 March 1927[42]
Reply to A.R. (*I haven't been able to establish who this is so far. HM.*)
   Ruthless exposure of shortcomings of the present time and the
invigorating revolutionary conclusions for the future – this is
not 'tragism', but genuine revolutionary optimism.
   To introduce ostrich-like politics, to shut one's eyes to
surrounding infamy, to smile blissfully or politely when you are
mocked and jeered at, to look gracefully and bow, on receiving
a gratuity in the form of a production or editing of a film – that
is not optimism and not 'tragism', that is 'lick-spittleism' (from
lick-spittle, toadyism, fawning, etc.).
   Such people (toadies), however high they may have climbed,
cannot become revolutionaries either in life or in
cinematography.
   Their pseudo-optimism, optimism of temporary well-being,
must be exposed just as much as their acted playing at
revolutionariness.
   The de-bunking of mystification both on the screen and in life
is obligatory for Kino-Eyeworkers. In the process of their current
work they must stubbornly unmask the pestilence in film
production (in life they hold the same firm line as in their work
on the screen). Not covering up shortcomings, injustices, crimes
and obstructions met in work, not afraid to show them, tell
about them, etc. – in order to overcome them, in order to destroy
them – that is the genuine revolutionary task, that is the
springboard for good cheer, for optimism, for the will to fight.

8 April 1933[43]
One says 'I' and thinks 'we', others say 'we' and think 'I'. One
speaks in an uncertain voice about that of which he is profoundly
convinced, and others, the opposite, speak with an uncertain
voice about that of which they are uncertain.

16 April 1933
I am accused of having spoiled Dos-Passos, infecting his
'Cinema-Eye'. Otherwise he would have become a good writer.
Others disagree and say that if it hadn't been for 'Cinema-Eye',
Dos-Passos would never have been known to us.
   Dos-Passos has translated cinemavision into literary language.
His terminology and structure is 'cinemaism'.
   'I work in the sphere of poetic documentary film. That is why

folk-poetry is near and dear to me, as is the poetry of
Mayakovsky. . . . I am a film writer. I write not on paper but
on cinema film.'

Vertov writes a lot about Mayakovsky because, of course, he was
his parallel in documentary cinema. And he loved him and his work
intensely and passionately. Somehow they never got together during
their lives and Mayakovsky's life ended very early by his own hand.
But what Vertov does point out is:[44]

Mayakovsky was at least successful in that he had his works
published in print. However, in one sphere he had complete
failure; he couldn't get on to the screens of the country, he
couldn't conquer the bureaucrats of the cinema. His scenarios
were either condemned or, even if included in the film studio's
theme plans, were never produced or were destroyed in the
process of the production. To our complete shame the greatest
poet of our time, having spent massive energy and time and
strength in order to try and appear on cinema screens 'at the
top of his voice', did not succeed. The talentless bureaucrats
stood by their 'principles' and Mayakovsky finally left the cinema
for good.

I need at my place of work to obtain my rights and if I don't
get them, if I can't achieve anything from the given directors,
from the given administration, all the same I will not surrender.
We all remember how in another situation Mayakovsky said,
'Administrations go – art remains.'

And in thinking about Mayakovsky and his suicide, Vertov
quoted: 'Still despite everything I don't need to "crush underfoot
the throat of my very own songs".' This quote is from the very
words Mayakovsky wrote in his last poem before he committed
suicide.[45]

26 May 1934
Without any pause, *The Three Songs of Lenin*, under very difficult
conditions without any holidays or days off. And yet I could
still work even more if the film wasn't held up for so long. If only
somebody would smile and say thank you or if they would praise
me, if they would only encourage me, or beat me with sticks.

Yet the last three months I have spent in the corridors of the
film studio continuously, today, tomorrow, waiting. In

continuous tension. It is the torture of an *indefinite* situation. The impossibility of answering questions, the anonymous telephone calls, and the slander – stifling mountains of slander. Even such trifles as not being invited to the opening of Domkino (The Club of Cinema Workers) or the refusal of Mezhrabpomfilm to give my photograph for the Domkino gallery.[46] And that is used as a springboard for the most savage fabrications which are disgusting to hear.

9 November 1934
I just heard on the radio that telegrams had been received from America about the extraordinary success of *The Three Songs of Lenin*. The leading newspapers published brilliant reviews. Yet only two hours ago the distribution head of Mezhrabpomfilm told me he was angry at the behaviour of the Moscow film distributors. They could not get *Three Songs* shown in any of the leading cinemas of Moscow. While I was present some foreigners came into Mezhrabpomfilm, complaining that they had been searching the whole day in the city to find the film. They eventually found one place, but all tickets were sold. They were told nothing could be done. They turned to me. 'You must protest,' they said. 'This is incredible. It's not only that the film is not shown in the large cinemas . . . but the public get the impression that the film is not being shown anywhere. This undermines faith in the film.'

When I read this in the diary of Vertov written exactly forty years ago, it was the same as when my wife and I searched all the cinemas of Moscow and Leningrad to find two modern film masterpieces which were being treated in the same way. One, Paradjanov's *The Color of Pomegranates*,[47] was shown only in a third-rate repertory cinema twice a day for a brief period in Moscow, and the other, Tarkovsky's *The Mirror*,[48] in one third-rate cinema in Leningrad.

And I was terrified at the thought that some minor bureaucratic despot, merely out of personal taste or other reasons, censors a film off the screen and thereby spits with impunity in the face of Soviet society. . . . What to him is the opinion of learned men, artists, political statesmen? He has his own dirty 'taste', his own petty 'opinions', his own hypocritical little 'thoughts'.

But of course, the 'minor-bureaucratic despot' was carrying out the orders of the 'great despot's' hypocritical little thoughts.

November 1934
About my illness. I began preparatory work on *The Three Songs of Lenin* in conditions of the savage slander on the part of the so-called cinematographic RAPP.[49] My sickness was induced as a result of a series of blows to my nervous system. And the history of this sickness is the history of discomfort, insults and nervous shocks, associated with my refusal to give up work in the sphere of poetic documentary film. At the moment I am completing the struggle for the film *The Three Songs of Lenin*. It was externally manifested in fatigue and the loss of my whole nervous well-being. Then, of course, RAPP was liquidated. Before that happened, the official organ of cinematography *Proleterian Kino* declared simply, 'Either you go over to the acted play-film or your mother and papa will cry; either you give up the documentary film or we will destroy you by administrative means.'

And so they did everything to sabotage his work until the day of his death. Vertov is left in the position of Kafka's tragic hero who cannot pinpoint exactly what are the accusations against him, or whether they love him or hate him. Everything happens yet Vertov can't explain why. And in his diary in September 1938, we read:

How to fight bureaucratic replies with instructions which are not decisions but postponement, decisions with an endless 'tomorrow'. How to explain impatience to the talented, patience to the untalented? How to play, poses from real experience, fact from invention? To suppress or pressing and not permitting? With conservation a charade . . . dragging out and slowing down to infinity. . . . Creative conceptions can be either destroyed or be immured for years and years, for one's whole life. What means can be achieved to save one's self. Must one use any means? All the usual disgusting means? Means that are scorned and humiliated. Shameful means in which one runs after business administrators. Can one on a matter of principle fight with unprincipled means? I obviously cannot. My hatred for such means arise. Meanwhile in truth I shall try to achieve the truth. Yet it seems everything that I have done was in vain. Once things were conducted in one way, now another. But now for one violinist there are a hundred conductors.

7 February 1940
It's one thing to play with talent on a wonderful violin. It's another thing – the ability and skill to get a violin.

It's one thing to produce a film with talent. It's another, the ability to get a production.

More often the most talented artist does not conquer, but the most energetic talker and operator (business man). . . . If one decides that the 'end justifies the means' then one could easily find a way out. But all one's hopes are to find a way out without such means.

12 February 1940
I don't isolate myself, but I am isolated. I am not invited anywhere. I didn't receive an invitation to a conference on historical films. For the film of Kisilev, *Our Cinema* (for the twentieth anniversary of Soviet cinema) I was not included. The article I was commissioned to write was not printed. There are no exhibition boards for me, they did not ask for my photographs or stills. My silence is taken to be because I keep silent, not that I am kept silent. I need nothing except work.

Now the most terrible variation comes. The transformation of the artist's poetic film into the educational technical. The destruction of all the work I have done in our whole group. Once I had iron nerves and an iron will. Of course there are other means but I am not able to use them. They can't make a 'business man' out of me. And I will not bow down to their feet, the feet of my enemies . . . The dead catch hold of the living.

One could go on to give facts and documentary evidence of how yet another creative biography was crippled by the Communist Party of the Soviet Union, but I think there is enough evidence about all these personalities, friends whom I knew well, great creative artists, to show that even though they did not land in the Gulag, they nevertheless had crippled biographies.

So one sees here that the fading out of this brilliant man, Dziga Vertov, was in a way even more tragic because it seemed to be conflictless, on the surface anyway. Only now when one reads his diary, extracts of which I am translating here, does one realize what tragic conflicts there were. How he felt himself, as it were, punching at someone or something shrouded in a mist, without knowing who or what to hit at. The parallel with Kafka's works keeps emerging when dealing with this aspect of the oppression of art and artists in Communist Party society. Vertov couldn't pin down who it was or what it was causing him to work less and eventually to vegetate completely. But in the final resort it was someone high up in the Central Committee, and possibly Stalin himself, who decided Vertov was not to be given the opportunity to produce any more films. That is why this policy continued even when he thought things would change, when a new director came in, or a new chairman of the Committee for Cinematography. But, as Droba-shenko points out, though the staff of the cinema industry changed, the treatment of Vertov never did.

It is a tragic dilemma Soviet biographers have with these virtually murdered artistic talents, when they try to explain, 'How did it happen?' Here is what Drobashenko says:[50]

> What is the explanation of the misfortunes in the creative life of Vertov? What causes brought him to the fact that when still a comparatively young man, full of artistic power, in the whole of the second half of his life he virtually remained silent? . . . Tortured with doubts, similar questions were often put to himself by Vertov.
>
> 'They don't love you,' said one of the leaders of cinematography in a moment of frankness. 'Who doesn't love me?' Vertov pondered over the phrase, when writing in his diary. 'The Party and the Government? No. The Party and the Government have given me high orders.'
>
> 'The Press? No, the press, beginning with *Pravda* and to the last newspaper in the Arctic Circle, have given me the highest praise!'
>
> 'Public opinion? No, Public opinion and its best representatives, leading writers, workers of the collectives, artists, all rose up to defend my film-work. So who is it then who doesn't love me? . . .'
>
> The artist didn't find an answer to that question.
>
> There was an answer. . . . If you carefully read his diaries you will see how gradually, the belt of the administrative pressure was tightened still tighter around him. Declared earlier by RAPP

to be a 'formalist', accused of 'groupism', 'social isolation', Vertov, more and more, with increasing difficulty, fought to make a path for himself to creative work. *The leaders of cinema organizations changed. But, essentially, the given situation remained exactly as before.* (My italics. HM.)

Here, of course, is the secret . . . for there was only one institution whose leadership did not essentially change, and that was the Polit-Bureau of the CPSU headed by Stalin. How could anyone dream that at the very same moment a Soviet artist was being loaded with State and Party honors a super-Machiavelli-Iago, Stalin, was planning that artist's assassination or incarceration?[51]

Yet Drobashenko tries to put the blame on the Cinema administration. He says:[52]

They didn't understand, and shrugging their shoulders, put on the shelf his applications, rejected his projects for a creative laboratory. Unceremoniously they interfered in his work and for months didn't release the films he had already made. . . . And all this time the artist fought with despair, with hopelessness and with pain in his spirit. In the changing conditions of life, he felt himself helpless.

This is exactly that helplessness, that defenselessness, that the poet Yevtushenko wrote about in his heyday[53] and was the typical situation of any Soviet citizen in the Stalin period. They know very well that any administration in the Soviet State apparatus only works to Party instructions – just as for over seven years all of Eisenstein's projects were 'put on the shelf' by the Cinema administration – under direct orders from Stalin.[54] And the bureaucrat who carried out these soulless orders was of a special type, chosen for such a job, an *'apparatchik'*: 'a soulless blockhead placed as a leader of art.' (Dovzhenko wrote the very same thing; see p. 169/171) Vertov meant the director of the Alma Ata Studios in the war years, Akhmedov. To this boss film directors were simply subordinate creatures whose 'secret' he had long ago discovered. 'It seemed to him that he was completely informed about everything in the cinema world, because when he shouted at these film directors, they kept silent.'

This was a phenomenon that Yevtushenko also wrote about in his poem 'Fear':[55]

When they should have been silent – to shout they were trained,
When they should have shouted – silent they were kept.

Once in a moment of spiritual suppression and fallen power,
Vertov wrote:[56]

All my life I have built locomotives that couldn't achieve a
railway for them to move on.

On which Drobashenko comments:[57]

Subjectively, unfortunately, that is how it was. To the end of his
life, Dziga Vertov remained almost forgotten. Not one of his
later ideas were created. In the post-war years, he was registered
as a director, only formally in the Newsreel Studio and there
all he could do was to edit the newsreels of the day but never
make any more films!

When he was but 57 years old he was told he had terminal
cancer. But the man with the movie camera went on working and
editing his humble newsreels until the last few weeks of his life. He
died on 12 February 1954.

Now, in 1966, Drobashenko tried to cheer up the dead Vertov
by saying that nevertheless, eventually (in other words after the
death of Stalin) his ideas *were* being carried out. And once again,
in the outside world, his name began to shine again, and in France
a group called themselves 'Ciñema Vérité' in honor of the creator
of Kinopravda, Cinema Truth. And this was only because the
slavish-Stalinist-Communist Party of France was following the
Moscow line. They didn't remember him during the Stalin period
either!

But again, as we see, like in the other crippled biographies, his
total work is more appreciated in the world outside the Soviet
Union. And with a lump in my throat, my mind goes back fifty
years to the first time I met my first Russian cinematographer,
Dziga Vertov, filled with passion for the Revolution and whose
Lenin Kinopravda beat in my brain, 'Lenin is dead!' 'Lenin lives!'
But Vertov's films, like Pudovkin's, Eisenstein's and Dovzhenko's
were Potemkin Villages. They gave an artistic image of a socialist
revolution that had never really taken place. The cinema of fact
became the cinema of non-fact. Kinopravda became Kino Non-
Pravda. And now, like the other great Soviet artists who were first

damned by the Communist Party 'with bell, book and candle' as heretics, they are now being beatified in the Communist Party Pantheon of Saints as 'socialist realists'!

Well, one could go on giving more facts and documentary evidence of how yet another creative biography was crippled by the Communist Party of the Soviet Union, but I think I have presented enough evidence about all these personalities, friends whom I knew well, great creative artists, to show that even though they were not executed and did not land in the Gulag or Lubianka prison, they nevertheless all had crippled biographies.

Alexander Dovzhenko

Writing about Dovzhenko on the seventieth anniversary of his birth, the director Gerasimov said, 'One thing about which he was always grieving was that he made two or three times fewer films than he could have made.' He had in mind those years of forced inactivity, the period of limited film production when, according to him, 'we all kept silent or made one film every five or six years.' Dovzhenko himself said, 'We were meant for something more, significantly more, than such an output!' In celebrating Dovzhenko's eightieth anniversary the critic Yurenev details this output: 'If one counts the films he directed one finds there are only thirteen documentaries, two shorts, and eight full-length features. One could add here his unfinished films, unrealized scripts and projects. Not much, in sixty-two years of life and thirty years of film-making.'[1] Dovzhenko himself says in his 1945 diary, on the twenty-eighth anniversary of the Bolshevik Revolution:[2]

> My basic aim in life now is not the cinema. I no longer have the physical strength it requires. I have made a pitifully small number of films, killing the best years of my life for them, through no fault of my own. I am a victim of barbaric working conditions, bureaucratic poverty of mind, and an ossified cinema committee. I know that the years will not come back and that there's no way to make up for them.

And in the introduction to this celebration a Party spokesman, in talking about the bad films produced in the Stalin period says,[3]

> In fact, if in the years of the Cult of the Personality all or almost everything was bad, even if good people became villains and considered that they couldn't be anything else, such an attitude dragged in, even if involuntarily, the idea that in those years

the decisive role in the life of the people was played by one single will, the will of that evil personality. Only then it was called 'good' . . . that was mystification only with a negative sign. It was the Cult of Personality inside out.

Dovzhenko began working with the revolutionary avant-garde of the Ukraine in the organization called VAPLITE – The Free Academy of Proletarian Literature, headed by the writer Mykola Khvylovy. But eleven years later they were liquidated by the Party, and the 'bacilli of Khvylovism' wiped out as Carynnyk says:[4]

Writing in the 'Autobiography' eleven years after Vaplite had been disbanded and the 'bacilli of Khvylovism' supposedly exterminated by the party, Dovzhenko naturally played down his association with the group. He did, however, publish his first article, 'Toward the Problem of the Visual Arts', in the Vaplite journal, and he became familiar with the most important manifestations of the new cultural upsurge: the pantheistic poems of Pavlo Tychyna and the chiselled verse of Mykola Bazhan, the plays of Mykola Kulish, the expressionistic productions of Les Kurbas's Berezil Theater, the fiction of Yuriy Yanovsky (a leading Vaplitian who became Dovzhenko's lifelong friend), the monumental paintings of Mykhaylo Boychuk and the short stories and polemics of Mykola Khvylovy. Today, when we know the fate of these artists – Khvylovy committed suicide; Kulish, Kurbas, and Boychuk died in prison camps; Tychyna, Bazhan, and Yanovsky were broken in spirit – their works smell of tragedy and suffering. They seem of a stature and richness that a mixture of elation and despair alone could have produced.

Dovzhenko had in fact applied for Party membership in 1920 and was accepted, but while he was at his diplomatic post in Berlin there was a so-called Purge (*chistka*) of Party members before renewing their Party card. This, at that time, was a regular procedure and I remember our group going through it in the GIK. Each member of the Party had to stand in front of the audience, like at a Salvation Army meeting, and confess his or her sins for the last year and what he had done to prove himself a good Party member. If he passed the Purge Committee then he was given his new Party card. While he was working in the Ukrainian Embassy in Berlin in the early 1920s, Dovzhenko didn't have a committee in Berlin and he had to send his card to the Kharkov Committee. He did this, but heard no more.

Then, on his return later, he found that he had been expelled from the Party for not passing the Purge Committee. He insisted that he had sent in his papers. They investigated but couldn't find the papers, therefore his expulsion still stood.[5]

Dovzhenko heard no more and himself considered his expulsion a formality and an injustice. He said, 'Can you tell a man from papers only? A man you can judge not by papers but by deeds.'

Then one day, Blakitny called him into his office and said, 'Sashko, we have found your papers. Your Party papers.' The papers which two years ago had been sent by Dovzhenko from Berlin to the Party Purge Committee.

'Well, you can be re-instated,' said Blakitny.

And he gave the name of a comrade from the Party Control Commission with whom he had spoken and to whom now Dovzhenko should go. So it seems that during those two years Blakitny hadn't forgotten his friend Sashko and himself had dug into the Archives and asked people, until he had at last found the papers and confirmed the truth of Dovzhenko's statements, and the basis for his tragic bitterness about it. But it seemed tragically that this last conversation with Blakitny was indeed the last in his life. For in a few days his friend died. However, Sashka had the telephone number of the Control Commission member he was to get on to, but it was always busy, he could never get through to that very busy comrade for at least a week. Finally, however, he was able to meet him. But the meeting was unsuccessful. It only increased the spiritual pain which never left him.

'Well, I understand you found my papers,' said Dovzhenko, entering into the cabinet of the high comrade.

'No,' said the occupant of the desk. 'We didn't find them; they were always here.'

'Well, nobody knew about it. I was told that I hadn't sent them, as if I had been lying to the Party.'

'Well, that was a mistake, they should have been searched for more attentively.'

'Well, what will happen now?'

'Well, you'll have to write and put in an application for acceptance into the Party.'

'But I've been a member of the Party since 1920.'

'How are you a member of the Party?' said the man behind the desk, in whose voice Sashka heard a haughty disdain. 'You didn't pass the Purge Commission.'

'No, but they lost the papers.'

'Well, now you see that they are not lost.'

At this Sashka left the room. Sashka never said anything to anybody and the new application he never gave in.

But for Sashka the justice of his cause was so obvious that it seemed stupid to attempt to prove it.

It is significant that Mykola Bazhan, the leading Party activist and poet of the Ukraine, was a lifelong friend of Dovzhenko. He was with him in 1925 when Bazhan worked in the Scenario Department of the Studios of Vufku, from which came brilliant films and directors like Dovzhenko and Vertov. Later Bazhan himself became a high-ranking influence in the Party, but not a word was ever mentioned of what he did to help Dovzhenko in his years of trial and attack from the Personality Cult and Stalin, and his banishment from his native land.

It is significant that when we criticize the philistines of the Central Committee of the Party for not understanding the artistic value of Eisenstein's, Pudovkin's or Dovzhenko's films until they were acclaimed from abroad, so Dovzhenko himself writes that even Maxim Gorky didn't understand his films. He says:[6]

> With all my deep love and profound respect for the greatest man of our epoch, the greatest master Alexei Maximovich Gorky, still there are a whole number of questions where I cannot agree with him and would like to clarify his position on the cinema front. For me it is even more difficult, for weighing down on me is the low evaluation Alexei Maximovich gave to two of my older pictures. . . .

And here the article printed in Moscow in 1967 has dots indicating that something has been cut out on his attack on Gorky. It must be realized how brave he was, because it was done at a meeting of writers, composers, artists and workers of the cinema with Maxim Gorky on 10 April 1935, when he was at the height of his influence and authority in Russia as the protagonist of so-called socialist realism, with the full support of Stalin. But he, like Stalin and the other leaders, didn't understand the great pictures of Alexander Dovzhenko.

The veteran writer and critic Victor Shklovsky wrote, 'Dovzhenko's path of creative achievement was beset with difficulties. How ill equipped we are to acknowledge the infinite value of a genius's time. How little help we give him as he climbs the path to the future!'[7]

But though Victor Shklovsky understated the difficulties, he made up for it in the latter part of the statement, for he is mourning the helplessness of a Soviet citizen in the Communist Party society, unable to help even his brother genius in the face of the total dictatorship that controls them equally.

At the famous 1935 film-makers' conference, which I attended, I remember vividly Dovzhenko's speech: it was so utterly sincere and dedicated and passionate and truthful; he still had his faith in the Party. He said about the mission of a Soviet artist:[8]

> Everyone knows the speedy growth of our cinema. It was determined by the special attention of the Party. One of a thousand areas and even here the genius of leadership is revealed. In command [of our Socialist state] stands the most advanced, the very best part of our society and of all humanity.

And later in the same speech he said:[9]

> The Party does not allow a state to be built within a state. And that is completely right and lawful. There is no autonomous art or autonomous criticism. The function of leadership in art is taken out of the hands of the individual.

And how wrong they were – for in the end the leadership *was* in the 'hands of the individual'.[10]

Just like his brother artists Dovzhenko voted wholeheartedly to entrust his whole art, his whole life, the art and life of the whole Soviet people, into these hands 'of genius.' Even the very thing Dovzhenko praised, the increase in growth of cinema, was proven untrue – particularly in his own Ukranian film studio.

The Ukrainian Film Productions in Kharkov, Kiev and Odessa were linked-up in a center known as VUFKU, a very experimental and adventurous center until the Communist domination. They published a journal, *Kino,* which kept them informed of avant-garde and other productions in Europe. They encouraged Dziga Vertov and his Kino-Eye Group, now famous as *cinéma-vérité,* until he was forced to work in Moscow, and eventual silence. They tried out Mayakovsky's scenarios until he too could no longer make films. And they gave Dovzhenko his chance of making films, including *Zvenigora,* until he too was forced out.

Dovzhenko comments on the bankruptcy of Ukrainian films in his diary:[11]

[In 1952] Before leaving Kiev I had a long talk with X, who wants me to come to work at Kiev Studio.

'Alexander Petrovich, the studio is dying. It's fallen so low that it can't exist any more. We need you very badly. Only you can save Ukrainian cinema. You can see yourself what's going on.'

Then we talked about the film industry executives, their indifference and obscurantism. The films are really terrible. The Ukrainian cinema has never fallen so low; it's never been so deprived of Ukrainian cadres.

'Why didn't you suggest I come home at least five years ago?' I asked.

And Dovzhenko in the same speech says that 'all the best films were made quickly,' and I have shown this in the case of *Potemkin, Mother,* etc. He made his first important film *Zvenigora* in three months. He wrote the script of his great revolutionary film *Arsenal* in two weeks and produced the whole in six months. Eisenstein, too, wrote the final text of *Potemkin,* impromptu, in two weeks. And Dovzhenko goes on to criticize the slowing-down process so that now he says, 'We work five to six times slower than American film directors.'[12] The USSR was then producing up to 100 features a year as against America's then production of 500–600 a year. I have pointed out that as Stalin's dictatorship tightened these were reduced to ten 'masterpieces' a year, during which no masterpieces could possibly be created, and were not.[13] Except perhaps for the unique exception of *Ivan the Terrible,* the reasons for which I give in my Eisenstein essay.

In this famous speech Dovzhenko spoke most honestly and forthrightly, at the same time paying the necessary lip-service to the genius of the Party and which then he no doubt believed in, like so many did.

He said, 'It seems to me that in our circles I present a figure on which the greatest number of various labels have been pinned. Pinned so many and so variously confused that recently I have ceased to read criticism and articles about myself.'[14]

He said the very first and only lesson he learned from his cameraman on *The Diplomatic Courier*, A. F. Kozlovsky, was, 'Sashka, I will give you one golden rule: never enter into a compromise. If you compromise for five kopeks, it will grow to 100 roubles and you will never know how to get out of it.'[15]

Dovzhenko added, 'That rule I have adhered to all my life, and seemingly, will continue to do so the rest of my life.' And he did so with the most fearsome and terrifying results, which he writes about in his diary.

He refused, for example, to apologize for his past errors as pointed out by the Party critics, and he even criticized Pudovkin at that same meeting for saying:[16]

'. . . it would be terrible to view my *Heir of Genghis Khan* (*Storm Over Asia*) today.' I don't understand that. I would never say that about your films, Comrade Pudovkin. No matter what Comrade Pudovkin would say today about his *End of St Petersburg*, I cannot forget, that at the time I saw that film it acted on me with mighty power, as it did on all those masses who saw the film together with me.

About confessing mistakes of the past Dovzhenko went on:

Pudovkin also flattened himself out in recantation; *The Battleship Potemkin* is now a wooden plow; *The Youth of Maxim*[17] is also unsatisfactory. A whole lot of other films are also bad. This whole pack of bitter words, self-depreciation, sounded very bad to me. I can't treat cinematography like that. I consider that it is our common great work. In that work we put the whole of our creative life. I treat our former films with respect. I do not wish to consider our creative history as a chain of errors and mistakes, on which I just spit. I wish to consider them as an approximation to the truth, in this respect even mistakes are dear to me, as are achievements.

And in the 1960s a modern Soviet critic, I. Metter, writes:[18]

One must not be afraid of mistakes. How much the whole world

of cinema needed the 'mistakes' of Eisenstein, and the poetry
and theater of Mayakovsky and Meyerhold! Look at the press
that accompanied these artists in the course of their whole
creative life: *continuously, totally, their mistakes were registered.* (My
italics. HM.)

But alas, following the attacks of Yutkevich and other 'socialist
realist' protagonists, Dovzhenko goes on to say about Eisenstein:[19]

We all know the role of Eisenstein in cinematography . . . we
await his further contributions. . . . But yesterday I was
somewhat terrified by his speech: on the one hand Eisenstein
revealed himself in his speech as a profound fundamental master
and thinker, investing his thought, his time on research, on
putting into order a tremendous accumulation (of material), on
the other hand – Eisenstein held something back. He does not
now occupy his proper place in cinematography. Standing
beside him, loving him immeasurably, I express to you – and to
him – my view on his creative work. I don't want Eisenstein to
tell us about Polynesian women. They are so far off, so many of
them, so scattered and so much has been written about them,
there is still so much to be said about them, quoted, researched
– that one lifetime isn't enough to do such work. I propose that
Eisenstein must look at 'living women,' which are here around
us. They are close to us, they are much more necessary for us.
Giving birth with them takes on a new course. Understand the
metaphor, comrades as you find necessary.
When I listen to a lecture of Eisenstein, I fear that he knows
so much, he has such a lucid mind, that is obvious that he won't
produce another film. If I knew as much as him, I would die.
(Laughter, applause) It's no laughing matter. I fear Eisenstein
might consume himself from the tail, I fear that the laboratory
of his mind might explode from the accumulation of that
complex, mysterious, unknown to all of us, compound.
I am convinced, that in many ways that very erudition of his
will ruin him. No, forgive me, that's not the right word to say:
it will disorganize him. I consider that the work of Eisenstein, i.e.,
a new film, is absolutely necessary for us and for him. . . . Your
film must untie all the controversial knots wrapping around your
figure, it must untie all those 'Freudian complexes'. . . . It is

unpleasant to me to say these things. . . . For me your film, *Sergei Mikhailovich*, is ten times dearer than all your theories.

How such a mind as Dovzhenko misunderstood Eisenstein, how tragic it all is in retrospect.

But then in another part of his speech, Dovzhenko admits his own errors:[20]

I didn't have enough organization, experience, precision. The conclusion is clear: the creativity of all our Soviet film-workers must be organized.

Here again is the 'naive' Soviet artist putting himself in the total power of the Communist Party of the Soviet Union to organize his whole creativity. And one sees now how such honest and sincere men created their own Juggernaut. . . .

The image is a real metaphor for the Communist Party machine.

My wife and I have actually seen the original Juggernaut, in Puri, Orissa, India. A vast chariot of really gigantic size, made of wood, with colossal wheels, so heavy that it needs hundreds of men to pull it. It was said that, during the holy festival of the Juggernaut, the devotees who had built it worked themselves into a frenzy until sometimes they threw themselves under its wheels in holy abnegation.

The machine they created and worshipped as the Chariot of the Goddess of Destruction became the chariot of their own destruction. They died with a prayer to this goddess on their lips.

How remarkably that is paralleled by the Juggernaut of the Communist Party of the Soviet Union. The very devotees, loyal Party members, who built up this gigantic structure, the monstrous apparatus of which they were the *apparatchiki*, were destroyed by it. Even if they survived being run over physically by its gigantic wheels, they were run over spiritually by its weight of cruelty, lies, self-deception and hypocrisy.

Dovzhenko wrote in his diary, 'Enjoyed seeing Okhlopkov. He's the only one who treats me well. But what can he do?'[21]

Okhlopkov was a People's Artist of the Republic, a one-time Deputy Minister of Culture, a winner of both the Stalin and Lenin Prizes and of other honors. But he was helpless to deal with the Juggernaut he too had helped to create, and about which he too had created works of praise as in his production about collectivization and the 'liquidation of the kulak,' the play *Razbeg*. And his praise of Gulag prisoners building the White Sea Canal in *Aristocrats*,[22] which was equal with Dovzhenko's film *Earth* as a great work of art, but alas, leaving no trace now except print and photos. He too was attacked by the Party dogmatists just like Dovzhenko, and yet did all that the Party could have asked for in falsification and the glorifying of villains as heroes and vice versa.

'But what can he do?' cries Dovzhenko in despair, as the Juggernaut plows on.

The ephemeral film

In writing about the artistic creations of this famous trio, one is faced with a formidable problem that one is writing about works of art that have not been seen by the reader, or seen perhaps decades after their first showing and initial revolutionary impact, and more likely than not, on a small television screen. So, I am forced to attempt to describe in writing what the films were about, to verbalize their visual expression (for, in the case of the trio, they were all silent films), and to convey the terrific impact they had on all audiences in their day. This is really most unsatisfactory, but there is no alternative. One cannot turn the clock back forty or fifty years.

Here we are faced with a terrible fact – that the art which Eisenstein taught us was the synthesis and pinnacle of all the arts, the 'most important of the Arts' for Lenin, quickly gets out of date – not only technically but also thematically and artistically. And this was pointed out first, I think, by Dovzhenko at the famous 1935 meeting of cinematographers in Moscow.

Here is what he said:[23]

The quality of the life of a film, the life of our productions is differentiated from the life of other arts. . . . A writer writes a novel, which is considered unsuccessful. . . . But he will comfort himself with the thought . . . that maybe in a hundred years this novel will be understood. . . .

He may so think. But we, cinematographers, cannot think like that . . . because the film, a fixed work of art, has however a certain illusory fixedness. It has shortened co-ordinates of breadth (space) i.e., the co-efficient of useful action of the film in the end is balanced. A film, equivalent to Raphael's *Madonna* is seen by the same number of people in ten years which sees Raphael's *Madonna* in 450 years, because a film can have 100 copies and can be seen by millions of people. If one can say that Raphael's *Madonna* has been seen by 200,000 people, then 200,000 have seen *Potemkin*. The co-efficient of useful action is the same. But I am convinced that if we, lovers of literature, can enjoy the first edition of Shakespeare, if old books smell with the aroma of the ages, delighting us with their print, type and other qualities and in general heighten our interest, all of this is not applicable to film, for even the greatest work of film genius, made ten or twelve years ago, does not now affect our consciousness in the same way other works of art do.

Comrades, the blemishes of time may be pleasant in old folios, in painting, sculptures, but the 'rain' on a film is unpleasant in the cinema.

I affirm, that each of us reading a drama of Shakespeare perceives it each in his own way, i.e., exactly in the same way we think about the world. But I also affirm that, if by some miracle we could see the productions of Shakespeare of his time, we probably would laugh at them. Our conception about expressiveness, of the expression of human feelings, are different from what they would have been at that time. Much we wouldn't have understood, and many profound, serious feelings would have been expressed in such a way that today would only have provoked the author. Eisenstein once said: 'Yes, but we look at old comedies with pleasure.'

I replied, 'Of course, old comedies are interesting not only because they are talented, and made comic, but because a whole series of tricks appear comic to us.'

Eisenstein, 'Even drama.'

Yes, and even drama seems comic. These circumstances have great significance. That is why I consider cinema an art of short-lived impact. The power of its action, the power of its impact, is concentrated into a tiny segment of time. That is what distinguishes cinema and in that lies its significance. It is necessary to understand this precisely and clearly, in order to properly evaluate old and new films, and in order to properly approach those tasks which face us today.

Since Dovzhenko's day, through Telstar satellites and international television link-up the impact of a film can be made simultaneously on the whole population of the planet! Plus the fact that all the classic films (that have survived) can now be seen on one TV program or the other, at least in the free world.

Today, not just the 200,000 Dovzhenko mentioned in 1935 but millions have seen *Potemkin*.

So when we see old films now, they are indeed quickly dated, or out-of-date – except, as Dovzhenko perceptively pointed out, for comedies and some melodramas that become comic to us. But I would point out one other feature that doesn't date and that is music, orchestral or choral.

Unfortunately, Dovzhenko's masterpieces had no sound, as he himself so often complained, or else the singing of village youth at the funeral of Vasily in *Earth* would still ring in our ears as eternally contemporary.

About *Zvenigora* he wrote, 'I did not so much make the picture as sing it out like a songbird.'[24] And Dovzhenko as a passionate Ukrainian had singing in his blood.

Some of the tales he told us showed this clearly. Here is what one of my fellow students, Ivan (now, alas, dead), told me:

'Alexander Petrovich said one day, "Ivan, have you ever considered why people invented songs?"

"Well, Alexander," I replied, "it's probably because they wanted to sing!"

To which Alexander replied, "Once upon a time three women plowed a field and found a skull.

The oldest one took the skull in her hands and cried out, 'A skull!' and wept.

The middle-aged one said, 'A skull!', and laughed.

The youngest one said, 'A skull!' and sang a song".'

That's how people invented songs.

And as for the atmosphere in the Stalinist period I remember Dovzhenko once telling me, 'You can always tell if a Ukrainian village is happy, it sings at nightfall. They don't sing like they used to.'

So only comedy and songs survive in films, and that, alas, is a sad commentary on the permanence of cinema.

Dovzhenko's films are songs and poems based on Ukrainian folklore and this stuck in the gills of his Russian masters. For he could never eradicate it, even if he had wanted to.

In the script of *Arsenal* Dovzhenko wrote, 'The mother is sowing, stumbling as she sows. And from all her pictures (shots) blows the breath of something songlike, and in the field she herself is just like a visible song.'[25]

In the script of *Earth* he wrote, 'The singers in their songs encompass whole eras of their lives.'[26]

And in writing about Vasily in the village night, he writes sound into this silent film: 'Everything is filled with the hardly discernible special sounds of night. Through the far-off song of the village girls, hardly reverberating somewhere in the silvery radiance, one seems to hear how the grass grows, the cucumbers. . . .'[27]

And his poetic metaphorical treatment permeates every film; they are Mayakovsky's poems in pictures. Let us look at the first shots of *Earth*.[28]

A wave runs along the wheat. How many times, since films were made, have we been shown these wheat fields, shot from so many different angles. But to this day that artistic image of Dovzhenko has not faded, nor lost its novelty. Because these shots were not filmed as a realistic presentation and not just for their beauty. This is a metaphor. This is *'a sea of wheat'*.

No matter how many times the final shots of *Earth* are repeated – drops of rain dripping from the fruit – Dovzhenko will not stultify nor his discoveries fade. Because for him this was not still life, but a metaphor: This is *a flood of tears*, these are tears, wiping away the grief and sorrow of man.

Dovzhenko's triptych

However, I must now try and give the reader some idea of the Dovzhenko triptych of films, so that he can follow the true story of this great Soviet film-maker's conflict with his Party and how it affected his creative work.

I am not dealing with his earlier attempts, because he himself has said they weren't really his own work.

The triptych consists of:

Zvenigora (1927)
Arsenal (1928)
Earth (1930)

Zvenigora was described as 'a film with blended allegorical and contemporary elements, combining the past and revolutionary present of the Ukraine.'[29]

Arsenal was described as 'a completely political film'. 'In making it I set myself two tasks,' said Dovzhenko, 'to unmask reactionary Ukrainian nationalism and chauvinism and to be the bard of the Ukrainian working class that had accomplished the social revolution.'[30]

Earth portrays 'the state of the Ukrainian village in 1929, that is, at a period not only of economic transformation, but also of mental transformation of the whole people.'

'In the three films together, I show our country its history, its way of life, its struggle and ideas.'[31]

It is significant that in that same brief period of this Russian Renaissance of the 1920s, criticism and analysis also had its freedom, so that a work of art had its protagonists and its antagonists, not like in the Stalin years when there was only the one or the other. There were the personal and group points of view and the Communist Party of the Soviet Union's point of view, but after the iron curtain came down there was only the Communist Party of the Soviet Union's point of view, however it may have been disguised under alleged personal points of view.

Let us look at how Dovzhenko's films were received.

Zvenigora

His first film was *Zvenigora* – it wasn't actually his first film but Dovzhenko considered it so because 'it was the first for which he had his own way, wrote his own scenario, directed the film.' He was to 'have his own way' for three films only and then it was 'the Party way.' He was never to have his own way again.

I have my notes recorded at the time I first saw this strange film, in 1930, from which the following is an extract:

Dovzhenko first called it 'A Cinema Poem', based on an old legend of Ukraine and the eternal symbolism of the hidden treasure. With that typical Dovzhenkian disregard for normal space and time it roams over history from the Viking invasion till after the successful revolution in the Ukraine. If Old Mother Russia is the archetype in Russia, in Ukraine it appears to be Old Granddad Mykola, who has two sons, the good and the bad, Timosh and Pavlo. Granddad tells them of the legend of Ukraine's hidden treasure, how Cossack and other robbers roamed the Ukrainian plains and hills searching for its hidden treasure. But a sub-title reads: 'Centuries passed. People were born and died – trains passed over the Ukrainian plains – but the hills and forests and rivers of Zvenigora kept Grandpa's secret.'

Another sub-title says: 'Soaked with blood, sealed in secrecy, shrouded in legend, treasures of the country have been buried for ages in Ukrainian soil.'

Pavlo, imbued by the idea of finding this hidden treasure, grows up to be a bandit; Timosh fights in the war and participates in the revolution. Then comes the inevitable – civil war between them. The over-tone of the Biblical parallels Cain and Abel is clear, as well as specific Ukrainian legends.

A heartbreaking scene, reminiscent of Stenka Razin, the Cossack rebel who also sacrificed his beloved for his cause, is where Timosh retreats from the village leaving it to the mercy of Pavlo. He is forced to leave his wife behind, she follows him barefoot, he shouts 'go back!' 'I cannot return Timosh. Kill me or come back!' she begs him. He leans from his horse, kisses her farewell; takes his rifle from his shoulder. We see her from his point of view and then in this silent film we seem to hear a shot – and she slumps to the ground dead. He rides on to save the revolution.

Pavlo is now an emigré in Prague/Paris and Timosh is at a Workers' school studying science and technology to find the true treasure of Zvenigora, the secret of the riches of the Ukraine. And in a grotesque parallel his brother Pavlo is before a public audience paying to witness his suicide! But he cons them and escapes with the box-office receipts. Now he has enough money again to find the treasure and rescue it from the 'fiery serpent that will crush the treasure underfoot' (i.e. the Bolsheviks) by counter-revolutionary sabotage. Grandpa now joins his good son, cursing his bad son Pavlo who finally does commit suicide.

It was a film quite unique in those days in its symbolism and overlapping space and time sequences and filled with all the technical experiments that Dovzhenko used later, just as Eisenstein did from his similar film *Strike*.

However, Montagu, the English Communist critic and 'friend' of Eisenstein said, '*Zvenigora* was an inspired mess.'[32]

But what did Eisenstein and Pudovkin think of this film when they first saw it? Here is what Eisenstein wrote:[33]

'However the film began to reverberate with irresistible fascination, fascinating in its original manner of thinking. The extraordinary weaving of real profoundly national poetic thought. Sharply contemporary yet at the same time mythological. Filled with humour and pathos. Something Gogolesque. . . .

The viewing has finished. People stood up. Silent. But in the air something hovered: in our midst was a new man of cinema.

A master with his own personality. A master of his genre. A master of his individuality.

And at the same time ours. Our own. Of our community.

Linked flesh and blood with the best traditions of our Soviet work. A master who did not go begging to the Westerners.

And when all the lights came on, we all felt that before us was one of the wonderful moments in the biography of cinema. Before us stood a man who had created something new in the sphere of cinema art.

I stood alongside Pudovkin. A wonderful task fell to our lot; in response to everyone in the auditorium watching us, we had to formulate that which no one could express, owing to the highly unusual phenomena witnessed, but which however everyone sensed. To say that before us was a wonderful film and still more a wonderful man. And we were the first to congratulate him.

Thus was Dovzhenko ordained as a regisseur. Today for a moment could the lamp of Diogenes be put out: before us was a genuine human being. A genuine new mature master of cinematography.'

It was after the official première of *Zvenigora*, while Eisenstein was still editing *The Old and The New*, that the trio met to celebrate and congratulate each other, in Eisenstein's words they discussed the problems of cinema that excited them and 'the sense of youth and creative repletion of the new Renaissance. The unbounded creative perspectives of the new art ahead of them. . . .'[34]

And then Eisenstein made the famous comparison I have already quoted of this trio of talents with da Vinci, Raphael and Michelangelo. Dovzhenko was Michelangelo, though physically he was more like the noble figure of 'David'.

This appraisal by the two masters of the new master and the unique contribution of his *Zvenigora* and *Arsenal* was supported by many critics, in those days of varying schools.

In particular, Piotrovsky wrote:[35]

The method of Dovzhenko allows the presentation of historical material, without lowering their significance, without distorting their social dependence on each other, without resorting to melodramatic adventures in order to achieve this aim. And at the same time by showing these historical events through generalizations, through artistic images that are humanly exciting and humanly emotional, they allow the artist to establish a mighty bridge of direct sympathy to the spectators.

But alas, Piotrovsky was immediately attacked by the hard-liners, the Party anti-formalists, 'class-conscious' school, that eventually predominated and eliminated any opposition, by all methods including physical elimination. As will be seen in all subsequent Party 'Marxist' criticism, particularly singled out for attack were the concepts of 'human', 'general', 'abstract', 'objective', etc., only 'class proletarian' categories were accepted. The official Party 'Film Newspaper' wrote in a front-page editorial:[36]

Not fully successful was the attempt to negate these 'nationalist-democratic' conceptions in the film of A. Dovzhenko, *Zvenigora*, in its artistic level standing much higher than all the previously cited films. But even in this film nationalistic romanticism was not dethroned, there was insufficient class differentiation of the villages (country folk); the treatment of the image-character of 'Grandad', the treasure hunter, was 'nationalist-democratic.'

Another attack came in a parallel journal, *Kino i Zhizn*, no. 25, 1929, typically from an anonymous author.[37] Piotrovsky had also defended Eisenstein's theories and this Party-inspired article said, 'Attempts were made to deepen the mistakes of Eisenstein, giving them a supporting theoretical base by formalistic and eclectic groupings, still existing in Soviet cinema, still not completely exposed.'[38]

He then goes on to deal individually with those back-sliding masters, characterizing the method of Dovzhenko as follows:[39]

[He is] a master of the left-fellow-traveller school, approximating his creative work to the tasks of revolutionary cinematography.
The creative method of Dovzhenko is significantly differentiated from others. For example, the 'thingism', the 'technicism' [sic] of Eisenstein is alien to him; Dovzhenko builds his artistic images by other methods, he strives to express the social motives and behavior of his heroes (e.g. the type of arsenal worker in *Arsenal* and Vasily in *Earth*).
This is undoubtedly a progressive trait in his art. But the artistic style of Dovzhenko is spoiled by a stream of biologism [sic],[40] breaking through, particularly in the film *Earth*, and reducing to practically nil the social significance of the film. This attachment of the artist to show in his work the days of yore, reveals the tendency of Dovzhenko towards pure painting, which also significantly lowers the social content of his films, despite their high artistic qualities. This was particularly revealed in the films *Zvenigora* and *Earth*.
It is quite clear that these tendencies of the artist prevent him mastering that creative method, which is able to reveal before the artist the mighty creative perspectives of cinematography.

Here are laid bare all the elements of the depreciation of art that the Party insisted upon and finally achieved, including even criticism of the artistic beauty of Dovzhenko's shots and sequences, their approximation to 'pure painting', their revelation of the unity of man and nature, of human and animal fertility, of life and death, past and present and future.

Such a Party is not worthy of such artists.

Arsenal

As I have written elsewhere, on the question of the prosaic and the poetic, Dovzhenko was always getting into trouble because he was the poet of the cinema, and his next film *Arsenal* also caused him much trouble.

Here are my personal notes made when I first saw *Arsenal* in Moscow in 1930.

Script and Direction: A. Dovzhenko
Assistants: A. Kapler and L. Bodik
Cameraman: Danyll Demutsky

Svashenko – a worker

1   Barbed wire. Woman in log-cabin. Still. 'A Mother had three sons.' Explosion.
Train – Soldiers – Trenches. Mothers still. 'War.' '*War.*' '*War.*' A legless cripple crawls on crutches.
Village. White Guard – touches a woman's dried breasts and goes on. Women take no notice.
'*But the mother no longer has three sons.*' The sons alone.
Cripple. Sons. Nicholas 1st. Czar writes his diary. Sons fall. Officer.
'*Today I shot a Crow.*'
Worker. Czar's Diary '*Weather was good*' signed 'Niki.' Mother. White.
Where shells fall. Grapple and horse. Mother and 2 kids.
Man in field – bad crop. Children cry. Peasant beats horse, Mother beats children.
Kicks. Exhausted. Child cries. Horse says to man, 'You're hitting the wrong one, Ivan!'
Trenches. War. Explosions.
Attack. Laughing gas. Soldiers move heavily. Dead hand sticks out of ground. Hand.
Face laughing – dead. Soldier goes to kill. Stop. Drops rifle. 'Where is the enemy?' Train. German soldier. Russian soldiers going home standstill. 'Who is the enemy?'
Hands out. Officer never aims. Hands out. Laughing gas. Man march. Clouds. German officer shoots German soldier in back of neck. Boots of dead soldier are silhouetted on ground.

2   Scramble. As old Bureaucrat crawls with lighted ikon lamp and sings: 'Pull off your Ukrainian boots and overcoats.' Suddenly Shevchenko angrily blows out the lamp.
Rev. soldiers deserting from White Army.
Laughing dead – Russia –v– Ukraine.
Old enemies. 'Three hundred years.' Train. Brakes give way. Timosha the mechanic fixes it.
'Surrender your arms in the name of the Ukrainian People's

Republic.' 'Who said,' asks Timosh. Civil War begins. Train goes. Concertina. Train. Goes downhill.

'Keep it going!' Concertina falls from train. Timosh decides, 'I'll be a locomotive engineer.'

Polish mother and child. Wait. Soldier returns. 'Who?'

German mother and child. '*Wer?*'

French mother and child. '*Ou?*'

A legless soldier crawls along the street, comes back to Kiev arsenal. 'A Ukrainian deserter.'

'Go back to barracks Timosh, be ready for the next call of the Revolutionary Committee.'

3 Crowd – Religious – 'Pray for Free Ukraine.' Ikons.

'Student searches orthodox' actions – (White).

'Long live! For 300 years under Russia.'

In midst of ikons, Shevchenko: 'Christ has arisen!'

National Poet of Ukraine, 'Who was Bogdan Khmelnitsky?' 'Some kind of General.'

Mass. Speaker 'Can we kill the bourgeoisie and officers if we meet them in the street?'

Answers: but a smile is yes and no.

Leader – former officer White Guard. Holds out hand.

Timosh refuses to take it. 'But you're a Ukrainian?'

Timosh says, '*I am a worker*' – goes to platform pushes off speaker.

'I am a worker, Timokey Stoyan.'

All get up at his call. A proletarian.

4 *Worker S and P Congress*

Word from Bolshevik Republic – they don't like it.

Leader. 'We are also workers – we demand the factories, the land and power!'

But they have been flooded with deputies – And all shout.

Peasant says: 'OK Ukrainian power, but whose land – Landlord's or peasant's?' General Petlura will reply. Timosh and Bolsheviks leave. 'We will return!'

Letter from Black Sea Fleet – Read.

Platform refuses, it is a mistake. Who is against? The Red Army – The Red Navy. Revolutionaries all against. And the Arsenal. Strikes. Revolt.

People try to leave but stop as soldiers led by Timosh arrive to help.

5   The Petlurovites want the Arsenal. 'Let's begin a worker's arsenal,' says Timosh.
Whites. Reds. Mothers. People listen and wait. Fear of Whites.
Red Sentry waiting. Woman knitting.
Attack. Whites surround arsenal.
Legless soldier crawls along street.
Quiet, all wait. Man on ground dead with smashed bottle and red cross. All wait.
Letter home, dictates.
Nurse writes for soldiers and 'What's the address?' He doesn't answer.
He is dead. Nurse rises and addresses his letter to everyone: Reads, 'Can I kill the bourgeois officer in the street if I meet him?'
'You can,' says Arsenal worker making the counter-attack.

6   Fights. Snow – riders. Dead or live. Marching. Riderless horses. Dying man. 'Bury me at home – I've been away for nine years.'
'Hurry or the Arsenal will fall.' They take him and ride and ride for the Revolution. 'Faster, faster horses!' The horses reply, 'OK, we are running as fast as our 24 legs can carry us!' Revolution.
Woman by the grave. They come. They give his body to the woman – 'Take him mother – no time to explain, the Revolution is our Life and Death.' And they go on to the attack.
White shoots worker. 'Turn with your face to the wall so that I can shoot you in the back.' But worker goes and turns around and faces him and comes nearer. White afraid. 'And you can't shoot into my eyes.'
'But why is it I can?' Worker.
Takes gun and shoots White.

7   Midnight 24-48-72 hours, after attack.
Attack again. Leader at machine gun. Army gone. Hardly any ammunition left. Gone.
Arsenal falls. Prisoners. Whites shoot workers.
Worker Revolutionaries die.

Widows. Mothers. Brides don't ask: 'Where is my father – husband – son?' 'Empty factories, where is the fitter?' 'Dead.'
'Where is my father – my husband – my son?'
'Where is the blacksmith?'
Killed in cold blood. Timosh. Machine gun has jammed.
Attack – Whites cry 'Who's at the machine gun?'
'A Ukrainian worker: shoot!' They fire and he does not fall.
He rises up and bares his breast.
They fire volley after volley. He does not fall. They cry out in terrified frustration: 'Fall, damn you, fall!' He does not.
They disappear.
Stands Timosh, Ukrainian worker.

Contemporary critics of *Arsenal* noted how in 1929, the Kiev Studios of Vufku had improved with the production of Dovzhenko's *Zvenigora* and *Arsenal* and Dziga Vertov's *Man with a Movie Camera*. But though *Arsenal* as a whole was hailed as a truly revolutionary film, at least one critic could not understand its poetry and imagery. Semyon Getz wrote this of the ending of the film, in which Timosh, the arsenal worker, is shot by Ukrainian nationalists but does not fall, no matter how many bullets they fire at him:[41]

The worker Timosh – this generalized type of a bolshevik-arsenal worker – after the train crash said to himself: 'I'll become an engineer!' A wonderful symbol! But as the film developed the engine driver burned with an impatient desire to go forward with Timosh to that moment when he becomes a fully-fledged engineer, truly and unswervingly driving the train to a new life.

But to our great disappointment, Dovzhenko didn't take us to this moment. His Timosh was shot by the Petlurovites. Shot – and full stop. At that the film ends. From whence comes such pessimism? Dovzhenko is not carolling the Paris Commune, but the history of the Kiev Arsenal, which not only lives, but is very healthy and together with us has taken an active part in socialist construction under the leadership of hundreds of thousands of engineer-Timoshes. In our opinion, the director hurried to finish the film, from which it suffered severely.

But that most brilliant and honest of Soviet critics, M. Bleiman, argues:[42]

Dovzhenko treats his material with complete freedom, concerned not with its correspondence with actuality, but with its expressiveness and its political clarity. And that is why in *Arsenal* horses reply to man, why shots of winter landscape are suddenly intercut with summer, and why a mother waits for her son at his already-dug grave.

This use of fantasy and folklore imbues the picture with a high emotional intensity, raises every one of its events to the status of a symbol, and finally, gives the film its completely original poetic character. If we can talk of a filmic poem, then we will find it in *Arsenal*.

Simultaneously, Dovzhenko uses the methods of American 'comic' films. In this lies his similarity to other of our revolutionary masters, raising the American 'comics' to the level of social pathos and imbuing every episode with exceptional significance. The old comic trick of bringing a portrait to life works in *Arsenal* with deep political significance. This is where in response to a bureaucrat of the old regime Taras Shevchenko's portrait suddenly comes to life and blows out the ikon-lamp flame the old man has brought to him with his prayer '*Sche ne vmerla* Ukraina. . . .'

Passing on to the reconstruction period, the development of the socialist attack still more sharpened the class struggle in the country and in particular on the ideological front. *Arsenal* was a powerful blow to the Petlurovsky-Vinnichenkovsky theoreticians of the non-bourgeoisness of the Ukrainian national.

Dovzhenko himself remarks with some bitterness in his *Autobiography* that a delegation of Ukrainian writers that travelled to Moscow with a protest and a demand to bar the film was not exactly reproached by the leaders of the country.[43]

He goes on, however:[44]

Making the film was an important step in my life. I became wiser and more mature as a political worker because of it. I was proud of myself and at the same time felt great pain. I realized that things were far from what they should be in our society. Life became hard.

1 Portrait of Vsevolod Pudovkin by E. Bieber, Berlin 1929

2 In his film *Mother*, Pudovkin played the part of a White Guard officer arresting 'Mother's' son Pavel (left, played by Fogel. Next to him is Savitsky)

3 'The End of the Demonstration,' from *Mother* by Vsevolod Pudovkin

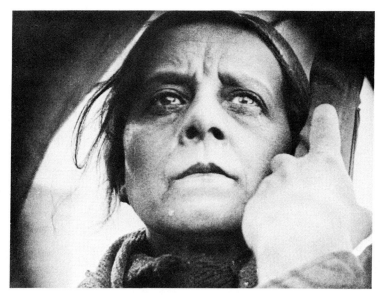

4 'Heading the demonstration with the Red Banner.' The mother, played by
Baranovskaya of the Moscow Art Theatre, in Pudovkin's film *Mother*

5 Caricature of Vsevolod
Pudovkin, Soviet film director, by
Isaac Schmidt. Schmidt was a fellow
student with the author in
Eisenstein's group at the All-Union
State Institute of Cinematography
(the VGIK), in Moscow

6 Caricature of Herbert Marshall by
Isaac Schmidt, at his German
exhibition in 1973

7 Caricature of Herbert Marshall by
Isaac Schmidt, Moscow 1962

8 Vsevolod Pudovkin and Herbert Marshall meeting after twelve years at the World
Peace Conference in Paris, 1949

9 Savitsky, the Party Secretary of the Institute of Cinematography, and former Red Cavalry Commander

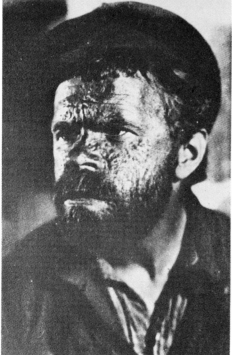

10 Savitsky as a strike-breaker in Pudovkin's film *Mother*

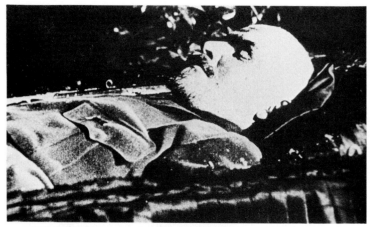

11 Lenin's body lying in state, from *The Three Songs of Lenin* by Dziga Vertov

12 Lenin's bench without Lenin, in summer, from *The Three Songs of Lenin* by Dziga Vertov

13 Lenin's bench without Lenin, in winter, from *The Three Songs of Lenin* by Dziga Vertov

14 Lenin sitting on his favourite bench in his country house (*dacha*). From *The Three Songs of Lenin* by Dziga Vertov

15 Lenin on a rostrum in Red Square (behind him is inscribed, 'Here will be erected a monument to victorious labour'—eventually it became the Lenin Mausoleum)

16 A squad of Red Army men marching with a banner which reads, 'We're going to see the cinema film *The Three Songs of Lenin*' (1934)

17 Stalin as a Guard of Honour at the bier of Lenin during his Lying in State, from *The Three Songs of Lenin* by Dziga Vertov

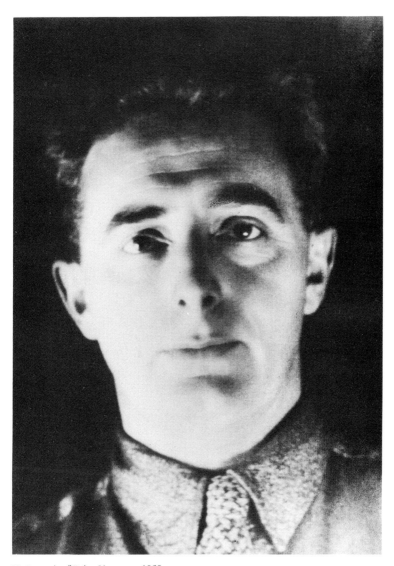
18 Portrait of Dziga Vertov, c. 1920

19 Dziga Vertov, 'The Man with the Movie Camera'

20 Caricature of Dziga Vertov by P. S. Galadjev, *c.* 1920

21 Caricature of Dziga Vertov, 1929. This caricature is a clear expression of the negative mood of Vertov, even the way he holds the camera, as compared with the two illustrations of earlier years

22 Alexander Dovzhenko (left) with Nikita Khrushchev (center) in Red Army uniforms on the Western Ukrainian Front during the war (1943)

23 Caricature of Sergei Yutkevich, Soviet film director, author of the term 'crippled creative biographies'

24 Alexander Dovzhenko, self-portrait, profile, in the 1930s

25 Alexander Dovzhenko, caricature by Isaac Schmidt, in the 1950s

26 Alexander Dovzhenko, caricature by himself, 1924

27 Sculpture on the grave of Alexander Dovzhenko in Novodevich'e Cemetery, Moscow

28 Caricature of Sergei Eisenstein by Isaac Schmidt

29 Caricature of Sergei Eisenstein by Boris Livanov, People's Artist of the Soviet Union and Artistic Director of the Moscow Art Theatre. It is inscribed, 'To Herbert Marshall in memory of our friendly meetings in Moscow, London, 1930–62. (signed) Boris Livanov, Moscow, 28 November 1962'

30 Eisenstein meets Paul Robeson with Herbert Marshall at the Belorussian Railway Station, Moscow, 22 December 1934

31 Caricature of Grisha Alexandrov by Isaac Schmidt

32 Bronze sculpture, portrait of Eisenstein, by Fredda Brilliant, acquired by the
Ministry of Culture of the USSR for the Eisenstein Museum

Earth

It is significant that of the four film directors I am writing about, three of them had their films chosen as among the best films of all time. This was at the World Exhibition in Brussels in 1957, when a conference of world cinema critics chose the ten best films ever made. Among them was Eisenstein's *Battleship Potemkin*, Pudovkin's *Mother*, and Dovzhenko's *Earth*.

This but confirmed all that we foreign critics had written about it, since my very first review of it in 1930. I am proud to have been the first, at least in the English-speaking world, to review and praise this film.

In his homeland it was a different story, which I will go into. As I write they have been celebrating posthumously the eightieth anniversary of Dovzhenko's birth, filled with panegyrics of this Soviet genius, and boasting that he, ardent supporter of the Communist Party of the Soviet Union, made one of the best films of all time. But just read my preamble to the review I wrote in 1930:[45]

> One film in particular had fundamentally a counter-revolutionary philosophy and was cut, and now I believe is withdrawn, though indeed a beautiful film. Its title, *Earth*, could not be bettered. The treatment imparts all the richness, the fecundity, the immutability of nature, earth giving birth to flowers and animals and men, feeding them, giving work for them, burying them. They who rightly live need fear no death.

And here is my review:

> Regisseur and Scenario for *Zimla* (*Earth*): A. Dovzhenko.
> Rich waving corn, cloud shadows moving in the wind, great open skies, growth of fruit, sunflowers and a sunflower maiden, luscious apples on heavy laden trees, ripe for the fall. On the thick grass in the orchard, an old man is lying, white and beautiful with age. He is smiling at three people standing around him, waiting, their dark hair contrasting with his whiteness.
> 'Son – I am dying,' peacefully they watch, the very young man with cleanshaven face, the father with dark beard and wife buxom; on the grass, two young children play.
> 'Yes . . . but you must die.'

The reply is as natural as the ripe apples and the corn and the children as they watch the old man's smile.

'For 75 years have I plowed the earth.'

'Father, if I were a Commissar, I would give you an Order for that.'

But the grandson interjects: 'They don't give Orders for that.'

'For what do they give them then. . . .?'

But the old man holds out his hand.

'I should like something to eat. Give me an apple.'

And as he slowly eats the ripe fruit, another old man, unobtrusive in the background comes forward.

'Brother, promise to tell me where you have gone, if you can, so I may come too.'

The dying man smiles and nods, and falls slowly back.

Dead.

The children are nibbling at ripe apples, the sunflowers and the fruit are growing.

Crying faces of women, angry Kulaks, resisting collectivization. One tries to kill his horse, but is stopped by his son. There is a great meeting in the village, all crowding under great white sky.

In the one cemetery old man kneels by grave of his friend.

'Brother, are you there?'

And he listens, ear to earth.

'Good health, grandfather,' comes the reply . . . from three children hiding behind another grave.

The crowd increases, ploughman stops horse to watch, three cows watch, three Kulaks, all chewing.

All watch the road that leads over skyline. On which appears figures marching, and in the middle, IT!

Crowd rushes.

The TRACTOR has come!

It stops. Kulaks deride: 'IT STOPS!'

Others: 'IT GOES!'

Men try to push it. Then driver finds radiator empty. No water anywhere.

'Did you drink well at the last village?' he asks of his company. And they fill the radiator with their urine.

'IT GOES!'

Triumphantly enters village.

'FACT,' admits one Kulak.

Driver addresses crowd as to what it can do. Kulaks jeer.

'WATCH . . . WE BEGIN.'

Then the machine is plowing, raking, sowing, reaping, threshing, sorting, breadmaking, machines over beasts.'

The leader of village Communists, the dead man's grandson, Vasily, is triumphant. His work bears fruit.

Then when work is done, twilight comes, lovers walk, older ones to bed, mists creep, darkness falls. Grandson and his love at last have to part.

And along the lane he comes home, strong with love and completed work. His joy bubbles over, he begins to stamp the dust, he dances, DANCES, dancing man and dancing dust.

Then suddenly Vasily collapses limp to the ground, still.

A horse starts with fear in the dark, and in the distance a white figure is running, running away.

Only the dust dances.

Night.

The father is sitting with bowed head, by his dead son. Knock comes to door, all look up. News of murderer? But it is only a priest.

'It's no good now,' the father says, 'and you too are no good now.' The priest goes back to his empty church.

'Bury him in the New Way,' the father says to head of village Soviet, 'Without priests or acolytes,' and so only a singing crowd escort him to his grave. But the older women fearfully cross themselves, muttering.

'God save us, without priests or crosses!'

But the people sing on. Past ripening sunflower fields. A pregnant woman labours in travail. Priest totters around his empty church and barren ikons. Youth sings. The open coffin almost seems to float along. The dead face is brushed by apple-laden branches.

'Strike them, God!' priest cries to ikons. And a white figure of a Kulak is seen running across the fields.

The baby is being born. Sunflowers growing. The body of the dead moves on. Life is singing.

Priest muttering.

A Kulak running amok, twisting his head round and round in the earth.

'Strike!' says priest.

'This is *my* earth,' cries the white Kulak. 'MINE!'

But the fruit grows, babies are born, sunflowers grow, men and women sing, the dead go on. The Kulak hears them coming near. He rushes to the cemetery between the crosses, towards them, crying,

'I killed him!'

The procession moves on, they do not hear him.

'I killed him at night,' he shouts.

Still they sing.

'At night when he danced like this!' and he too dances among the graves. There the dying living and the living dead. But no one hears him.

They are listening to a speaker on the new life.

'He died on the dawn of a new life.'

'He died for the dawn.'

Then comes the rain and the lovely fruit and trees are made yet more beautiful by the silver rain brushed with the wind. Corn, apples, melons, fruit, shine as the rain ceases, triumphant nature.

Function – In contrast to the majority of Soviet films and to Dovzhenko's last film, *Arsenal*, this is a meditative film. A philosophical meditation on the immutability of nature. Nature grows, man dies, is born, struggles, dies, part of that greater Nature. Death is even more beautiful than life when it is of the rightly lived. Theoretically, this film is not of strict Communist ideology; it is rather the resignation and acceptance by man of immortal, immutable Nature. Fear no death. 'Yes, but you must die,' is said quite calmly. Deep-meaning too is the old man's request, not for an 'Order' but 'something to eat.'

The original film had two other threads which were cut out by the censor, but are of great interest in that they emphasize more the philosophy of the film. One part is that of the lover of the dead man who, when she heard of it in her room, tears off her clothes and goes 'berserk' with sorrow, deep animal sorrow, the cry for a lost mate. And the other is the end, where this girl is in the arms of another man; Nature consoles herself always with the living. (Reminiscent of part of Sean O'Casey's play, *The Silver Tassie*.) It is not really tragic, it is just life, nature immortal. Another part too that will probably be cut out is the filling of the radiator by the men. Interesting attempt to link up man organically with his machines. They grow from each other, part of a Whole.

Form – Due to its meditative quality, it tended to stillness of action, that at times seems suspiciously photographic and not cinematic. The 'suspended action' of *Arsenal* was here almost 'non-action.' The fact that Dovzhenko was once a painter may help to explain this tendency. The shots of the fruit are the most beautiful I have seen. Several continuing compositions were interesting: a plowman between two cows, and the driver between two great tractor wings, but the contrasts of cows and people has been done before! But to me undoubtedly the loveliest moment in the film is when the apple-laden branches brush the face of the dead man in his coffin. Here, death really *was* beautiful. Throughout the composition of narrow earth and wide expanse of skies gave the impression of nature overall. But – and here is an important point – Nature in its best clothes. Bedecked with jewelry. Nature in one mood.

An original and beautiful film. The man that can make two such divergent films as *Arsenal* and *Earth* is a master to be studied. The subject of his next will be DNIEPRESTROY, which will be, when completed, the largest electric power station in the world, with Turk-Sib the pride of the Five-Year Plan thus far achieved. With such a variety of subjects, can one wonder at the versatility of the Soviet cinema?

Dovzhenko was the first Soviet cinematographer to bring the theme of collectivization on to the screen, but then it was still voluntary; later armed force was used and the 'liquidation of the Kulak' began after his film was made, with all its vast tragedy. Parallel was Eisenstein's *The General Line* (*Old and New*), which was an intellectual exposition as compared to an emotional, passionate exposition.

Later, I learned the Party had damned this film as counter-revolutionary. I couldn't read Russian then, but years later I was to dig out the initial attack on Dovzhenko that signalled the overall attack on the revolutionary artists by their Party. It was by Demyan Bedny, the popular Party poet, and obviously officially inspired and published in the official Party newspaper, *Pravda*. Here are some extracts of this vitriolic attack:[46]

PHILOSOPHY

Concerning home-grown philosophers
Cinema simpletons,
About political apathy
and about the cinema film *Earth* in particular.

So now, on our name day, we are presented with a good-for-nothing film . . . a newly announced motion picture called *Earth*.
Cinema specialists in Moscow now show *Earth*. Fatuous viewers are virtually being told that the latter 'don't understand' or 'don't properly apprehend' it, that this film-miracle is not clear to everyone. . . .

Earth is a Kulak cinema film. It shows us a Ukraine of healthy, growing Kulaks, well-fed, drunken, corpulent, tough, smart, juicy, with violently rebellious bodies, sensuous, 'anecdotal,' unnatural. Completely theatrical with a vulgar operetta-like spirit, Gopak folk-dances, loving couples, stereotyped props. The age-long tenor of life, an old man. There, that is its background.

The tractor in it is a novelty. Like the old man by the elderberry tree: lying on his backside. But in reality: the method of *mastercraftsmanship for masking its essence.* . . .

And here – why go further afield? On the cinema screen a scene is presented of this very same satisfaction. A new lad kisses the lass full on the lips. The murdered lad is made a fool of with an apple on his nose. But the murderer, Kulak, is somewhat alarmed and can you imagine calls forth pity for himself! He torments himself, the poor Kulak torments himself! He has pangs of conscience, the poor Kulak. He gives an angry push to his own father. It may be the funeral has frightened him. But on the morrow he will confidently emerge from his cottage. His forthcoming retribution is not seen in the film, there is not a breath of this in the whole picture.

No misfortune whatsoever threatens the Kulak. What then does the simple-minded viewer see in the film?

Through the 'gloss,' through the fancy shining lacquer, simply that *ONLY ONE VICTOR ON EARTH AND THAT IS THE KULAK*!

'An experiment' [Note this as the start of the Party-inspired attacks on 'Experiments' – see *Eisenstein* and *Pudovkin*.

Everything must be controlled – there can only be 'Experiments for the masses'. HM.]

Connoisseurs plead: 'It's photogenic!' 'Wonderful!' 'Filmic!'

But for me it is simply *cynical*.

Just see, marked cards are already in the pack and they are beginning to pick out the red suit for us:

And by the graveyard's gateway
young let life play unconfined,
awhile indifferent nature
with eternal beauty shines.[47]

Already they try to aim Pushkin at us. Anyway, what has our wise poet got to do with this? Such 'hot stuff' is not written à la Pushkin, but they present us with a salacious limerick.

Come my love into the courtyard
for a little loving courtship!
without delay I'll make a blitz!
Let me rattle little tits!

Before us the hero of this very limerick is engrossed in playing with the rattles, pawing away at the girl. Hurry up and send this film abroad! In our children's class let teenagers lick their ruddy lips, exciting them sensually before they have matured spiritually.

'How very interesting!'

Particularly beautiful is the delirium of the naked girl.

Where there is something to show, it was shown.

Right on!

In genuine anguish!

The girl is stripped of her chemise.

Publicly, before the whole world!

What is this? Not cynical?

What is this? Permissible?

Isn't it forbidden on the theater stage?

But permissible on the cinema screen?

Is it clever?

It is necessary?

How many times have we quoted Lenin's words:

'For us the most important of the arts is the cinema.'

But the most important words have not been noticed,

The most significant have not been noted;
The 'most important' is self-evident.
But '*for us*' in our crucial battle,
Showing *no pity* to our enemies,
'See how far we go with a naked girl!'
But didn't Lenin instruct us, didn't he decree:

> 'Organize supervision over cinema-performances and
> systematize that activity. Entertainment films are specially
> for advertising and profit (of course without obscenity and
> counter-revolution).'

Without obscenity and counter-revolution!
And already amongst us, somewhere, resolutions are proposed,
buzzing cinema bumble-bees, advertisements cry out
unceasingly, in honor of the cinema film *Earth*.

Counter-revolutionary obscenity!
That's how low we have sunk.

Our film-front remains without attention, a crew of master-
touch-me-nots has formed amongst us, not permitting us on to
the forbidden threshold.
Bloatedly-boasting with its cheap philosophy, stupid, dirt-
cheap.
A genius gives himself airs.
The devil knows what he doesn't grab on to,
At times what a mish-mash he produces,
He raises a dust in advance, glorifies himself, and afterwards
what does one get?
One gets a cinema *Earth*!
That the film-thing *Earth* would not have pleased Ilyich.
He would have appraised it with words of short shrift:

'insufferable muck!'

and that would have been the end of it.
*The end of that cinema film. The more so because of where the Kulak
cries out in victorious triumph.*
And I can't imagine Ilyich any other way!
And after all I did know Ilyich!

Here are Dovzhenko's own words about how his masterpiece was
damned by the Party's official spokesman:[48]

Earth I directed at the Kiev studios. My joy in having creative success was cruelly squashed by Demyan Bedny's horrible article, *The Philosophers*, in *Izvestia*. I was so stunned by this article, I was so ashamed of walking the streets of Moscow, that I literally aged and turned grey in several days. It was a real emotional trauma. At first I wanted to die. But a few days later I found myself in the honor guard at the funeral of Mayakovsky, with whom I had always been on good terms. Bedny stood in front of me in the guard. I stared at his balding head and passionately thought, 'Die!' But he was immune. So we left the crematorium alive and unharmed.

14 April 1945

Today is the fifteenth anniversary of the death . . . of Vladimir Mayakovsky. How sad it is to recall that the greatest poet of our epoch forsook our epoch. I remember, on the eve of his suicide, we sat together in the little garden of the Dom Herzen [House of Writers] both in a very despondent state of mind – I because of the way my film *Earth* had been savaged – and he exhausted because of the RAPP-speculator-cannibalistic worthless riff-raff and rogues.

'Come in and see me tomorrow, let's get together, maybe we shall be able to gather together a small group of creators to defend our art, because that which is going on around us is unbearable, impossible.'

I promised to come and shook his great hand for the last time. The next day, on the Sunday, I prepared to go to him with Julia, when I heard the terrible news. . . .

Now 15 years have gone by. Not long ago in the Kremlin Hospital the aged [. . .] Demyan Bedny met me and said: 'I don't know, forgotten even, why I swore at your *Earth* so in those days. But I can tell you now – neither before, nor after, have I ever seen such a film. What a great work of art that really was.'

I said nothing [. . .].

And who was this Demyan Bedny? He was the favorite poet of Nikita Khrushchev! In fact, a mere versifier, an agit-prop poet of the Party. He was used by the Party and its secret police to attack anyone they wished to be calumniated. This was open knowledge but proof was eventually given by Khrushchev himself in his memoirs, *Khrushchev Remembers*.[49] Here is what he wrote about Bedny:[50]

Soon the political terror started. I caught only an occasional, accidental glimpse of its inner workings.

While the trial of the Leningrad oppositionists was going on, Kaganovich and Sergo Ordzhonikidze were left in charge whenever Stalin and Molotov were out of Moscow. Once I went by the Central Committee office to see Kaganovich about some matter relating to city administration. When Kaganovich was informed that I was outside, he asked me to come into his study. He had Sergo Ordzhonikidze and Demyan Bedny with him. They were conferring about the trial of the oppositionists and the presentation of the trial in the press. A series of articles condemning the oppositionists was being published in order to prepare public opinion for the harsh sentences which actually had already been decided upon.

I remember the scene well. Sergo and Kaganovich asked Demyan Bedny, 'Well, Comrade Demyan, have you written a poem that we can use?'

'Yes,' said Demyan, and he recited the poem.

When he finished there was an awkward pause. Kaganovich spoke up first: 'That's not quite what we had in mind, Comrade Demyan.' Sergo, who had a fiery temper, didn't beat around the bush. He heatedly exhorted Demyan to do better. Demyan Bedny was an obese man, and he was completely bald. His head looked like a huge copper cauldron. He looked at them with good-natured eyes and said, 'I'm afraid I can't do any better. Much as I've tried, this is all I've been able to squeeze out. I just can't raise my hand against the oppositionists. I can't do it. I'm impotent toward them.' Actually, he used a cruder, more manly expression.

I don't know if what Demyan wrote was ever published. He obviously wasn't completely convinced that the oppositionists were criminals. That's why he couldn't muster the inspiration and the Party spirit to rip them apart in his poem. He just wasn't sure they were enemies. To mention my own attitude, naturally I was on Kaganovich's side – that is, on Stalin's side.

Therefore, at the time I glared at Demyan disapprovingly. But now I understand why Demyan had his doubts.*

And such men as Khrushchev, with their primitive level of culture, decide the fate of all artists in the Soviet Union, great or small.

Apart from the revelations during the Khrushchev period, it is interesting to have confirmation of the treatment of the 'Kulaks' in a recent Soviet critic's review of Dovzhenko's work – that of Irakli Andronikov, called *The Poetry of Dovzhenko*, which I have quoted from.

I have the Russian text and a Soviet version in English. It is interesting to note the eternal censoring that goes on, even from a Soviet Russian version to a Soviet English version.

Here is an extract: 'The juxtaposition of contrasting scenes and ideas in Dovzhenko's work is based on the principles of antithesis in poetry.'[51] (And here with the typical Communist Party cover-up, a paragraph is censored out, without any indication that it had been there.)

I translate what was omitted; it reads: 'Let us say Lermontov speaks: "And reigning in the soul is some kind of secret cold, while fire burns in the blood.' "[52] Cold is contrasted to fire. "Farewell, unwashed Russia, land of slaves, land of masters."[53] Slaves are contrasted to masters.'

Now why would the censor have a guilty conscience about these famous quotations of a Russian classic, long dead? Maybe his words would find a reverberation still in Russian souls? Andronikov goes on:[54]

Let us turn once more to the film *Earth*. In the opening scene we are shown an old man dying with a smile on his lips and in a second the Kulaks are weeping. A man dies and reverent silence reigns while his kin stand around the bedside and bemourn him. This silence is then rent by thunderous noise, women shrieking, dogs whining and horses rearing in the stables – *the peasants are plundering the Kulaks' property.*

Yes, that is the recent Soviet translation. The Kulaks are weeping,

* D. Bedny, a hack versifier, may have had his doubts at this time. He soon recovered, however, and produced a series of nauseating 'poems' vilifying the accused (including the main victims of the subsequent purge of the Red Army) and demanding savage punishment. (Original footnote)

the women are shrieking, the horses rearing, because their property is being plundered.

And Andronikov goes on (with another bit censored, with errors): 'He [Vasily] plows up the furrows left by the Kulaks and his forefathers.'[55] But the Russian original says, 'He plows up the boundaries of the Kulaks. He plows up the boundaries of his father.'[56]

Andronikov says Dovzhenko endowed Vasily with 'high moral principles' and this is true. Dovzhenko believed in those principles, and yet ignored, even in this film, men and women weeping as their hard-earned homes were plundered and stolen by other peasants, aided and abetted by all the Young Communists and Communist-like Vasily, with guns, and the *Cheka*, which was to arrest them all, men, women and children, and send them to prison, exile, slave labor, and deaths by the millions.

It is for us to realize that the works of art we have been talking about remain so, despite the factual falsification of their content and the fact that the tragedy was on the other foot – not of Vasily-Vartan-Sasha but their fathers and fellow-farmers and that the heroes were the villains, and the villains the heroes, whether in *Earth*, *The Old and The New* or *Bezhin Meadow*.

Here is where the genuineness of an artist is tested, his portrayal of truth, and the artist uses his artistic means to show *that* truth even against all superficial appearances or initial overt statements that seem to present the Party line.

So Vasily in *Earth* is a genuine, sincere Party activist, one of those the Party used to 'liquidate the Kulak'. He is killed at the height of his happiness doing his Party duty. And the other youngster who killed him is shown in the depth of his despair, having done *his* duty, defending his family and his people against liquidation, exile and death. And what emerges when seen in retrospect, and the reason the Party senses something was wrong, despite the overt pro-Communist Party treatment?

The Party critics labelled *Earth* 'biologism,' 'pantheism.' And it was just that, as I clearly realized in my original review. For now that the whole basic tenet of the Party that Dovzhenko ostensibly expounded, the justice of collectivization and the liquidation of the Kulak, is shown to be the colossal crime it was (however sincere the Vasilys may have been in doing the Party's dirty work), yet the film expounds a vaster theme, a profounder truth, that one called 'pantheistic'.

In fact, these are the tenets more of the *Bhagavad Gita* than of *Das Kapital* – that, in the long view, life and death are the inextricable opposites in unity, no matter what labels they wear, Communist or anti-Communist; for mankind it is the same.

That is heresy to the Communist Party of the Soviet Union and for that they crucified Dovzhenko. And it is ironic that the Communist Ivor Montagu sees this and now tries to adopt it as the Party line – as 'sound Marxist dialectic: the union of opposites!' Here is what he wrote:[57]

> For the key to all the poignancy in Dovzhenko's film is death. Just that, the simplest thing of all. Death apprehended never as an end, a finish, dust to dust. But death as a sacrifice, the essential one, a part of the unending process of reviving life. . . .
>
> Pantheism? No. Nature Worship? Not at all. Sound Marxist dialectic: *the union of opposites.*

So what the 'Marxist' Party *then* damned as pantheistic, as anti-Marxist, as anti-dialectic, is now the opposite!

And when they now write about these films or film-makers nothing is said of what really happened to them.

Being Communist or anti-Communist, Kulak or informer, is irrelevant on the great canvas of existence. Thus both Eisenstein and Dovzhenko as artists had the last word – against the Party they were apparently supporting with their works of art. The didacticism, the 'Party-mindedness,' the class-consciousness disappears, the art remains. The particular dies, the universal survives.

And as George Bernard Shaw so brilliantly pointed out:[58]

> Effectiveness of assertion is the Alpha and Omega of style. He who has nothing to assert has no style and can have none: he who has something to assert will go as far in power of style as its momentousness and his conviction will carry him. Disprove his assertion after it is made, yet its style remains. Darwin has no more disproved the style of Job nor of Handel than Martin Luther destroyed the style of Giotto. All the assertions get disproved sooner or later; and so we find the world full of magnificent debris of artistic fossils, with the matter-of-fact credibility gone clean out of them, but the form still splendid.

Here is a 1930 article by S. Tsimbal on Alexander Dovzhenko's
Earth:[59]

The latest work of Dovzhenko has aroused a most lively
argument, the spectators are sharply divided into passionate
supporters and no less passionate opponents. That alone signifies
that we here have to deal with a very significant work of art,
which demands the long and genuine attention of the mass
spectator. The point here is not in the talent of Dovzhenko
(which is obvious to everyone) and not in the creative power of
his *Earth* which is indisputable. The principle around which
public opinion surges is the problem of world outlook
(*Mirovozzrenie*) in art, a problem put forward by Dovzhenko with
unexpected sharpness, head-on, unequivocally.

Somewhere in the Ukraine, on a small plot of warm fertile
earth, the fury and despair of the dying Kulak class brought to
a stop the young happy militant human life dancing from an
excess of life force. A Kulak rifle shot the village activist, a
collective farmer. A collective farm tractor plowed over the Kulak
boundaries. This is the beginning of a war. This is what decides
the fate of the tractorist Vasily. And after he has been murdered,
a terrible conveyor of human passions comes into action. In her
unspent woman's love, the wife of Vasily thrashes around in a
frenzy. Twisting around like a wolf the Kulak murderer tears
his hair and twists in his unquestionable fury. The village, the
youth of the village, sing with gladness over the coffin of Vasily,
and the heavy laden apple boughs bend over the coffin, also
voting for the new oncoming life into which so passionately and
gladly Vasily was striving. On that the picture finishes.
Immediately after that discussion begins.

Dovzhenko is one of those few artists who serve the new themes
not out of fear but out of conscience. And if his wonderful film
will not turn out to be a popular keynote lecture on the theme
of the class struggle in the village (and such cinema lectures
incidentally we badly need) *it will be undoubtedly the greatest creative
document of the greatest creative epoch. Earth* is not the path of Soviet
cinematography. That is true. But *Earth* is a stage on that path,
a stage on which no one suggests halting. But not to point it
out would be of the greatest thoughtlessness.

[Signed] S. Tsimbal.

What happened here? The Party was supposed to be rejecting this film because it was *not* of value to the proleteriat or the class struggle, but in the very same magazine we have the following evidence of the kind of reception even such a complex film as Dovzhenko's *Earth* received amongst the industrial proleteriat, the cream of the workers of the Soviet Union, who were supposed to be the cream of the Party. Here is what it said:

The comrades participating characterized the film as '*A most valuable contribution to Soviet cinematography and the director Dovzhenko as the proletarian master closest of all to the workers.*'

Tsimbal's criticism was written as soon as the film was released in the early part of 1930, but I quote the Party film newspaper some four years later, where now Stalin had taken over complete dictatorial control, and this is what the critics said: 'The next work of Dovzhenko, *Earth*, ideologically was a step backward. It was significantly influenced by bourgeois philosophy, in particularly the influence of biologism.'[60]

This of course is fantastically interesting to read, because what happened eventually was that the Party censors cut out the scene of the frenzied naked wife going berserk over the murder of her husband.

And as if to add the last touch of the absurd – Dovzhenko's own father was ejected from his collective farm because of participating as an actor in his son's counter-revolutionary film *Earth*! Dovzhenko himself wrote, '*Zvenigora, Arsenal, Earth*. The uproar at the reviews. Disputes. Father expelled from collective farm for *Earth*. Ostracism for *Arsenal*. Ostracism for *Ukraine in Flames*.'[61]

Ivan

Ivan was Dovzhenko's first sound film. He was urged by the Party to make a film on the industrialization of the country and the transformation of the peasantry into workers.

The film begins with a prologue – the paysage of the mighty River Dniepr filled with calm and quiet beauty. Starting with the spring, which means the breaking of the ice, ice goes slowly floating downstream. Then the bright blue sky is reflected in the waters. Vast scope and distances. Slowly the picturesque Dniepr shores move past the viewer. The distant lyrical music slowly merges into a distant song. All is wrapped as it were in ageless somnolence.

The paysage changes. The tempo quickens. Then rhythmic voices of the oarsmen are heard. They approach the rapids. The water begins to foam stormily. The roar merges with explosions from the shore. This is the beginning of a great panorama of the mighty Dnieprostroi Dam (built, like Magnitogorsk and other mighty Soviet industrial constructions, under American engineers, of which of course nothing is said in any film).

Now the action changes to the village. A peasant family are discussing the need for workers on the construction. The father of Ivan urges the villagers to join. But there are three Ivans, each with different fates. The village Ivan was educated on the construction work and joined the Communist Party; the second Ivan, a shock-brigade worker, was killed at his work; the third Ivan, a Young Communist, took an independent path and was considered a truant worker.

Two original Dovzhenko episodes in his script were not included in the final film – one where a worker speaks directly to the audience (a favorite technique of Dovzhenko) and pleads for better quality work; and the second where the Pope of Rome in full dress robes sits behind the 'black' pay desk reserved to pay those 'lazy' workers and shame them. Here he joyfully greets the third Ivan – the truant!

In one scene Dovzhenko tries to justify the loss of life, like the second Ivan, caused by carelessness and lack of safety precautions, the disregard for human life, so typical of the mad rush of construction during the Five-Year Plan. Here the mother of this shock-brigader rushes through door after door of the bureaucracy to demand greater care for their workers. But on finally reaching the chief's office she hears him already demanding better conditions and greater safety precautions and at that ceases her complaint. And now all is care and concern as work goes on, building socialism.

Thus did Dovzhenko attempt to follow the Party line. But nevertheless his film was severely criticized and the present-day critic in the official History of Soviet Cinema says the film was difficult for his contemporaries to understand. He goes on to say, 'Now the distance of time separating us from the film's creation allows us to understand better its significance as one of the most profound works of the First Five-Year Plan.'[62]

But in all the reviews of Dovzhenko's films in this latest 'History' there is not a word about Stalin and the true reasons for this 'lack of understanding'.

Unrealized film projects

In his autobiography, Alexander Dovzhenko writes:[63]

> After returning from the foreign assignment I suggested to the directors at Ukraine film a screenplay about Arctic explorers based on the tragedy of Nobile and the death of Roald Amundsen. The directors turned down the idea and demanded that I immediately write something about our present-day life in Ukraine and not about the Arctic. I put Amundsen out of my mind and in twelve days wrote the unsuccessful screenplay *Ivan* and began shooting. I found it difficult to work on *Ivan* because Bedny's article continued to oppress me.
>
> *The film was cut and considered half forbidden.* I was listed as a pantheist, and Spinozist – a doubtful fellow traveler who could not be tolerated. Even the students from the Film Institute who were working in my group were considered as Dovzhenkoites, that is, counter-revolutionaries in cinema. I was deprived of the opportunity to train a crew. And because I wasn't even invited to lecture at the Kiev Film Institute I was sure that they did not want anyone to study with me. Later the director of cinema, Shumyatsky, stated this very definitely. The proletarian wave in films was taken over by Party members, directors Arnold Kordium and Mikhailo Kapchynsky. I was relegated to the camp of the petit bourgeoisie as a gifted but politically limited fellow traveler. The higher political powers lived in Kharkov, I in Kiev.

He was obliged to deliver *Ivan* in time for the fifteenth anniversary of the Revolution, 7 November 1932, and found the deadline[64]

> almost impossible to meet. It was my first sound film, made with very bad equipment which the sound technicians had not mastered yet. Nevertheless I did manage to turn the film in on time, although at the end I had to work at the cutting table without sleep or rest for eighty-five hours. The film came out raw. The leadership received it badly. Kommunist[65] published an article by Fedir Taran, full of threats and malevolence.[66] Mykola Skrypnyk,[67] the People's Commissar of Education,

wrote an article accusing me of fascism. I fled to Moscow in order to put an end to this life in Ukrainian surroundings where I was hated and continually harassed.

But what is terrifying is the naivety of such intelligent and honest men as Dovzhenko, realizing the falsification about themselves spread by the Party, yet taking at face value all its falsifications about the outside world, and about America in particular. Almost everything Dovzhenko wrote about the USA has a totally negative character. He prepared an anti-American film at the behest of the Party – but even that he never produced. He wrote this in his diary:[68]

16 June 1949
The American Government refuses to send grain to the starving people of India. 'Give up your resources and starve to death.'
    Neomalthusians, slanderers, ravishing the earth and hoping to kill a third of the supposedly overpopulated and exhausted planet's population.

In view of the subsequent rescue by the USA not only of India from famine but also, by the sale of wheat, of the USSR when in dire need, this is typical of the Party-induced anti-American lies that are persistently propagated, which are not only anti-foreign in general. His précis for a story entitled 'The Swedes' is a case in point.[69]

8 June 1951
Write a story. Captured Swedes during the reign of Catherine the Great are driven into exile from islands of the Baltic to Southern Ukraine. Some of them die on the way. The village is called Swedovka. 200 years go by. Swedes are now in collective farms. German occupation. The Swedish collective farmers are neutral.
    After the war, the Swedish Government demands reparations. Our Government agrees. A plebiscite. Agitation. Patriotism. Mixed feelings. Back to the motherland!
    Sweden. A meeting at the port. The purveyors of patriotism. The Swedes are settled in the mountains in poverty-stricken stony plots. Squalor and the absence of perspectives. And everything gradually settled down. Everything is small, but above all – there is no amplitude of life, no flight, no great aim.

They become spiritually impoverished. And then they understood what they had lost. Youth revolts.

Back to the fatherland. '*Hai Zhiva Radyanskaya Ukraina!*' [Long live the Soviet Ukraine!] Once more the steamship, but this time it is Soviet, *SS Ukraine* carries the Swedes back from Sweden to their fatherland. There are meetings in the ports of Europe, only this time completely the reverse. They arrive in their fatherland and begin to build Communism.

It is heartbreaking to read this proposed story – not written in the optimistic, idealistic 1920s or early 1930s but in 1951!

First, there is the total ignorance of the standard of living of the proletariat in Sweden, the highest in the world. Second, what happened to the foreign minorities in the USSR during the war is completely ignored. Take the Volga Germans who had lived there since Catherine the Great, and had their own Volga Autonomous Republic with its capital city called Engels, its German theaters and cultural life, and both indigenous Soviet-Germans and Communist emigrés. They were all exiled, Communists, workers, collective farmers, men, women and children – and the Volga Autonomous Republic was wiped off the map of the USSR – and hasn't returned. Even though it was eventually admitted, grudgingly and almost in secret, that such an event had taken place, no retribution or rehabilitation was allowed in the land of their forefathers. The same with the Tartars of the Crimea, who still remain in exile.

And now the Soviet Germans want to come home to their fatherland – and it isn't the Soviet Union, it's Germany – and not East Germany but West.

Dovzhenko writes further:[70]

23 June 1951
All the forces of nature, including the insects, work toward increasing crop yields and creating plenty. American Imperialists introduce the Colorado beetle to Europe. The transformation of nature for mankind's benefit has become a reality in our country.

Branched wheat as a symbol of abundance for liberated mankind. Dealers in hunger at a convention of agricultural experts in Canada. They demand that as a condition for signing an agreement with the USSR the Soviet government stop

Lysenko's research on branched wheat because it could cause a drastic fall of wheat prices.

Professor Wider of Cornell University proposed sending ships with special equipment to the Atlantic and Mediterranean to produce premature rain and then drought in Europe and Asia.

The capitalists have their own way of transforming nature: 'Thanks to the scientific research in biology, no one can deny the possibility that entire continents will die of hunger in the future. The Americans and the Japanese have been successful in developing bacteriological means of destroying crops. They can kill an entire nation by poisoning the soil.' What an abomination!

Look through all the materials for *A Measure of Life* and adapt them to the contents and plot elements. Look through the notes for *The Golden Gate*. Find literature on the subject. The history of agriculture. The history of wheat. The politics of wheat. Hunger. The dying father's testament to his son.

Ukraine – wheat – Lysenko – the construction of communism – Stalin. Lysenko – Siberian strains of wheat. Vernalization.* The phasic theory.

He accepts Lysenko – the charlatan whose Party-imposed theories retarded genetic science in the USSR and contributed towards its agricultural and horticultural backwardness, from which it still suffers.

In his proposed film *Dawn Over China*, he includes China of that time as a positive character:[71]

Transformation of nature in China. . . .
India's nature in chains.
Africa.

But then adds:

The murderous fertility in America.
Venereal soil. America.

How much of this false information about America he still believed! For example, Dovzhenko writes in his diary:[72]

* Trofim Lysenko claimed that his vernalization processing of seeds of spring wheat endowed them with qualities of winter wheat. (Original footnote)

9 April 1944

America has refused to see my *Battle for Our Soviet Ukraine*. She didn't even want to look at the blood she is buying with her canned bacon.

Curses on you, ladies and gentlemen of America, with all your prosperity and your gentle smiles. My father and mother and I and all the Ukrainian people curse you.

Of course probably what happened was the same problem I had when I was in charge of Soviet films during that war period of distribution in England. The endless films about the war and the wrongly chosen documentaries of terrifying bloodshed and loot and strife were too much for any cinema box-office. But we *did* have showings of these films in special meetings in the Soviet Society for Cultural Relations and others but of course they did not always get commercial release.

A Soviet critic writing in 1964 said:

Before Dovzhenko there were Ukrainian films, but there was no Ukrainian national cinema. For it's not a question of national landscapes, and not of national types. Gogol spoke to this point very precisely: 'True nationality consists not in describing a sarafan but in the very spirit of the people. A poet can even be national when he is describing a completely alien world, but looks at it through the eyes of his national poetry. With the eyes of all his people, when he so feels and speaks that to his brother nationals it seems as if he feels and speaks for them.'[73]

Eisenstein noted that accompanying Dovzhenko's *Ivan* one could declaim Gogol – his *The Beauty of the Dniepr*. The poignant expression of emotionality, the lyricism, the elevated style was not the result of imitating Gogol – the Director didn't stylize his material according to the great writer. Their similarity was given birth to by one and the same national basis.[74]

And this essential nationalism Dovzhenko could never shed, much as his masters, Stalin and Beria, threatened him. And that is why he made so few films.[75]

Before I made *Michurin*, production of *Chronicle of the Flaming Years* was halted, although it had been approved by the Ministry of Culture. Since *Michurin* I have not succeeded in completing a single picture.

Dawn Over China was set aside. My half-finished *A Farewell to America* was shelved. The script for *Discovery of the Anarctic* was not put into production. Apart from these scripts I have also written two plays: *Life In Bloom* and *Descendants of the Zaparozhe Cossacks*.

No doubt the *China* film was halted because of the serious back-stage conflicts that began to take place between Khrushchev and Mao Zedong, and at the same time the anti-American wave stopped when Khrushchev began a kind of temporary *détente* with America. That is always the danger for an artist in the Soviet Union trying to make a film on the current general line, that it can alter before he even starts shooting, as so many have found out to their bitter cost.

In fear of arrest he left for Moscow and personally appealed to Stalin. He was sent to Mosfilm Studios and now assigned Russian tasks. His first was a film about Siberia, *Aerograd*. His other two films were personally proposed by Stalin: *Shchors* and *Michurin*.

In Moscow: Directly Under Stalin

Aerograd

Now Dovzhenko had taken refuge in Moscow, escaping temporarily from those Ukrainian anti-nationalists, who seem always to be more virulent and intolerant and cruel than their Muscovite bosses. But now in reality he had less leeway than before. For his next films began his downward slide as it had for Pudovkin, when they both tried to carry out Stalin's orders and create 'socialist realism'. The poet had to try and be prosaic and it was a failure. Above all, for the first time he was ordered to take material which was non-Ukrainian. And if ever there was a nationalist artist it was Sasha Dovzhenko, whose previous films were saturated with folklore, the poetry and the singing of his mother Ukraine. Now he was in a foreign land, indeed an artificial land, *Aerograd* not yet created, on the Siberian frontier – indeed, the English title of the film was *Frontier*.

1930. Siberia. The Soviets want to establish the city of Aerograd

on the shores of the Japanese Sea for defense purposes. The
title: *Hurrah For The City*. Vladimir, a pilot, sings of the city about
to be built, of joy, and of fraternity. Title: *Hurrah For the City of
Aerograd that we, Bolsheviks, plan to build on the shores of the Pacific*.
Churkcha skis toward the city. Throughout the film he
approaches. He wants to study there. At the end he arrives,
'after skiing for 80 suns.' He finds the city still unbuilt. 'So I
will build, and *then* I will study,' he says.

Title: *Between the Bering Sea where there is ice and squadrons of our
whales, at the mouth of the great Amur River*. A group of eight men
are smuggling dynamite over the Amur border to sabotage the
Soviet efforts. Title: *Through the Amur borderland people come bearing
dynamite – six Russians and two who are not Russians*.

Stephan Glushak, an old partisan and the father of Vladimir,
sees them and shoots. Title: *Watch out! We'll kill them just now*.
The two Japanese escape. Glushak pursues and captures one of
them, who speaks of his country's hatred for the Soviets before
he is shot.

During this sequence the following titles appear:
On the shores of the Japanese Sea.
The old light dims and sinks beneath the Pacific Ocean.
A typhoon comes from Japan.
*Seen from afar there is a man in the Taiga, who knows how to read the
Taiga.*

This last refers to Khudiakov, another hunter and an old
friend of Glushak. Glushak has come upon him in his search
for the other Japanese saboteur. Khudiakov denies seeing any
strangers. Vladimir, meanwhile, is flying to visit his father. . . .
Khudiakov, it turns out is lying and has hidden the Japanese.
With the aid of Shabanov, who fled from the Revolution into
eastern Siberia, Khudiakov is trying to stir up a revolt among
the 'Old Believers.'[76] Shabanov exhorts the widows to remember
their dead husbands in his reactionary speech. When he calls
out the name of Maria Kudina, who does not know her husband
has died, she calls him a liar. He produces the dead man's hair
and throws it at the grieving widow.

Van-Lin, a friend of Glushak discovers the plot and spreads
the word. Glushak forms an army to fight Shabanov and his
Japanese allies. His son leads the attack from the air. Glushak
discovers that his old friend, Khudiakov, is a traitor. He takes

him into the forest and kills him. Dying, Khudiakov calls for his mother.

The prisoners are given over for judgment to the widows of the men who were misled into uprising. Van-Lin has been killed. Glushak carries his body into an airplane. Vladimir and his Korean wife have had a child. The sky fills with airplanes. Titles announce the parts of the Soviet Union from which they fly. Below are seen the masses of people who have come to help build Aerograd.

The one powerful, typically Dovzhenko scene, was when the old partisan Glushak finds out his lifelong friend Khudiakov is a traitor. He is inevitably condemned to death. Glushak asks that he himself be the executioner. They walk into the taiga, the jungle they had lived and hunted in together all their lives, and then comes the moment for him to shoot and he turns and looks straight into the camera and speaks to the audience: 'I am killing a traitor and enemy of the people – my friend Vasily Petrovich Khudiakov, sixty years old. *Be you witnesses of my sorrow.*' And he turns. His victim lets out a animal cry of agony: '*Mother!*' and is shot dead.

But the danger to Soviet power in the Far East coming from the tiny group of Old Believers in alliance with the Japanese is completely unbelievable – particularly in view of their incorruptibility as a religious group, however small. But now Dovzhenko was subject to the new rules, i.e. he had to write a 'cast-iron' scenario, no longer the 'emotional scenario', i.e. the poetic springboard for his imagination; furthermore he had to submit it allegedly to the 'masses' by a public reading to the Union of Soviet Writers, and to his fellow-workers in the cinema industry. He could only now work on 'experiments understood by the masses'. And he received approval on every side – once the Big Boss had approved who could not approve? A whole page of the *Kinogazeta*, the Soviet cinema newspaper, is full of praise for him and for 'the greatest achievement in our cinema dramaturgy – a new stage for Soviet cinematography'. For indeed it had been approved by the most high, Stalin himself.

The influence of D. W. Griffith is still seen when Dovzhenko inserts poetic subtitles throughout the film. And the influence of the old masters of the Renaissance on the composition of the shots is noted by the film historian[77] – a Soviet figure is represented as a 'Madonna and Child'!

It is well known that the subject of Dovzhenko's next film was proposed by Stalin. Their meetings extended over a number of years; it was during the writing of *Aerograd* that they first met. Mosfilm's bureaucrats were making obstacles for the *Aerograd* script; Dovzhenko wrote directly for advice to Stalin and was given an appointment twenty-two hours later, at which he read his scenario to Stalin, Voroshilov, Molotov and Kirov. The *Aerograd* difficulties were straightened out and production started briskly with the expedition to Siberia.[78]

For me, the film has personally tragic overtones, apart from its failure for Dovzhenko, because one of the leading characters, the Chinese boy who became a Soviet partisan, Van-Lin, was played by my fellow student and friend, the Korean, G. Tsoi. We studied together in Eisenstein's group and lived together in the same students' dormitory. His parents had been revolutionaries who took refuge from the reactionary Korean government in the Soviet Union. Tsoi had worked in a theater group in the Far East and then came to the GIK to study film directing and acting. This was his first (and last) big part. He appears in the climax of the film and I translate from a review of the original script by L. Indenbom.[79]

The character of Van-Lin is unforgettable. He doesn't manage to do much in the scenario, but in that limited action and limited words – is all the love of a Chinese coolie for the country which became his real motherland. As a reconnaissance tracker, Van-Lin follows in the footsteps of the enemy. Carried away by the chase he falls into the hands of the enemy. He is tied to a tree. Now Van-Lin will cry out. That will be the last cry of Van-Lin, 'People Arise! Arise! Arise!'

'Volodya, my winged brother, bury me in *Aerograd*. I laugh in their faces.'

And over the plain circles the airplane of Volodya Glushak – son of the old partisan, who finds the lacerated Van-Lin. He carries the dead Van-Lin in his arms. He carries him to his fellow fighters. He carries him to the airplane. The airplane takes off. The airplane flies. Three airplanes fly. Many airplanes fly. Apotheosis – the might of the Soviet Union.

So Tsoi was acting his own life – he had all the love of an

emigrant for his real motherland: but what happened to Tsoi in real life?

I learned that during the Stalin terror he had been arrested and exiled to the Far East – someone said he had been in a prison camp, others said he was released and working in an Eastern theater group. In the USSR, you can't find out the real truth without danger of being called a spy. What happened to most foreigners who adopted Soviet citizenship is now well documented by Solzhenitsyn, Medvedev and others. Such is the real end of Dovzhenko's dream of *Aerograd*.

Shchors

Now that socialist realism had achieved success with the Party and above all with Stalin in *Chapayev*, in 1934 it became the official line which all artists were now obliged to follow. *Chapayev* was the history of a legendary Red Cavalryman and presented a more lifelike character than previous attempts at socialist realism.

So Stalin proposed personally to Dovzhenko that he make a Ukrainian *Chapayev*. Here is what Leyda says of this meeting:[80]

> At the February 1935 session of the Central Committee, at which the film-makers received their decorations, Stalin remarked, while pinning the Order of Lenin on Dovzhenko, 'Now you must give us a Ukrainian *Chapayev*', and briefly proposed that Dovzhenko look into the Civil War activity of Shchors as a film subject. Dovzhenko naturally agreed and the press carried considerable publicity on Stalin's suggestion.
>
> While *Aerograd* was still in production Dovzhenko was again summoned (as usual, at night) to the Kremlin. After asking him how the work was going, Stalin came to the point:
>
> 'The reason I wanted to see you is this. When I spoke to you about *Shchors* last time, I was merely making a suggestion. I simply thought of what you might do in the Ukraine. But neither my words nor the articles in the press place any obligations upon you. You have a free choice in the matter. If you want to do *Shchors* – go ahead and do it, but if you have other plans, then keep to them by all means. Don't think that you are bound to anything. I called you in to tell you this.'

However, there was little choice here. Once Stalin suggested someone do something, it virtually became a law which had to be carried out.

One of the major reasons was of course the result of the Purges and the Stalinist Party terror and the ferocious attacks on so-called nationalism, particularly Ukrainian. Stalin's hatchet man in the Ukraine had been Khrushchev. And Dovzhenko's problem was compounded not only by having to submit to the apparatchiki's total scrutiny and censorship, but by being unable to use the real names of Shchors's fellow revolutionaries, as, for instance, the Vasilievs had done in *Chapayev*, because they had all been arrested and either imprisoned for life or executed. On top of that they were forced by torture to confess to crimes they had never committed (part of Communist Party terror), including a deputy commander of Shchors, Ivan Dubovoy, who 'confessed' to murdering Shchors!! It was lucky for Dovzhenko, Shchors had died naturally. Here is what Leyda says: 'The old ghosts of Ukrainian nationalism rose around the dramatized figure of Nikolai Shchors. His own early death protected him from accusations of complicity, but many of his comrades' names were now taboo in the purest political circles.'[81]

But luckily bits of the truth were given by Khrushchev himself:[82]

I was personally very close to Ivan Naumovich Dubovoy.[83] He came from a proletarian family. His father was a miner on the Don. Dubovoy finished officers' school during World War I. When the Civil War broke out, he was made deputy commander of a division commanded by Shchors. . . . I was very pleased that we had commanders like him in the Red Army – men devoted body and soul to the Revolution, to Soviet Power, and to Socialism.

When the enemies of the people were exposed, Stalin distributed the testimonies of Tukhachevsky, Yakir, and the others to the Politbureau. Among these testimonies was a confession written in Ivan Naumovich Dubovoy's own handwriting. He wrote that he had killed his commander Shchors during the Civil War. Here is what he said in his confession:

'Shchors and I were lying on the ground watching the battle. Suddenly an enemy machine gunner opened fire in our direction. The bullets sprayed all around us. Shchors was in front of me. He turned his head and said, "Vanya, Vanya, the Whites have a good machine gunner. Look how accurately he's firing on us."

A few moments later he turned around again and started to say something else. Then and there I killed him. I shot him in the head. I killed him in order to take his place as commander of the division.'

You may imagine how disgusted I was when I first read this confession. I had always respected Dubovoy, and suddenly I discovered he had done something as vile as that. I rebuked myself; how could I have been so blind? Why hadn't I known that Dubovoy was Shchors's murderer?

But at the time of the Twentieth Party Congress in 1956 – when we opened the archives and looked into the files of all the people who had been declared enemies of the people and shot or strangled – I found out that Dubovoy's testimony was all a lie. I had been deceived a second time. The first time was when my regard for Dubovoy as an honest man was shattered by his confession to Shchors's murder. Now I had been deceived again, this time by Dubovoy's own murderer – Stalin himself.

But in the 1973 *History of Soviet Cinema* Dubovoy is never mentioned, and a quote from Dovzhenko's instructions to his film crew has now ironic overtones. He wrote, 'Prepare your purest colors, artists. We shall depict that long outsung youth of ours . . . refine only the pure gold of truth.'[84] And he proceeded to falsify history in his film.

As a result Dovzhenko had to find a way around, and in effect it gave him a chance of avoiding the censors, because none of Shchors's fellow-revolutionaries were allowed to be the real-life figures, so Dovzhenko had to create his own imaginary ones. Leyda goes on to say:[85]

Most of his comrades in the finished film were inventions by Dovzhenko, who was actually happier with an invention like his emotional Bozhenko (drawn again, from Dovzhenko's grandfather) than with the morally god-like figure of Shchors, whose every word and gesture had to be approved by microscopic censorship. . . . The scenario took eleven months, the filming twenty. In Dovzhenko's words it seemed 'a lifetime'.

The film is memorable not for its Civil War story, which is close of course to the Soviet pattern, but for the fact that perhaps because Dovzhenko had participated in most of the military and political

battles of the time and known personally many of the actual protagonists in the Civil War in the Ukraine, *Shchors* transcends the
prosaic socialist realism of *Chapayev*. As Leyda observes, '*Shchors*
leaves in the memory burning images of death and passionate life.'[86]
I shall never forget the opening. Like all of Dovzhenko's scenarios
– at least all those written by him alone – that of *Shchors* is a work
of literature in its own right. This is the opening:[87]

> The year, one thousand nine hundred and eighteen, the day
> June 29th, the time three o'clock in the afternoon, in the
> Ukraine, in the village of Vorobyovka. A northern Novgorod
> carpenter Severin Chernyak slashed with his sabre the neck of
> a German soldier of the army of occupation. The German fell.
> Chernyak slashed another.
>   And so it began. . . .
>   Men and horses got all mixed up. One hundred eagles surged
> on to the German-Gaidamaksky detachment. Piercing into their
> very camp on the village square, stabbing, firing, at point-blank
> range, hacked from their horses, killing.
>   The foe rushed around in panic amidst the sun-flowers in the
> kitchen-gardens, in the wheatfields, cried out, howled, cursed and
> died at the hands of the rebelling poor. . . .
>   A log-cabin burned, blasted by hand-grenades. From the
> flames of the cabin there rushed out, like a bird in the smoke,
> someone's old mother, who wept bitter tears.
>   And at the same time into the flames a German soldier flung
> himself followed by two Gaidamakis.
>   Cherries smoked by the burning eaves. . . .

The script alone reveals Dovzhenko's splendid use of counterpoint,
from the slow, detailed narration of time and place to the sudden
change of rhythm with the abrupt surging action in the very heart
of the battle. But in the actual film Dovzhenko far outstripped this
literary outline. In the very first shot, in close-up, sways a vast,
peaceful sunflower, as if drawing into itself all the sun's rays. Then
there is a sudden explosion, a smoking black cloud of earth, and
shrapnel wells up and men are slashing and hacking each other in
the midst of those peaceful sunflowers.
It was a masterpiece of an exposition. And all the didacticism of
the film script was balanced by Dovzhenko with his wonderful
poetic moving images – which so cried out in those days for cinema-

scope and cinerama. Dovzhenko himself said, 'One cannot paint a great canvas with a little brush. Metaphorically speaking, a scenario should be written with two hands: in one hand: a tiny delicate brush for delineating eyes and eyebrows; in the other: a sweeping big brush for wide strokes of a hundred kilometre spaciousness, passions, mass movements.'[88]

So many unforgettable pictures: a riderless horse in a smoking sunflower field; through a bombardment an unprecedented wedding procession on sledges, jingling with bells, surging through a snowy ravine; and finally the death of Shchors's *alter ego*, the anarchistic, brave Ukrainian warrior, Bozhenko, when over the burning Ukrainian black earth, over endless fields of rye, slowly move his comrades-in-arms, bearing on high the body of their commander on a rudely constructed bier, and in the background his cavalrymen surge at full gallop.

But, although Shklovsky was to write of *Shchors*, 'Just as Eisenstein in *Alexander Nevsky* infinitely deepened the screen, so has Dovzhenko broadened it,'[89] the film brought bitter disappointment for Dovzhenko. He wrote in his diary on 4 July 1945:[90]

I am a film director. In all my working years I have not seen a single one of my pictures in a decent theater on a decent screen, printed on good film by qualified technicians. The film theaters are miserable, the screens the size of postage stamps. It never seems to occur to anyone that screens can be large and the effect of the picture quite different – grand and beautiful. The sound is scandalous, and the film quality is disgraceful – dirty and full of reflections. The very thought of seeing one of my pictures makes me sad. The film is always worse than I conceived and made it.

This has been one of the misfortunes of my life. I have been a martyr for my work. Not once did I obtain satisfaction or even peace from seeing the results of my immeasurably difficult and complex work. As time goes by I become more and more convinced that the best twenty years of my life have been wasted. What I could have done!

But on the other hand my old colleague Paul Rotha, pioneer historian of the cinema, who saw the film almost as soon as I did, wrote:[91]

Moments in this film achieved again the summits of *Arsenal* and *Earth*; intellectually it went deeper than either. *Frontier's*[92] nationalism stemmed from environment, character and political clash. As much cannot be said for his next film, *Shchors* (1939). But as an example of Dovzhenko's style, or any film style at all, *Shchors* was non-existent. It had very beautiful photography, by Ekelchik; a memorable opening sequence of battle among the sunflower fields; and a few moments reminiscent of the old Dovzhenko, especially in the scenes of horses; but all this was overweighted by the 'policy' line. As in *Chapayev*, as in them all, the 'development of class character', the nature of friend and enemy, and even the strategy of the battles, was lost in a maelstrom of words. In this pseudo-epic there was little trace of the passionate poetic creator of *Arsenal* and *Earth*.

And in truth because of the strict political control and endless censorship it could not achieve the universality of Dovzhenko's films made in a freer period; the 'development of class character' and socialist realism means the distorting of truth and the demeaning of the universal and the poetic, which made Dovzhenko the greatest poet of the cinema.

Ukraine in Flames

It was Dovzhenko who first clearly saw the transitory nature of cinema and under the relentless hounding of the Party in this area, he decided to give up films and write stories and books instead. And instead of joining the general cinema evacuation to the safety of faraway Alma Ata in Uzbekistan he decided to stay in the battle zone in Moscow and the Ukraine.

And basically the reason was, I think, that the kind of total censorship over every stage of film production was far more onerous and soul-killing and ulcer-inducing than writing short stories or novels and eventually making documentary films out of newsreels.

He himself experienced everything on all the front lines of his native Ukraine and wrote of it with terrifying passion. The incredible suffering during the war shattered him. But his truthfulness got him into trouble, just like Constantine Simonov got into trouble over his diaries of the war. The Party does not want truth, it wants Party-mindedness, and in his diary Dovzhenko writes:[93]

X read my article *Ukraine in Flames* and he said to me, 'One place is unrealistic, you write there was great weeping, that is not true. No such weeping took place. They looked sad but they didn't weep. Nobody wept, you understand?'

'You lie, I thought, you lie, you blind bureaucrat! They poured out tears over your very pathway and you looked at them through your glasses and through the windscreen of your shut-in automobile and you saw nothing, because you didn't want to see anything. Blind one! They wept, oh how they wept! No other country in the world wept like that. Even old men cried so that their eyes puffed up from tears.'

In a letter to his wife Julia he wrote:[94]

June 4, 1942
Because of our long and painful separation, I find it very difficult to explain to you in detail the great changes that have taken place in my life. They have come upon me quite suddenly, and I will not be free of them, apparently, as long as I live. What are these changes? My dear Julia, they are the unprecedented troubles that have fallen on my people's heads and that will destroy them. In any case, more than half of them will perish, and the rest will either be physically or spiritually crippled or be treated as inferior, suspect elements because they did not go to Asia for lack of suitcases. What I have learned has made me so sad that at times I choke. Hitler will undoubtedly be routed – that's true, but he has ruined the Ukraine. Therefore, I cannot leave here. I need nothing now, neither money nor living quarters. Nor do I need the cinema with its mean, shallow, and paltry people, without kith or kin, petty and generally stupid or half-witted mongers.

I have made a firm decision. If I still have the strength, I will devote myself to something more durable and lasting, something more intelligent than ephemeral, illusive, transitory film.

I will write about the sufferings, heroism, and tragedy of my nation. I have thought and planned much, and I shall undoubtedly be able to accomplish something before I die.

Despite what the high Party man said, Dovzhenko went ahead and produced the film script based on his stories and experience of *Ukraine in Flames*. Prior to the war, he had been practically banned

from his native Ukraine and from working in the Kiev film studios.
But now that the war was on he was allowed to return and participated actively as much as he could. But then came the bombshell.
When he wrote the proposed script for the documentary film *Ukraine
in Flames* he was summoned to the Kremlin.

26 November, 1943
Back in Moscow today. Brought my elderly mother with me
from Kiev. Bolshakov gave me distressing news today:[95] Stalin
took a dislike to my story *Ukraine in Flames* and has forbidden it
to be published or screened.

I don't know yet what to do. My heart is heavy and anguished.
Not because more than a year of work has been wasted and not
because all my enemies will rejoice and all the petty functionaries
will disdain me, but because I know that *Ukraine in Flames* is
true. It is my concealed and forbidden truth about my nation
and its calamity. This ban means that no one needs my story;
evidently only panegyrics are needed.[96]

28 November 1943
The banning of *Ukraine in Flames* terribly depressed me. I wander
around despondent and can't find a place to exist in. And yet
I still think – let it be banned. God be with it! It is written all
the same. The speech has been spoken. . . .

I wrote the story honestly, just as it is and as I see the life and
suffering of my people. I know: I will be accused of nationalism,
of Christianism, of all forgivingness. I will be accused of ignoring
the class struggle and of religionism in relation to the training
of youth, who are now fighting heroically on all the terrible
historical fronts – but that isn't what lies at the base of my work
and that is not the point. . . . The point is the destruction. It is
bad enough that we gave to the Hitlerites the whole of the
Ukraine but it is also bad that we liberate its people with ill
treatment. We the liberators, to the last man, have all forgotten
that we are somewhat guilty before those we are liberating and
that we already consider them second category people, unclean,
guilty in our eyes, deserters – capitulators – opportunists. We
are glorious warriors but we don't have the normal human
goodness to our own kith and kin. . . .[97]

5 December 1943

I feel so bitter when I am accused of nationalism for *Ukraine in Flames*. Lord, how long will You shun me? I am almost mortally ill; my joints have been racked, my blood long since drained out of me. What are You afraid of? I can no longer stand on my feet. I [illegible]; I become numb, and You are still afraid of me! Do not be afraid. I need nothing from You. Everything will be as You desire. Not as I wanted it, but as You wanted it, want it now, and will want it.[98]

I am sick. My main artery and my whole body hurt. My head aches badly. The banning of my story and everything around it has destroyed in me the full significance of that work. I don't know how I can even live through such sorrow, if it hadn't been for mother and Julia I would have died, in order not to live and be tortured so. The artist it seems must be tormented all his life.[99]

And then years later we get the inside story from Dovzhenko's diary, and from Khrushchev's memoirs.[100]

One episode was characteristic of both Shcherbakov and Stalin. It happened in 1943. Aleksandr Petrovich Dovzhenko – a remarkable film director and an excellent journalist – wrote a scenario called *The Ukraine in Flames*. Many of the scenes in it were based on articles he had written exposing the faults of the Red Army. Dovzhenko, who had a sharp mind and a sharp pen, was especially critical of the people responsible for the ill-preparedness of our army on the eve of the war. He sent the scenario to the Central Committee, where Malenkov and some of the other comrades read it. During one of my trips to Moscow, Stalin asked me if I'd read it. I said yes, I had. Actually, I hadn't really sat down and read it, but Dovzhenko himself had read it to me during the German offensive of July, 1943. Naturally three-fourths of my attention had been taken up by the enemy attack, and I hadn't been able to concentrate on the text of Dovzhenko's work. I explained this to Stalin. He said I was trying to weasel out of my responsibility for what had happened, and he started a blistering denunciation of Dovzhenko, criticizing him up and down, accusing him of Ukrainian nationalism and all kinds of other sins. At that time it was very fashionable to accuse Ukrainians of nationalism, regardless of whether there was any evidence for doing so. This practice had started during Kaganovich's term in the Ukraine. He was fond of saying that every Ukrainian is potentially a nationalist – which is, of course, nonsense.

Anyway, Stalin called a meeting to discuss Dovzhenko's scenario. Shcherbakov presented the case for the prosecution. He was obviously trying hard to fan Stalin's anger against Dovzhenko by harping on the charge that the film scenario was extremely nationalistic. Malenkov sat silently through this whole discussion, even though he had already given the scenario his blessing.

Stalin didn't let the matter drop there. He told me to convene a meeting of the Ukrainian Party and government leaders, including the Central Committee secretaries in charge of propaganda. He told us to prepare a self-critical resolution about the unsatisfactory state of affairs on the ideological front in the Ukraine. Then he called Dovzhenko himself on to the carpet and gave him a fierce dressing down. *Dovzhenko was put on ice as an active man in the arts for a long time afterward.* [My italics. HM.]

This whole disgraceful affair was mostly the doing of Shcherbakov who had wormed his way into Stalin's confidence and did everything he could to make life miserable for everyone else. It might sound as though I'm saying all this because I have some special grudge against Shcherbakov. That's not true. I've given Shcherbakov the evaluation he deserved, and he deserved the worst. But the main culprit was Stalin. It was Stalin who made the mischievous influence of people like Shcherbakov possible.

Of this Dovzhenko wrote in his private diary on 19 June 1944 and in July 1945, only extracts of which were published by his widow, in the period of the thaw:

19 June 1944
Horrible things are happening within me. I cannot write articles. It's as if all the wiring had been torn up in my head, and not a single thought can escape outside to the readers. What has happened to me? I think that the public is not reading me; it hates and distrusts me in these days of World War II. The leaders have suggested to the public that I am an enemy of the

people, a dangerous and harmful person, a nationalist and counter-revolutionary, in league with Hitler and Lucifer. I have become spiritually ill. They ought never have done what they did to me. . . .[101]

Comrade Stalin, even if you were God I would not have believed, even then, that I am a Nationalist, who must be stigmatized and maltreated . . . surely love for one's own people isn't nationalism? . . . Why have you transformed my life into torment? Why have you taken away my happiness? Crushed my name under your jack-boots?

   Still I forgive you. For I am a part of the people. Despite everything, I am bigger than you.

   Being quite small, I forgive you your smallness and evil, because even you are imperfect, no matter how much people pray to you. God exists. But his name is Chance.[102]

During the latter part of the war he had been an artistic supervisor at the Kiev Film Studios while he was making his documentary films. But as his proposed *Ukraine in Flames* was banned he didn't work in any studio except the Central Newsreel Studio and there he produced *The Battle for our Soviet Ukraine*; technically directed by his wife Julia Solntseva and Jacob Ovdeyenko, but of course the whole imprint of Dovzhenko is on this mass of newsreel material so brilliantly compiled and edited.

   Then, near the end of the war, the same group made another feature documentary called *Victory in the Ukraine* on the expulsion of the Germans from the boundaries of the Ukraine.

   Jay Leyda quite truthfully said, 'These two documentaries are the least known and the least studied films of all Dovzhenko's work, though with great significance for both his career and for this period of Soviet film history.'[103] He had found a greater degree of freedom in making these films than if he had been in the studios in Alma Ata.

   During the war, of course, the official Party-mindedness encouraged friendly gestures to America and the allies, and Eisenstein, Pudovkin, Dovzhenko, Roman Karmen and all the others made great speeches of friendliness to allied film-makers and particularly to those from America. There were greetings from Samuel Goldwyn, Warner Brothers, Darryl Zanuck, David Selznick, Walt Disney and others in support of the grand alliance and friendly relations and genuine *détente*, as we now call it.

And then Dovzhenko gave a pronouncement which in fact, though addressed to the movie makers of the world, was above all addressed to his own film producers. He said:[104]

> Film workers: do not varnish the world today, do not put 'make-up' on the world in your pictures. The world is now very ill. Do not divert your art to trivial individual matters. The cinema can and must serve great aims. The cinema must give answers to the sorest sharpest contemporary problems. It must honestly help suffering mankind to find its bearings.

And, of course, we know only too well who had done the varnishing of Soviet and Russian history more than its film-makers.

Then came another bombshell. He was dismissed from his job as artistic supervisor at the Kiev Film Studios, sent back to the Mosfilm Studios, thrown off the Stalin Prize Committee and forbidden to return to the Ukraine. And this is what he writes in his notebook:[105]

> Yesterday X brought me the news from Kiev that I have been dismissed as artistic supervisor of the studio*. . . . So I'll return to Kiev with even more gray hair, impoverished, beaten, and wounded. I'll bear my shame for a long time before it's forgotten.
>   Enough suffering and repenting of my sins against Stalin. I must get down to business and prove to him with my work that I am a Soviet artist . . . and not an odious talent with a 'limited ideology'.
>   I must take myself in hand, clad my heart, my will, and my nerves in steel and, forgetting everything else, create a scenario and a film worthy of our great role in a great historical age.
>   Yesterday at Kozlovsky's† Samosud‡ told me that when

---

* Dovzhenko was appointed artistic supervisor of the Kiev Studios in 1940. He was planning to return there to film *Ukraine in Flames*, *Chronicle of Fading Years*, *Taras Bulba*, and *The Tsar*. (Original footnote)
† Ivan Kozlovsky (b. 1900): Ukrainian-born lyric tenor, soloist of the Bolshoi Theater since 1926. (Original footnote)
‡ Samuil Samosud (1884–1964): conductor of several theater orchestras, including the Bolshoi Theater, 1936–43, and the Nemirovich-Danchenko and Stanislavsky Opera Theater, 1943–50. (Original footnote)

Moskvin* heard about my being dismissed from the Stalin Prize Committee, he said, 'What a pity. They've taken the heart and soul out of the Committee'.

It grieves me.

But of course, it was not unexpected because Dovzhenko saw the truth of what was happening to his mother Ukraine, and then after the war there were those who had suffered cruelly under the oppression of the Nazis, who had desperately tried to help their country, often risking death against the occupying usurping power of the ruthless German army. People who had been captured, made prisoners unwillingly and fighting to the last, are now herded into echelons to go to Communist concentration camps. And of course, to criticize this would have been a deadly sin and yet, in his diary of 23 May 1942 he says:[106]

People have had let loose on them sufferings of such a scale, such a new unheard-of scale, which mankind has not ever suspected. One must not send embittered, ignorant, cruel youngsters in the tribunals that follow the army but healers of the spiritual wounds and mutilations, sensitive and wise, knowing the value of a grain of goodness in the times of evil.

And there is something left out in the published version because clearly these embittered, ignorant and cruel young fellows were the Secret Police in the army of the advancing Russians.

And then some years later, on 31 January 1948, he is still sick at heart and says:[107]

Today is the anniversary of my death. 31 January 1944[108] I was brought to the Kremlin. There I was hacked to pieces, and the bloody fragments of my soul were thrown to the mob. Everything that was evil and vindictive trampled and abused me.

I was born and lived for goodness and love. I was killed by the hatred and evil of the great at the very moment when they were at their smallest.

Yes, these are the heartfelt tragic words of one of the greatest poets in the cinema and one of the greatest artists Soviet Russia

---

* The Moskvin referred to could be either Andrei Moskvin (1901–61), the distinguished cameraman, or Ivan Moskvin (1874–1946), the equally distinguished stage and screen actor. (Original footnote)

produced and this is how he was treated. And the one whom he so castigates is now being rehabilitated alongside the naming of streets and studios and squares after Alexander Dovzhenko. And of course, he asks the fundamental questions that get all genuine artists in Russia into trouble to this very moment. Again, in his notebook he says:[109]

> My republic. My world. My future! But how long must I speak by rote and think only what is prescribed? Desire only increased production? Live only a rich and happy life?
>
> Where is my happiness? Who has exalted me in my suffering?

And of course there is only one answer. To say that would mean you become a 'dissident.'

Now the official Soviet film historians (see the last *History of Soviet Cinema*, op. cit.) say not a word about the banning of this film and the condemning of Dovzhenko by Stalin and Beria.

Michurin

As we know, Dovzhenko's love of nature reached such a degree that he was accused of pantheism. He saw nature and human nature as one whole, and loved all of it, both in its life and its death. It was only natural therefore that one day he would do a film about Ivan Vladimirovich Michurin (born 1855, died 1935). According to the Soviet Encyclopedia,[110]

> Michurin was a Soviet biologist and an honorary member of the Academy of Sciences from 1935 [just before he died].
>
> Guided by the principle that we cannot wait for favors from nature we must grasp them ourselves, Michurin was the first in the history of biology [sic!] to prove the possibility of guiding the evolution of plant organisms and their hereditability and variations . . . developing the teachings of hybridization he developed over 300 sorts of vegetable and fruit growth.

In fact he was preceded by the American Luther Burbank (born 1849), who was the originator of many new flowers, fruits and vegetables including the Burbank potato, the pineapple quince, and the stoneless prune. And he developed the very same methods that Michurin allegedly was the pioneer of. Historically, Michurin was only a pioneer in Russia, despite their chauvinistic claims.

And of this, Victor Shklovsky, in writing about Dovzhenko, gave his version of what Dovzhenko told him about Michurin and I quote:[111]

> Happiness is not always reaped from rich earth, tilled in the time-honoured way.
>
> Near Kozlov station there stood a flowering orchard. During his working hours, the man who tended the orchard repaired clocks along the long stretch of railway line. He had a season ticket and he used to sell little pamphlets to the passengers as he travelled to and fro on the train, which told not only of the different sorts of apples he grew but also of how he cultivated them in his orchard.
>
> The orchard brought forth good fruit from the rich land. Everyone admired the orchard. It was the pride of the town.
>
> Once the old gardener decided to select new varieties of plants on a plot of land that had not been cultivated before. That would ensure that the saplings would grow sound and strong. He wanted to select plants which would be able to live and bear fruit anywhere – a new variety of pears and apples that would be better than the old ones.
>
> The old man bought a plot on the riverbank which had not been used for cultivation before, where the soil consisted of gravel and river deposits.
>
> He dug up the trees in his garden and, together with his wife, carried them to the new plot of ground. They walked down the dirt road. The old man walked along, trying not to stoop under the weight of the big apple trees; and his wife tried to forget that all that was left of the old orchard was a row of holes.
>
> The neighbours watched them over the fences of their own little plots, where well-known kinds of apples were growing in neatly tilled earth, and they said that the old man had gone out of his mind.
>
> Nevertheless the new orchard flourished and brought fame to the old man, Michurin.

'One day I shall make a film about *Michurin*,' Sashko announced. This he was later to do, together with Solntseva.

When Lenin died terrible frosts were raging. At such times people usually burn bonfires to make a protective coating over the fruit trees; the smoke sticks to the branches like flowers and the trees lose less of their inner warmth.

Of course what the encyclopedia doesn't mention are the difficulties and tragic struggle that Michurin had under Tsarist society and at the beginning of Soviet society. As will be seen, it was only in 1935 just before he died that he was elected an honorary member of the Academy of Sciences. In other words, he was then 70 years of age. And the bitter lonely struggle that Michurin had paralleled Dovzhenko's who clearly put himself in the film. He said:[112]

I do not hide the fact that in the art of the cinema I am in the poetic camp. I always convey some part of the chronicle of my personal family life. For example in *Shchors* I represent myself and in *Earth* it was my granddad who was dying.

Michurin in the film, was also Dovzhenko and this was known to his friends and colleagues and was confirmed by Dovzhenko himself, who said:[113]

This is also revealed in my admiration of *Michurin* in so far as I also loved Gardens [Dovzhenko planted an orchard at the Kiev Film Studio which is now flourishing. HM.] and well organized public service and in my position in society as an artist I dream of the beautiful designing of our socialist actuality. Naturally I strive to express some of my pedagogical opinions and therefore in my treatment of *Michurin* I brought into the film certain oddities, possibly even bitterness . . . the problems of difficult, complex creativity . . . may have come to the forefront.

But now of course, he had to go back to Moscow and work in the hated Mosfilm Studio, Potylikha.
This is what he said:[114]

I work now in Potylikha [Studio]. This studio now has all the rights and obligations to be the first and best film studio in the Soviet Union, if only because it is in the capital of the State, *if only because the workers at this Moscow Film Studio have all the chances, all the bases, all the possibilities of finding themselves under more concrete and everyday Party leadership.*

Sasha was building the Juggernaut – and eleven years later he was to write in his diary:[115]

The orders for filming *Life in Bloom* (*Michurin*) at Mosfilm (Potylikha) have been issued. Leaving Mosfilm after making *Aerograd* eleven years ago, I swore to myself, 'Praise the Lord that He has freed me from this hideous den of iniquity! Never again, under no circumstances will I return to this house of cretins where everything is twisted and perverted.' And here I am again.

'Under Party orders and everyday Party leadership!'

One of my fellow students, who worked with Dovzhenko, insisted, 'Michurin was Dovzhenko himself, don't forget that,' and it is ironic that the Party defender, Ivor Montagu, wrote:[116]

In *Michurin*, the stubborn tree-breeder, with the troubles of Job on his head, faces every conceivable obstacle, frustration and disappointment. To cap it all, his wife, his one comfort and stay, the one being beside himself, who believed, dies of a long illness. *Michurin* steps out into the night. It is an extraordinary imaginative effect as Dovzhenko, in this, his first color scene into blackness, a darkness beset with howling wind and drifting autumn leaves, a horror of death and loneliness and nullity matching and reinforcing the blackness in his soul.

How that is matched by Dovzhenko's cry of black despair:[117]

5 April 1948

My *Life in Bloom* has been dragging for several years now. I brought it out as a color film. Then when the film had been completed with the utmost effort and it came to life and pleased even trained snobs, I found myself in some mystical zone where the film was completely cut up and naked; it was shown to the Great Leader, the greatest mortal since time began. The Great One rejected my labor.

Zhdanov saved me from asphyxiation. I revived after the meeting with him. And although the play was asphyxiated, in spite of his views, I did rest at Barvikha* for about three weeks and came back from there sick again.

O cruelty, I have come to know you.
Terrible misgivings oppress me.

* Barvikha: a sanatorium near Moscow for top Party leaders only. (Original footnote)

But Montagu goes on, 'But this loss is again a prelude to an issue leading to a finale of blossom and children and triumph.'[118]

In the film a Soviet happy ending – but not for its creator! For this did not satisfy the Party and Stalin and Dovzhenko was forced to remake it, and my student friend said the result was '*poshlyie,*' 'banal,' 'meretricious.'

But now, having been dismissed from the artistic directorship of his previous studio, he apparently is only given a third-category monthly salary, that is, the lowest in the hierarchy of the cinema studio! He found this so insulting that on 25 November 1948 he wrote:[119]

> To the Director and Chairman of Cinematography:
> Making use of the preparations for producing the film *Life in Bloom*, I respectfully wish to inform you that as of today I will no longer accept my salary. Please do not take this action as something that is meant to irritate you, or something like that. I have no intention of making a demonstration or displaying any disobedience. On the contrary, I wish in this manner to emphasize my loyalty toward my salary. At the same time, however, I cannot help thinking about the quality of the picture that I am beginning to film. Until now I have thought of myself as one of the best film directors. I have become accustomed to this idea, and it has helped me to stay on a high moral level during production. The third-category monthly salary that has been given me oppresses me and makes me doubt my abilities. Hence, in order to preserve myself from unnecessary and harmful hints about my artistic inferiority, I am asking you to take my request into consideration, that I may calmly give myself over to the dominion of my dreams without disturbing my usual conception of my dignity. Please make arrangements to pay me for the work in some other way after the film has been completed, in accordance with its quality.
> Respectfully,
> A. Dovzhenko

But now the tragedy began to be intensified because the new biologist to follow Michurin was the notorious Lysenko, Trofim Denisovich (born 1898). This biologist charlatan would become the hero under Stalin and able to do miracles far beyond Michurin and Luther Burbank! He was responsible not only for removing the great genetic scientist Vavilov as chairman of the Academy of Sciences but also for his imprisonment and death. Even under Khrushchev, Lysenko still had an ascendency and it was a bitter battle the Soviet scientists had to wage before he was eventually exposed and rejected. But Dovzhenko was caught in the middle of it and was forced to bring Lysenko's theories into the film. And this caused complete chaos in his work. And he writes:[120]

28 December, 1945
One must have nerves of steel, a soul of stone, and the heart of a slave to endure what I endured today. Conferred at my house today with S., A., and S. We worked on the corrections to *Life in Bloom*, according to X's demands. I haven't the strength to describe what sort of a conference it was. A picture worthy of Gogol's, Shchedrin's,* or Swift's pen; a live documentary *Satyricon*. The most horrible thing was that S. and S. and A. (the latter, by the way, remained silent the entire time) are all cultivated and intelligent people. All three know that they're · doing absurd things, and yet they can't help it. They have no minds of their own, no taste, no dignity. How can one even talk about art in these circumstances?

And not only were there the problems of the imposed theory of Lysenko but also the problems of Dovzhenko's own style and pantheistic deviations. Because not only was the film made all over again, but the scene that he loved was cut out of the second version. This is where there is a parallel death scene of old age surrounded by serenity and mellow fruitfulness just like in *Earth*. Here the lifelong friend of Michurin, Terenty, 'dies in an orchard on a fair summer's day, surrounded by buzzing golden bees, wearing a typical white shirt, his calloused hands folded on his chest.'

Here is the eternal pantheism of Dovzhenko that the Party always fulminated against, and this time the Party cut the scene out of the film. And then finally the film was banned. However, eventually one version of *Life in Bloom* was made for the home market, and a second version made for export, called *Michurin*, which he finally refused to work on. It ruined his creation.

It is interesting what arose out of the battle for *Michurin*, because

---

* N. Shchedrin (pseudonym of Mikhail Saltykov, 1826–1889); Russian satirical writer whose many sketches, novels, and stories were concerned with exposure of social and political conditions. (Original footnote)

it seems that Stalin gave an important indication there of how biographies of great men had to be dealt with by the Soviet artist. This is what Dovzhenko writes:[121]

> *18 November, 1954*
> I think it was after seeing *Michurin* Stalin ordered that the
> private lives of important people not be shown on the screen.
> 'We ought to be interested only in the scientific and civic aspects
> of their lives.' Why did he do so? Because in his private life, no
> doubt, there was something very cruel. . . . Everything that
> came within the orbit of his private life was oppressed and
> unhappy. So the criminal career of Beria, his most loyal pupil,
> was no accident.

From 1948 to 1956 – eight years – he made no films, and only finally started on *The Poem of an Inland Sea* just before he died, leaving it unfinished.

He wrote scripts which were never produced or taught at the GIK, which always seemed at least a refuge for those artists and directors who could not make films but only teach how to make them.

Ivanova also confirms that the *Michurin* image was, of course, a reflection of Dovzhenko. She writes:[122]

> In the film were reflected obliquely the major slogans of the
> campaign carried on at the time, which embodied the conviction
> that all our sciences had original and unquestioning superiority
> over foreign sciences.
> With this went the falsifying of Michurin as Lysenko with the
> aim of establishing in our biological science a peculiar, and now
> already non-existent monopoly of the latter, which forced the
> viewers to search for 'the genuine Dovzhenko' in other spheres.
> The original figure of the great natural scientist himself was
> expressed on a mighty canvas with exhaustive completeness, the
> merging of the fate of the hero with nature, was given in the film
> with a poetic power never yet seen on the screen. But now we
> are astonished by something else. How was it possible not to
> notice how the tragedy of the conflict of the creative work of
> *Michurin* with arbitrary rule, with neglect, with the negating of
> the great folk talents' right to create, to dare, to transform
> nature. How close this tragedy in the film paralleled those

torturous collisions which in those years experienced the mighty Columbus of folk cinematography, Alexander Dovzhenko. Yes, Dovzhenko put into *Michurin* his doubts, his disagreements, his pain, and belief in the victory of justice, just as Sergei Eisenstein did his in the second part of *Ivan The Terrible*. And the experience and feelings of the artist at that time made an unmistakable impression on every one of the creative works in the years to come.

Then soon after the tragedy of this film, what did the leaders of the Ministry of Cinematography propose to this great poetic artist? That he make an anti-American film of the Cold War, based on a book by Annabella Bucar, called *The Truth about American Diplomats*.[123] The Soviet critic Vlasov himself admits that this story about intrigue in an American Embassy and its intelligence operations vis-à-vis the Soviet Union was not of course a subject for Dovzhenko. But orders were orders and he tried to carry them out. The tragedy is that he spent two years on this scenario, trying honestly to make it into some kind of genuine Dovzhenko film. Vlasov admits that Dovzhenko couldn't avoid the well-known stereotypes in the presentation, representatives of American capital, of diplomats and intelligence officers, the trade union bosses, etc. This superficiality and straight-line characters in many of the American scenes was self-evident. And he says, 'Obviously here, insufficient information about life in the USA played a part, which of course, is explained by the politics of the Cold War, in which particularly, the right-wing leading circles of America carried on in relation to the Soviet Union.'[124] And of course, he doesn't say that the boot is also on the other foot.

Now Dovzhenko threw himself into another story, *The Discovery of the Antarctic*. He finished it in the spring of 1952 and spent eight months writing. In a way, this is rather an interesting contrast; it is the totally opposite extreme of the rich, luscious *Earth* and *Life in Bloom*, being instead the year-long searches of the sea explorers. Here, probably under demands of socialist realism, he didn't write in his usual style of the 'emotional scenario', but as a straightforward narrative taken from the book of F. Bellinghausen, the double search for the southern Arctic Ocean. But again, this typical socialist realism of Russian one-sidedness revealed itself, in that it was the triumph of the great discoveries of the Russians; they, of course, were the only ones to discover the Antarctic! And in the introduction Vlasov comments:[125]

> The scenario however seems to me to be not free from shortcomings. Perhaps the most serious one, is the over-exaggerated caricature of representing the English with their total desire to prevent the success of the Russian expedition by any means in their power. And the deliberate playing down of the role of foreign explorers in the discovery of the Antarctic.

So, again, the Soviet artist is bending over backward to placate his Communist Party masters: to give the Russians all the credit and to make it a film of the Glory of Russian Exploration. And he got the same thanks. The film was excluded from the production plan of the studio, just like so many other projects by so many other Soviet directors.

Once more, in bitter disappointment, Dovzhenko returned to his most beloved theme, *The Enchanted Desna*, which he called an autobiographical cinema novel. This he had been writing ever since 1942 and finalized in 1955. The memories of an artist about his far-off childhood, about his mother, father, grandfather and neighbors, simple peasants who, despite their unhappy and limited existence, still remained spiritually beautiful and generous in their goodness to people. And around them enchanting mother nature and the songs and stories of his people.

The world in which little Sasha lived was full of wonders and miracles. His grandfather is just like God and is able to catch fish from the river with his bare hands and loves to carry on long conversations with horses, birds, and rivers as if they were real people. And there are the terrible curses of the old women, and that journey with his father to help the inhabitants of the village flooded by the River Desna in spring. There in the old tree trunk lives a wise and cunning crow who guides the weather. And there before sleep, one could hear the endless stories of granddad about the good ol' days, when everything was bigger, grander, when even the mosquitoes flew healthy as bears and a lion appears on the banks of the Desna! There one could enjoy the work of that great mower, Uncle Samoilov, who, 'If you would let him mow with his scythe straight on, he would have mowed the whole earth.'

And then, underneath this magic world of Sasha, we see as if in a double exposure the second stratum of the scenario: memories of a man who is correcting his own children's impressions with his grown-up experience.

Then there is yet another triple exposure, another stratum permeating the whole scenario that is passionate confirmation by the artist of his aesthetic program, polemizing directly and indirectly with those opponents of romantic art, the art of inspiration and heightened pathos. This includes discussions on 'common sense', alluded to by his editors (who were his censors in the script department of the Ministry of Cinematography), who proposed that he should cut out 'the absurd lion on the banks of the Desna' and 'somehow generalize' scraggy and ugly horses. And they discussed the 'untypicality' of the prophetic crow and the fairy-tale character of the horse in the apple orchards from the old Christmas carols, which so astounded the imagination of the little Sasha and became for the artist a symbol of the indivisibility of common creation with the people and with its fate, its hopes and high aims.

And these attempts of his Party editors and censors to somehow make commonplace 'socialist realism' of his epic poetry remind me of an occasion when a similar editor-censor was sent from the Committee of Art to check on my wife's sculpture of Pavel Morozov, which she made at the same time as Eisenstein was making this hero in his film *Bezhin Meadow*. And she made him, of course, as he was in the days in 1921, in a shirt and short pants, no stockings and no shoes, and I remember the censor saying, 'Don't you think we in the Soviet Union can afford shoes and stockings!' And it was no good Fredda trying to point out that she was doing what was historically correct in the 1920s. When we were back there in the 1960s, Fredda's sculpture had disappeared and in its place was a Soviet sculptor's figure of that same peasant boy of the 1920s, now immaculately dressed, complete with stockings and shoes! 'Socialist realism'!

What was fact is not what the Party wants. It wants 'socialist realism,' that is, the facts as they should have been. And for this Dovzhenko suffered all his life.

Suffice it to say that his dreams of childhood in *The Enchanted Desna* were never allowed to come to the screen. There were so many ideas, conceptions, sketches, notes and stories that Dovzhenko was working on, that he hoped he might be able to make into films. He wanted to do an epic work which he called *The Golden Gates*, creating a character inevitably larger than life. The synthesis of all the characters he had used in his works up till now would be *Taras Kravchin*, a simple Ukrainian peasant, worker and warrior who Dovzhenko proposed should be a participant in all the basic historical events of the Ukraine. He would be a soldier of the two World Wars, a participant in the Revolution, a builder of the Five-Year Plans of socialism and Communism. And Dovzhenko dreamed of him being a neighbor of such characters as Don Quixote, Colas Breugnon, Till Eulenspiegel, Nasreddin and the Good Soldier Schweik.

And each of his family, suffering one or the other positive and negative aspects of socialist Soviet society. One of his sons would die in his arms, mortally wounded in the battle with the fascists. Another, a fearless aviator shot down by the enemy and unconscious, falls into the hands of the enemy. He escapes from prison but on reaching his homeland he is greeted with insulting mistrust. He is not taken back in the Army, is accused of having been taken alive as a prisoner whereas he should have killed himself (such as happened under Stalin). His beloved daughter, Kravshna, also suffers the torture and humiliation of imprisonment. She is dishonored and, though wanting to live, also wants to die. And yet another of his sons becomes an opponent of Soviet power following Benders's National Army and old Taras himself kills his own son, the traitor.

He wanted to include in it also the satirical story called 'The Twilight of the Gods,' the basis of which is the history of a certain Ukrainian village icon painter who is doing the frescoes in the church, and uses as models, for representations of the saints and even of God himself, his fellow villagers. And for this he is subjected to the strictest inquisition by a bishop who arrives and is determined to stamp out blasphemy. Here Dovzhenko developed the theme of the problem of the artist, of the nature of art and the relationship of art to life. It came to nothing except sketches and articles. One of the stories, which I translated long ago and which was published in wartime England, gives an example of his work.[126]

At the same time, he often wanted to produce a sharply satirical film, and in his notebooks we find sketches for a play called *Vice-President to the Blockhead*. The leading character was a director of a doll factory, with a Gogol-like name, Turokti Makagonovich Kabavoknuverni. With devastating irony Dovzhenko characterizes this man as completely 'positive' – who, however has one, only one, shortcoming; he is a blockhead. In the opinion of the co-workers of Turokti this shortcoming can be put up with and it even can be not a shortcoming at all, if the chief has a pair of very good, clever assistants! Other characters with insinuating confidentiality relate how his superiors had long considered where to assign him. And they eventually decide he would head 'The Committee of our village'. And he signalizes the directorship by 'forbidding this and forbidding that, forbidding the singing of folksongs, forbidding the bandura, forbidding the embroidery of *krestikom*, etc.' And in one of the sketches of 1949, he creates an ambitious and tenacious bureaucrat who is appointed to the post of chairman of a collective farm. His office is always filled with petitioners, because he considered lines or queues the necessary attribute of power. He creates around himself a bodyguard 'in order that he wouldn't be killed by international counter-revolution.' In his office there hangs a map of the world but there is not a map of his own collective farmland.

But suffice it to say that such caricatures and satire on Soviet bureaucracy would be no more welcome to the establishment of Stalin at its worst in 1949, than they were even in the early days of the 1930s, in both of Mayakovsky's banned plays, *Bed Bug* and *Bath House*. So, of course, they never got anywhere near the screen.

Then came his final attempt, *The Poem of an Inland Sea*. He wanted to show the creative labor of his people, the Ukrainian people, by which not only is man changing his surrounding nature but changing human nature itself. He wanted to show 'a beautiful man in struggle for his fatherland, beautiful in his suffering and his death for it. But the brightest beauty is in his labor.' So said Dovzhenko.

At the same time he wanted to show another aspect of this problem. The labor is necessary but not the only condition for the bright beauty of man. So in the scenario arises the image, the character, of a foreman, 'a handsome fellow with the brain of an engineer and the conscience of a bed-bug.' His name is Valery Golik – an energetic worker and at the same time a narcissistic egoist, capable of hypocrisy, villainy and treachery. 'He is not an educated person,' one old collective farmer says of him. 'He had no spiritual sensitivity, no respect for people, no compassion for someone else's sorrow, nor readiness to sacrifice himself for anyone else.' Golik considers himself an avant-garde builder of Communism. 'I always marched forward,' he said. 'You handed me the Banner of Labor, you awarded me the Red Banner, but my built-in blemishes will outlive Communism.' The point, is of course, built-in blemishes of Golik and Communism are phenomena contradicting each other.

'If we can do such things to each other, corrupt, slander, degrade, why then do we need such a sea?' passionately declares Saba, the father of the girl Golik has deceived. 'Why do we need a new sea? In our spirit are not sea waves but swampy decay.'

And this of course is a criticism of Stalinism which appears in different forms in the script. There is even a deputy Minister who comes back to her native village in a posh Soviet automobile, but pretends not to know her former friends. There is an opportunist and a demagogue and other negative characters. The basic story is about the creation of an artificial sea in a valley area, with its old township, church, centuries-old traditions, the homes of thousands of Ukrainians who loved it and now had to leave it and see everything swallowed up in flooded waters, that will eventually become an inland sea – part of the new industrialization of socialism.

Dovzhenko tries to justify this modernization and industrialization as being the basis of the new kind of life that has to be lived. But he deals with such things as the after-effects of the war, of the colossal tragedy of ten million widows and the fantastic destruction by the Germans. Then the more modern, difficult problem that all the youth flee from the land, from the countryside, from the villages.

Dovzhenko saw that life in the Soviet collective farms, without clubs, without music, even sometimes without light, couldn't possibly satisfy the cultural and spiritual demands of youth. One of his characters says, 'Either we need to stop education or else the villages must be transformed.' And then he attacks the Stalinist type of architecture that is notoriously in such bad taste and so ugly. He has an outstanding, fully approved-of government architect who presents a project for a club which none of the collective farmers like. Dovzhenko says from long specialization in the sphere of pantheons and pavilions his art became cold and passionless. And he isn't able to design a club 'which would lighten the spirits, where beauty will be heightened and necessary.' And the old carpenter of the village says, 'Who gave orders to build cottages all in a row along a straight piece of string? Cottages, stand to attention! By the right, number! The devil with bureaucrats!'

And in real life too, Dovzhenko gave in his plans for the beautification and reconstruction of his beloved Ukraine and found himself up against the Russian Stalinist bureaucrats, with plans for all the USSR laid down in Moscow with rigid 'cast-iron' scripts.

Then, of course, there is the sadness of leaving the beloved past. A beautiful new dam is being built on the Dniepr and the nearby towns and villages must be cut off from the river and must become the bottom of the new sea. The bulldozers will carry away the old log cabins, people will live on the shore of a sea. No one will be able to come back to their cottages, the cottages of their grandfathers, where many generations have lived and died. And so the farewell is sad and sometimes bitter. But, according to Dovzhenko, it is a bright sadness. The parting takes place in the name of a new, more sensible and beautiful life on the shores of an inland sea created by men.

In the finale are the final words of those beloved of Dovzhenko, 'Love the earth, love labor on the earth, otherwise there will be no happiness for us and our children on any kind of planet.'

And what Eisenstein was so fond of, the internal monologue, is here developed to its fullest audio-visual expression in scenes played out to express inner character. So the father of the betrayed girl imagines what he will do with Golik who seduced her. We see such a scene as he imagines it would be, where he judges Golik, a man with a brain of an engineer and the conscience of a bed-bug.

Vlasov comments, 'Here of course not only the character but the author himself strikes crushing blows at the egoism, hypocrisy and villainy of Golik. Here Dovzhenko attacks the petty bourgeoisism, [sic] the philistinism, as passionately, angrily and irreconcilably as Mayakovsky did in his time.' And as futilely, one may sadly add.

But again in understatement Vlasov says, 'The originality as described was not at once understood and not by everybody. The opinion then prevailing was that *The Poem of an Inland Sea* was beautiful, significant, but not a film script. The inertia of thinking, the power of conforming to the normal approved forms of art, prevented us seeing in *The Poem of an Inland Sea* a masterpiece of cinema dramaturgy.'

But of course now Vlasov ends with his valedictory hindsight (so typical of Soviet critics), 'The years have gone by, Dovzhenko is not with us, but his good and wise art continues to radiate with the light of thought and beauty and today particularly clearly is seen the power of his originality. An artist prophetically for the path along which contemporary cinema in our day now moves, which pays attention to the inner spiritual world of man; with still more daring attempts to express on the screen the process of thought and its complex dialectics.' But alas, it was too late for Sasha Dovzhenko.

Dovzhenko now a socialist realist

In the celebrations of A. Dovzhenko anniversary, I read in the *Radianska Ukraina*, the newspaper, on the Jubilee of O. P. Dovzhenko, 24 August 1974, the following:

> September of this year marks the eightieth anniversary of the birth of the Soviet film director and writer O. P. Dovzhenko. [Ukrainian, Oleksandr] The memorial museum in the birthplace of the creator of *Earth, Arsenal, Shchors, Sosnytsia in Chernihiv Oblest*, is preparing a new exhibition depicting the life work of this brilliant master of socialist realism. [!]

Such is the new Communist Party *nakhalstvo* (impudence). *Hutzpa* – I suppose the Yiddish word would be correct.

This is a clear example of what I am trying to show. The Party decides on a new truth and then automatically all its *apparatchiki* repeat, parrot fashion, the new 'truth' about those artists who have been attacked as anti-socialist realists in the poetic school, in the metaphorical school, in the formalist school, but are now all considered socialist realists, and automatically anyone writing about them now takes that for granted without question. So much for the truth of the Communist Party of the Soviet Union.

Then Dovzhenko leapt to a totally different atmosphere, that of a science-fiction script called *Depths of the Cosmos*, originally called *A Flight to Mars*. This was at a time when flight into outer space was still in the far-off future and he dreams a story about the flight of Soviet astronauts to Mars. But he didn't want to keep it in the usual tradition of story form or plot. Like all of his own works this one should have been a cinema poem in which his favorite subjects, man and nature, man and beauty, and creative art, take on new depths, new scales, dictated by the very scale of the cosmos. He conceived the picture as being both color and wide screen, in the possibility of portraying 'the might of space, and time and movement in outer space'. Only some sketches were made, nothing more was done and again the film idea was buried, only to be eventually recreated in a totally different era, the post-Stalin, post-

Khrushchev days, through Tarkovsky's science-fiction film *Solaris*. Ironically its theme was diametrically opposite to the progressive scientific optimism of Dovzhenko, even in the depths of pessimistic Stalin days.

Thus does Dovzhenko's film *A Flight to Mars* with its 'new poetry, new heroics and lyricism of a new world outlook', in which any intelligent beings elsewhere in the galaxies have 'all arrived at Communism', *after* the Communist Stalinist terror, turn into . . . *Solaris*. Communism isn't even mentioned in the whole film, and the human dream is for the old pre-Soviet Russian landscape and Chekhov's *dacha*. And the American science-fiction film *2001* becomes a paean to human scientific-technical process – just what Dovzhenko dreamed his Soviet film would be – but wasn't.

It is also significant how all Soviet citizens and particularly its most articulate intellectuals, change like a barometer according to the demands of the Party. So here, in 1943, the Americans, English and the others are allies and Dovzhenko is allowed to say good things about America and in particular about American cinematography. Here is what he said in 1943:[127]

> Cinematography determines the general moral and aesthetic levels of Americans. I've heard over many years the hypocritical opinions of certain of our cinema workers about American cinematography. Even any positive evaluations they give are frequently formulated with a hidden disdain for them. I confirm that everything that is the best in mankind we must have ourselves. Why must we hand over beauty, courtesy, friendliness to our friends and allies and leave only for ourselves rudeness and poverty? That is not right. I can say that today American cinematography is a mighty weapon of culture and is the basis of the moral power of the United States. The shortcomings of our activity over many years comprise some kind of strange underevaluation of this role of cinematography.

And then of course he goes on to complain about the very small quantity of Soviet films produced, without which you cannot do what the Americans do on a world scale. And so again, despite the fact that Stalin repeated Lenin's words: 'Cinema for us is the most important of the arts,' in actuality it doesn't seem that they treat it like that. In fact, elsewhere he complains bitterly that he has never been able to see his films in a decent cinema and from personal experience I know that the cinema theaters in Russia are very poverty-stricken, very bare, very uncomfortable and even in Moscow there are only one or two really good cinemas, and in other capital cities it's the same.

Then again he puts his foot in it when he complains now at the absence of so many journals that once existed. He said:

> At one time there was a Ukrainian journal *Kino*, other cinema newspapers, both Russian and Ukrainian, and even Leningrad had its own, and now there are no such journals and newspapers. This is bad. For all the Soviet Union there is one general literary newspaper into which everybody tries to fit in.[128]

He said, 'We must resurrect our newspapers and our journals.' And here of course again is where he gets into trouble because this would be considered Ukrainian nationalism, that he wants again to have more and more Ukrainian newspapers rather than just the Russian.

Then he gets into trouble again because he goes on to say that 'we must finish with the "all-rightism," the unprincipled criticism of bad pictures. We cannot call bad pictures good. If the film *Partisans in the Steppes of the Ukraine* is a bad picture, we should say so . . . because why should anyone do good films if the bad ones are also praised?'[129]

Dovzhenko's scorn for the *apparatchiki* – Party bureaucrats – is everywhere evident in his diaries and notebooks:[130]

19 November 1945
He was a Chairman and therefore knew more about art than anyone else.

And the work of those who manage things, the Party secretaries, the Party chairmen and directors, who are the bosses of Soviet society he summed up: 'To manage: to ban, hold back, forbid, guard, conceal, refuse'.

One of my fellow students who knew Dovzhenko well, told me once:[131]

> I was very fond of Alexander Petrovich Dovzhenko: and he often walked with me through the city [Moscow] and one day we were strolling through Red Square and he put his hand on my shoulder and said 'Ryzhaya Bluza',[132] he called me that because I was ginger and I was wearing a blue shirt and blue jeans.

'Ginger blouse,' he said, 'Let me tell you a fable. Once upon a time there was a village, it was a good village, and everyone in the village spoke the truth to one another. No one ever lied.

Now on the edge of the village grew a birch tree. People came under this birch tree and remembered their youth.

Lovers came and pondered on how they would live.

Pregnant women came and wondered what names they would give to their babies.

Then trouble came.

First came a storm and then a thunderbolt hit the birch tree and smashed it.

They had to decide – what to do with the birch tree? To chop it into firewood would be a pity. So they fashioned it into a speaker's platform.

And then do you know what happened? Up till then everyone in the village had spoken the truth, but as soon as that platform appeared they began to lie. And the whole village turned upside down. Then one day a collective farm bull was being led through the village. He of course knew nothing about all this but suddenly, in the middle of the village he ran berserk and smashed the platform to bits.

Having been smashed by the bull the platform now was only fit for firewood.

And henceforth everyone started to speak the truth again.'

And then Alexander Petrovich said to me, 'Kolya, now why was that, eh?'

Years later I found a note on this by Dovzhenko.[133]

To describe the tribunal. It was constructed by an unknown carpenter from some kind of special wood and he, apparently, cursed it, bewitched it.

It differentiated from all other platforms in that once on it no one could speak the truth. Already some bold spirits had ventured on it sometimes. But something twisted their tongue, and they said something else. For as soon as one finished speaking and got off the platform again everything was in its proper place. For no matter what they said it was bewitched and they spoke on it as if in a dream. They all spoke in the same tone. Some, once they stood on that bewitched place, changed so much that they were unrecognisable. That's the reason, probably, that even the stenograms had to be corrected – they were as much like speeches as a log is to a tree.

Once again Alexander Petrovich is using his eternal Ukrainian folklore to point a moral. With the coming of the Party agitator-orator to the village, with the coming of *partiinost*, party-mindedness, truth disappears. For truth is what the Party decides, not what the people express. They had to lie to live. Only when that party-minded platform is smashed will truth return.

But as early as 1942, Dovzhenko felt all that he suffered under the Communist Party regime:[134]

10 April 1942

I often think about how my life has been wasted. What a great mistake I made when I went to work in films. Sixteen years of penal servitude in this . . . bourgeois dustbin where I am forced to co-operate with pitiful wretches who hate me and whom I profoundly despise as unqualified and amoral brutes without a shred of decency or holiness, wretches who hate my nation and make it miserable. How much health and happiness have I lost because of people whom I can't stand! If I had applied all my strength and passion in these sixteen years to writing, I'd have at least a dozen volumes of real literature behind me. As it is, my unwritten books are like unborn children. What a great pity that they will remain only as plans.

Here is a letter I wrote to Dovzhenko in Russian (which I now translate). It was the autumn of 1935 and Fredda and I were on our honeymoon!

Dear Alexander Petrovich;

At this moment I am on a holiday in Piatigorsk with my wife, and in a quiet moment decided to write you: as it was impossible in noisy Moscow.

I remembered our conversation in Potylikha [the Moscow Film Studios. HM.] when you proposed that I come to work with you in Kiev (for myself as a film regisseur and my wife as a sculptress). But as almost all my contacts live in Moscow, I waited to see if something would come off with cinematographists in Moscow – but nothing emerged.

My wife still has not received a studio where she can work.

Because of that she got ill – but you will understand, as an artist, what it is in the Soviet Union to be without means of production.

I had concrete plans in Mezhrabpomfilm – everyone said that in so far as I am a foreigner it was necessary for me to work *there* on a foreign theme.

I began to work together with the scriptwriter, Rakhmanov,[135] on a scenario adaptation from an English book, a satirical novel. A very interesting theme and merry (how we need comedies. I long for the comedies of Chaplin – God knows!).

But the matter dragged on – as always – and the Studio director proposed that I make a short colour film – while they make the full-length script. I agreed and began work – when suddenly the Mezhrabpomfilm was liquidated! And everything went to the lower depths! [An allusion to the title of Maxim Gorky's play. HM.]

To the bottom, both the full-length scenario and the film! And for which they don't want even to pay me!

In bitter disappointment, I took my holiday leave and temporarily turned to literary work, writing poetry and translating Mayakovsky. At the moment, I am almost the only translator of Mayakovsky in the English language. I am compiling an anthology of Soviet poetry. I also want to translate Ukrainian poetry. Incidentally, I like Taras Shevchenko very much, as far as I can judge from the Russian translations. I want to translate him and am now reading his diary.[136] His works are completely unknown abroad – even less than Pushkin. I am invited to work on an English edition of Pushkin for his centenary.

I have almost decided to go home and take up what I can there in the cinema, if not, then in theater, and if not, then in literature – and all the time of course to do political work. [This I did just two years later and in that order – of that in another place. HM.] I am pulled there very much now, particularly in relation to the events in Spain. [The oncoming Spanish Civil War – for which I eventually did make films. HM.]

But it is almost insulting to leave here not having made one film! [And I never did – in my adopted socialist fatherland – whereas in bourgeois capitalist England, my then class enemy – I made films and produced plays and wrote books!!! HM.]

And so I am turning to you, remembering your proposal, and want very much to discuss with you this, for me, very serious problem. In any case, I must see you. In so far as one has to reserve a ticket twelve days before departure and I must leave here about the 14th or 15th, I would ask you please to reply at once, if at all possible.

In any case, I very much want to see Kiev – the Ukrainian Exhibition in Moscow was wonderful. [I didn't see Kiev till some thirty years later, when Sasha was dead – and then I came to translate Taras Shevchenko by official invitation of the Academy of Sciences Shevchenko Committee under the chairmanship of the Ukrainian poet Mykola Bazhan. And my wife was commissioned to sculpt a statue of Taras Shevchenko, which is now in the *Shevchenko Museum* in Kiev. The Kiev studios and a street and a ship were now named after Alexander Dovzhenko! HM.]

No doubt Venyarsky is with you – greet him for me. [He was my fellow student at GIK from Kiev, who always went to work with Dovzhenko on his practical work and after he graduated from the Institute. He came to meet me with Grisha Lifschitz, another fellow student who lived in Kiev, but that was also some thirty years later. HM.] Maybe he can arrange a lodging for me for a few days, as it is difficult in general to get a room and very expensive.

Greetings to Solntseva, [his wife]
to a swift meeting,
Herbert Marshall

But alas nothing happened – he didn't make any films in that very period and, in relation to this, Dovzhenko spoke at the famous Cinematographers' Conference in Moscow, at which, *inter alia*, he said the following:[137]

What happens to the growth of our new recruits? The students of the GIK have greater perspectives and rights studying in the GIK, than the same student finding himself in a film studio after graduating from the GIK, i.e., his status as to rights and perspectives end when he receives his certificate. [Laughter] There attention is paid to him, he studies every day, he is trained in a whole series of perspectives, he is trusted. But he comes to the film studio – and is forgotten. They wander around like shadows, without perspectives, working with regisseurs quite accidentally. . . . In any case, the position of youth in film studios at the moment is bad beyond words. We must draw conclusions from this situation. Obviously the situation in Leningrad must be better. [From the floor: 'Worse!']

I can't imagine it.

But as to Moscow, the position here is wretchedly bad, bad.

The honesty of Dovzhenko is clear – but nothing was done, except to make it worse with Stalin's new 'production of masterpieces only' plan!

So we had no contact until over a year and a half later, when I last saw Alexander Dovzhenko in Moscow. I went to bid him goodbye. This was in the late autumn of 1937. My decision to leave what was now my second homeland was occasioned by the demand of the Party that every foreign citizen must take on Soviet citizenship or else go home and work in his own country. Of course such offers were only made to Party members or to fellow travelers trusted by Party comrades. But one thanks fate that Fredda and I decided to stick to our British citizenship and go home to England. Those of our other foreign comrades who stayed, in the end, found themselves in concentration camps, or were executed or so ill treated in the camps that they came out wrecks. I know of examples which I won't go into here.

Having decided to go we began to bid farewell to friends. And as it happened there was an extraordinary parallel farewell made on the one hand to Alexander Petrovich Dovzhenko and on the other to the dramatist Alexander Afinogenov. The parallel was strange.

I met Sasha Afinogenov quite by accident on what was known as Okhotny Ryad (now Marx Prospect) and it was just outside that great block building of the Soviet of Ministers of the USSR. At one time Sasha and I were friends and I had introduced him to the beautiful girl Jeanya who became his wife. They moved to some apartment in some special building and I learned from my student friend Vartan that this was the building owned by the NKVD (the Secret Police). Later I learned that Sasha was under the special protection of the head of the NKVD, People's Commissar of Internal Affairs, Yagoda. Of course at that time this was considered a very lucky thing for him. What greater protection could he have than the head of the Secret Police, who everywhere was lauded as 'The Flaming Sword of the Proletariat,' head of the most powerful organization next to the Party.

However, here by chance I met him with his great comrade and friend, the dramatist, Kirshon. Kirshon also was a favorite of the Party and Stalin. He was the one who wrote the kind of 'socialist realist' plays the Party approved of and which were produced even in the citadel of conservatism, The Moscow Art Theater. And so, as I bid farewell, I asked Sasha to come with Jeanya to visit us in England on his way to America some day, and he said he would. He had promised Jeanya they would visit her home one day. But then somehow, I seemed to notice a shadow on his countenance and Kirshon was very glum. I had met them from time to time at the Soviet writers' meetings and so on and they were usually the most chirpy and cocky even of the bunch of older stagers, who were much more under Party criticism than these two favorites. Somehow, there was a somber feeling as we shook hands and said, '*Do svidanya*.' I only realized later that their protector, 'The Flaming Sword of the Proletariat' had been extinguished as a spy and 'enemy of the people.'

Then I rang up Dovzhenko and found that he was staying at an equally inaccessible building called *Dom Pravitelstva* (Government House). A great grim high-rise building just across the river, Zamoskvarechy, as it was called.

Alexander Petrovich left word downstairs, so I was allowed by security to see him. He was staying in the apartment of Mikhail Koltsov. Koltsov, like Kirshon, was a favorite of the establishment. He was a leading journalist, quite often prompted by Stalin, and was sent by Stalin to be special Party correspondent during the Civil War in Spain. Alexander Petrovich commiserated with me that he hadn't been able to have me working with him on his films, as I had written him earlier, but of course what could he say. He couldn't complain to a foreigner, just leaving the Soviet Union, about the difficulties he was having in getting or making another film, let alone worry about having a student of the GIK working with him. Indeed the letter I had sent him (see p. 177) brought no reply, because he wasn't able even to finalize his next film. So too, there was an air of sadness about Alexander Petrovich; here he was unable to make films despite all his international prestige and his great talent.

Now I said it was a strange parallel, because years later what transpired was that very soon after I saw them, Kirshon was arrested as an 'enemy of the people,' though he apparently passionately defended himself. The Union of Soviet Writers of course voted unanimously to expel him and he was executed.

Mikhael Koltsov came back from Spain as an honored Stalinist correspondent of the Party and was also arrested as an 'enemy of the people' and he too was executed. But my two friends escaped by whatever quirk of fate. Afinogenov was expelled from the Party, but eventually reinstated.

Then he died, what in the Soviet Union would be considered a natural death. He was killed accidentally by a German bomb that hit the Central Committee Headquarters of the Party in Moscow during the war. But tragedy seemed to dog the family, for beautiful, dearest Jeanya was going with her two children after the war to take them at last to see her family in America. As they were crossing the Black Sea in a Soviet ship, it apparently caught fire and in rescuing her children she was burned to death.

Alexander Petrovich Dovzhenko, though bitterly attacked by both Stalin and Beria, nevertheless did not experience a concentration camp. Only internal exile.

And so one by one those 'luckier' fellow-artists of mine and friends died their natural death, but they were broken-hearted men.

It is significant that Ivor Montagu, in writing of the death of Dovzhenko, admits the way Dovzhenko was received. He said that his films called forth hot discussion:[138]

> Feeling its power, outside their narrow range, mistaking for pantheism its truly dialectical perception of the oneness and continuity of the Universe, the puritans and careerists, alarmed, were nervous. Without that same passionate love of man all nature was misunderstood and applauded as a sign of indifference toward the contemporary struggle or the standards of the artist's socialist homeland, a sign that he was not engagé. Nothing could have been more false. This artist was the most engagé of all the talents in all Soviet art.

Note that Montagu puts the blame on the pundits, the puritans and the careerists! Not once in the whole of his article does he pin the blame on the one power in total control, the Communist Party of the Soviet Union.

Montagu went on to say about these critics who were attacking Dovzhenko:[139]

> . . . and so some reached the cheap suspicion – approving or disapproving according to their political bent – that beneath the revolutionary surface 'document' lay a consciously introduced smuggled primary interest, nature worship, eroticism or the like, nothing could have been more remote from the truth. I doubt whether Dovzhenko consciously knew or could have explained what he was doing any more than Shelley could have written on a blackboard the 'how' of being a poet. Dovzhenko himself tells us 'as far as I was concerned there were no questions of style or form involved. I worked like a soldier who fights the enemy without thought of rules or theory. I dare say if I had been asked then what I was thinking about I should have answered like Courbet to a lady's question, "Madame I'm not thinking – I'm excited." '

All the panegyrics now on his seventy-fifth or eightieth anniversary praise Dovzhenko inside the Soviet Union but, of course, in all the praise there is hardly any mention of his tragedy.

But Dovzhenko had something of his own to say about this and in his diary and notebooks is sufficient evidence to show what happened to this great genius in the 'socialist' society he so enthusiastically helped to create.[140]

22 January 1949
To X and Y:
  Farewell, comrades, friends and foes, farewell. Go on trampling my name if you have to, let me die quickly. I wish you a long life. For each of you I wish with all my ruined heart that you accomplish much more than I have. May you fold your hard-working hands some day in the wonderful distant future when you are neither built up nor condemned, when you look back at your own road and our people's broad fields that will be sown with honest words and not ravaged by lies, hatred, greed, cruelty, and careerism. May you sigh easily and happily with the thought that I, who dreamt all my life about creating good, was not fated to have: blessed are labor, and the day, and the house. . . .

With what will I comfort myself abroad? Where will I rest my gray head? In distant China, under foreign skies? Farewell.

Or will the evil that you, my happy, faultless foes, have perpetrated catch up with me even there?*

As compared to Eisenstein, who scintilated intellectual wit, and Pudovkin, who was a passionate, volatile man, Alexander Dovzhenko, who was considered the Michelangelo of the trio, really was more like Michelangelo's 'David.' He had such dignity, such poise, such beauty and what in Russian they call *oboyanie*, which one might call radiance. He seemed to have an aura. Eisenstein had intellectual passion, Pudovkin emotional but Dovzhenko had poetic passion.

In these essays about them, I have tried to give a more truthful picture of their lives and their struggles and their creative work in Communist Party society than the Communist Party gives.

I have tried to show by my montage of facts, quotations, actual documents, and printed works of the Soviet Union, to prove that what I am saying is not my imagination or prejudices, but facts.

We have seen how these three musketeers, these three revolutionary artists, started out with such high hopes in the new Renaissance in which they equated themselves with da Vinci, Raphael and Michelangelo. And all three reacted to the terrifying period they had to go through under Stalin in their own characteristic ways.

Pudovkin remained, as Eisenstein had cast him, as the Holy Simpleton; the sacred fool of Russian iconography. Never in any of his works, published or unpublished, has there been any overt criticism or blame in any fundamental sense attached to what the Communist Party did to him or to Russia.

In Eisenstein, of course, we have the reaction of the intellectual *in excelsis*, who said his say indirectly, through his films, through his lectures and his drawings, particularly, in that figure of implacable fate that dogged his footsteps even in the so-called Renaissance of socialist society. But it remained for the poet Dovzhenko to cry out at the top of his voice in his diaries and notebooks the truth about what kind of regime he served so faithfully.

---

* Dovzhenko was planning to go to China to film *Dawn Over China*. The project was canceled. (Original footnote)

And this would be the proper thing for Russia. For always, in Russia, the poet has been the conscience of its people, whether a Pushkin who first openly fought the autocracy or Nekrassov, the poet of rage and grief, or Pasternak, the crucified Hamlet of Russia, or Akhmatova, who cried out, 'A hundred million people speak through these lips of mine', or even a Yevtushenko who dared to speak out in his time and say, 'A poet is more than a poet in Russia.'

And in the cinema, its greatest poet, Dovzhenko, spoke out the truth in all of his scripts, despite the terrifying onslaught on him by the Stalinist *apparatchiki*. Nowhere has a cry of despair and pain been made so manifest as in these works and writings of Dovzhenko.

What is terrifying now is to see how all of this is being hushed up. I notice in the four-volume Russian edition of his *Selected Works*[141] that all his attacks on Stalin in his diaries have been censored out. Not just his criticism of the Party but his specific attacks on Stalin have gone. The rehabilitation of Stalin is progressing in this way, by smothering the truth, as was expressed in this case by Dovzhenko. And now the attempt to equate all of these great artists, who were bitterly attacked as formalists and anti-socialist realists, under the common umbrella of socialist realism.

It is an incredible situation, and yet that incredible situation of the cover-up, far beyond anything Watergate ever dreamed of, is part and parcel of Communist Party life and work. I remember reading recently how Yevtushenko was shocked to the core when he was in Siberia and at dinner with young students who toasted, of all people, the great Stalin! And he found to his horror that they did not know of the anti-Stalin poems he had written in the Khrushchev days, which are now no longer reprinted or republished. The vast cover-up continues, so that the works of all those who died most tragically at the hands of the Party are now all great creations of the same Communist Party.

Well, I've done my bit to show the truth about these men as honestly as I can and as factually as humanly possible. And if the world does not learn by it, so much the worse for the world. I remember reading in the *History of Civilization* the difference between those nations who choose democracy and those who choose tyranny. And I quote:[142]

Hardly any of these surrounding nations (Persians, Goth, Carthage) cared for what to the Greeks was the very essence of life – liberty to be, to think, to speak; and to do. Everyone of these peoples except the Phoenicians lived under despots, surrendered their souls to superstition, and had small experience of the stimulus of freedom or the life of reason.

Greeks called them *Barbaroi*, Barbarians. A barbarian was a man content to believe without reason and live without liberty.

And I suppose in the end, the people get the government they deserve. If they choose to be under a Stalin, a Mao Zedong or an Andropov and if even countries far removed from Russia choose the same Communist Party apparatus which will eventually trap and hold them by their jugular veins, in order to keep their power, then what more can I say? Those whom the Party will destroy they first make mad.

Sergei Eisenstein

It is the irony of fate that Sergei Eisenstein's fame and appreciation was primarily abroad. I quote from his autobiography:[1]

In 1941, the first bulky volume of the American film index was published. In a survey written on the Cinema's first forty years, according to the introduction, the boy from Riga occupies fourth place for the quantity written about him. First is Chaplin, second Griffith and our boy follows straight after the third place which belongs to Mary Pickford.

And in the tragic last chapter, 'P.S.', (which he knew was the postscript of his life,) he says:[2]

P.S., By all the laws of science, I should have died, but for some reason, survived. Therefore, I consider everything that happens as a postscript of my own life. P.S., And indeed at the age of 48, I had to read this about myself: 'one of the greatest directors of his time.'

This was in the foreign press – not his own.

In 1956, in the journal *Iskusstvo Kino*, the Soviet critic S. Ginsburg writes:[3]

Our cinema authorities and critics are in an insolvable debt before S. M. Eisenstein and V. Pudovkin. The creative and theoretical researches of these wonderful artists of the cinema, laying the foundations of revolutionary cinema art, over a whole series of years have either been distorted or suppressed. The articles of Eisenstein and Pudovkin, scattered through old journals and brochures, have been translated into all the leading languages of the world and in certain countries have even been published in special collections (anthologies). For our readers they have been hardly accessible. . . . For many years our critics have written almost nothing about the researches and achievements of these cinematographic innovators. And if they did mention these masters, it was most of all to condemn the mistakes they had committed. There actually existed specialists in 'working over' these artists, whose creative work constitutes the national pride of our native cinematography.

Let the critic answer the 'cinema authorities', by which Ginsburg means the Party.

It is ironical that today, the Communist Party of the Soviet Union tries to take full credit for the genius of Eisenstein; it is clearly shown that what he achieved was done in spite of them and even the world-shaking success of his great *Potemkin* (which was declared by an international jury to be still the best film ever made), was not at first appreciated and accepted by the bureaucrats of the Communist Party of the Soviet Union.

'And that morning he woke up famous,' Eisenstein quotes Zola, and the same thing happened to him, with the première of *Potemkin*, in *Berlin*! But I have written fully all about this in my compilation *Battleship Potemkin – The Best Film of All Time*, to which I refer the reader.[4]

One must remember that for all the noise the CPSU now makes about its geniuses and their successful films, in their own country hardly any of the classics were widely shown successes. Pudovkin's classic film *Mother*, Dovzhenko's *Earth*, Vertov's *Enthusiasm*, and Okhlopkov's *Way of the Enthusiasts* were all first acclaimed abroad.

And to bring this history up to date, I quote from a fellow student of Eisenstein:

I went to the première of *Ivan the Terrible, Part 1*. A film on which had been put a lot of work and effort. . . . In the cinema theater, if I said there was 30% capacity it would be a lot. It was more than half empty! That was embarrassing, shameful and insulting. I went to Sergei Eisenstein and said: I have just gotten a copy of your newly published scenario *Ivan the Terrible*. Inscribe it for me please. I treasure this book. He wrote: 'To Dear Kolya. In memory of the première of *Ivan the Terrible*. *Vkalyvai sam*. [Dig into it yourself.] SME.'

Zorkaya is the Soviet critic I have read who honestly pinpointed the taste of the new ruling class, who wanted nothing of left fronts, factualism or constructivism or abstractions or cubism or modern art.[5]

> Meyerhold wanted his spectator to come not to the theater, but to a meeting. Spectators didn't want to come to meetings, they preferred the theater, unattainable to them in Tsarist days. They wanted to sit in red velvet seats, in gilded loges, where previously the bourgeois had sat. They wanted to see famous artists who now played not for the gentry, but for them. In the theater now, too, he felt he was the boss, as the leaflets explained, and demanded that the same damned 'LEF'[6] should sing to him in baritone. *So arose the gap between those artists who were attracted by revolutionary creative form and spectators who, meeting for the first time with art, were fully satisfied with the traditional public fare.*

This was the artistic taste of Stalin and Khrushchev, not of Luna-charsky and Bukharin and Trotsky and the intellectuals, all of whom were wiped out. Even in the late 1960s Khrushchev, in attacking the 'modernists' of that decade, said he preferred Demyan Bedny (a versifier and Party hack and hatchet man)[7] to poets like Pasternak or Yevtushenko, as Stalin preferred Alexandrov's slapstick film *Volga Volga* and Chiurelli's pompous aggrandisement *The Vow*, to Pudovkin's, Dovzhenko's or Eisenstein's films.

In England, where I have been intimately involved with the showing of Soviet films from 1929 until 1945, the classic Soviet films have not been 'box-office,' but they have had their effect on the intelligentsia and world film-makers. That can be vouched for, as I have written elsewhere.[8]

In London, when a group of left-wing avant-gardists, headed by Ivor Montagu, tried to show *Potemkin*, it was banned by the British Board of Film Censors, and attempts to show it were under the surveillance of the British Special Branch detectives. Eisenstein quips about the stupidity of the British censors[9] but says, 'It is true, though, that this in no way prevented our films from not being shown anywhere in London, even though the censor is not consid-ered a State organization.'

Here Eisenstein prevaricates. He wrote this in 1949, yet he knew very well that his and other Russian films *were* shown in London, and indeed throughout the United Kingdom, despite censorship, even if only to limited audiences. The London Film Society, a voluntary organization, mainly influenced by the Communist Party, was the spearhead of these showings. Every loophole in the law was used by us all. Ivor Montagu worked in England as Leon Moussinac did in France to show Soviet films. Eisenstein himself writes that Moussinac was like a D'Artagnan, engaged in a practical struggle to ensure that the West saw Soviet films. 'The chain of Communist film clubs using their right of "private meetings" to stay free from the censor, was one of those channels.'[10] So, in England, the Communist Party used every channel.

But unlike the democratic world, there are no rights of 'private meetings' in the USSR for any purpose, and to attempt to stay 'free from the censor' would have meant arrest, prison camp and probably death. No 'avant-garde' or any other foreign films were ever shown privately in the Soviet Union, and only to a very limited audience publicly.

As to Eisenstein's appearance at the Paris Sorbonne and many places in the world where he lectured, he writes:[11]

> I gabble addresses and lectures in three languages in Zurich,
> Berlin, Hamburg, London, Cambridge, Paris, Brussels,
> Antwerp, Liège, Amsterdam, Rotterdam, The Hague, New York
> (Columbia University), in Boston (Harvard), in New Haven
> (Yale), at the Chicago and California Universities, before
> Negroes in New Orleans and Dorchester, at countless meetings
> and lunches, and in Mexico City. . . .

However, no such reciprocal facilities were given to any foreign person of eminence within the Soviet Union; even if they were against the government in power in their *own* country.

'The novel,' says Eisenstein[12] 'by Theodore Dreiser, *An American Tragedy*, was banned for having given moral offence.' Nonsense, of course! Yet, because of the monolithic censorship and strict control of the CP in the Soviet Union, over almost every aspect of life, it is almost impossible for any Soviet citizen to believe that such censorship doesn't exist everywhere else. One of the fundamental problems in dealing with the Soviet Union is this lack of understanding of what individual freedom is. They just don't know.

On the other hand, there is a great deal of hypocrisy, also, in the fact that Eisenstein (like others) complains about the difficulties that at times Soviet films had in getting shown abroad. Nevertheless, they *did* get shown in most countries of the world. What he never troubles to mention is that no foreign films ever got similar showings throughout the Soviet Union!

The only time was when some film, asked for by the State Film Organization, was sent to Moscow 'on approval.' In fact, it was never intended that it would be purchased, only that it could be shown either to the higher-ups in the Party or to the film specialists. I know, because I worked for the Soviet Film Agency and its organizations, at both ends. After a foreign film was shown to such limited film professional and high Party audiences in Moscow or Leningrad, it would then be sent back as 'unsuitable.'

Even during the war, when we were widely showing Soviet films in England on a reciprocal basis, I later learned that our films, which were supposed to be equally widely shown, were by and large only shown to limited audiences in Moscow, and not at all to wide masses, except in a very few cases where films had a negative aspect or a purely comic or romantic tale. It seems that among Stalin's favorite films was *The Great Waltz* and *Waterloo Bridge*, so they probably might have been shown.

As Eisenstein's itinerary shows, in those days (up to 1930) Soviet citizens had more freedom of travel than ever since, even after the death of Stalin. But finally, the Stalinist iron curtain descended even on the leading Communist artists. One of the causes of the great poet Mayakovsky's suicide was the Party's refusal of a visa to visit Paris in 1930. After Eisenstein came back in disgrace in 1931, he was never allowed out again until the day he died. And I know personally how much that irked and depressed him, as it did and does so many other members of the Soviet intelligentsia. Yevtushenko wrote of this in his poem 'Prologue': 'Frontiers hinder me. . . . I'm embarrassed not to know New York, Buenos Aires.'[13]

Yet in those early days it was different.

As I have written, my first contact with Soviet film-makers was the memorable meeting with Dziga Vertov at an avant-garde film conference in Stuttgart, Germany, in 1928, then in 1929, with Pudovkin, who came to London and showed his two great films through the Film Society.[14] In 1930, Eisenstein, Alexandrov and Tisse came to London *en route* to Hollywood. Ivor Montagu writes of this:[15]

Sidney Bernstein threw a party for him. Jack Isaacs took him to the theaters and browsing amid books. Herbert Marshall, just then beginning in cinema as an amateur, took him to see the city and the more ordinary sights. (Bert was later to become the only foreign student to go through the whole course of the Moscow Film School and graduate there, as an Eisenstein pupil. Eisenstein then thought highly of him as a comic actor – talent Bert has since concealed – but I remember that, at the time, Eisenstein, who cannot be said to have exactly disliked admiration, nevertheless returned exhausted at the end of the day, exclaiming in wonder: 'He is so very worshipping.')

Six months later, I received an invitation through Eisenstein's assistant (and later wife), Pera Attasheva, from VOKS (the Soviet Society for Cultural Relations with Foreign Countries) with a scholarship for the All-Union State Institute of Cinematography in Moscow, but I had to learn Russian. I started, but couldn't! I decided the best thing was to go there. At that time, diplomatic relations between Britain and Russia were broken. I could only book a train to Warsaw. So with a tin trunk, unabashed, and with about £10 in my pocket, I left for the unknown.

I was met by Pera Attasheva and Valya Milman, her co-worker in VOKS. I stayed with Pera and worked as an assistant editor to Anna Louise Strong, starting the *Moscow News*, the first English newspaper in the USSR, until I was accepted at the cinema institute. I then moved into the students' dormitory, wooden barracks, with just bedsteads, straw mattresses, and two shifts of Box and Cox, students who studied in daytime and who slept at night, and vice versa. Thank goodness I was a daytime student! The place swarmed with bugs and enthusiasm. But I was told that soon the Five-Year Plan would give us our 'students' town.' I was skeptical. But in six months we moved into the new dormitory blocks, four or five in a room, designed for two. But to us it was luxury!

We studied at the institute, known as the GIK:[16] it was housed in the former notorious Restaurant Yar, haunt of Rasputin and the gypsy choirs.

Eisenstein's lectures were like a magnet. Numerous visitors to Russia came to listen. Eisenstein's erudition, his humor, his free and easy approach, contrasted so strongly to the dour officialdom of Stalinist bureaucracy.

From 1932 to 1935, I was a student-director in Eisenstein's

Research Group of the GIK. There were four departments in the institute: directing, acting, script writing and cinematography.

Eisenstein was Dean of the directors' department. The institute was equipped with its own studio (but hardly ever had any film stock), and had a very good library of international films. The course at that time lasted four and a half years. Three years were devoted to theoretical and practical work inside the institute, and a year and a half to practical work in the studios and on location. The film director's curriculum I studied covered nearly thirty subjects, including philosophy, political economy, sociology, the fine arts, history of the world cinema and theater, scenario writing and editing, acting and psychology, theater, radio and film production, as well as the technical subjects directly concerned with cinema production.

A student's greatest pride was to work in Eisenstein's Research Group. This group was an instrument in the fulfillment of Eisenstein's dream. He said, 'I want to create a work which will be to Art what Darwin's *Origin of Species* has been to Nature and Marx's *Capital* to Society. I want to lay bare the nature of artistic creation.'

But Eisenstein's main problem was the philistines in the government and Party – the Stalinist bureaucrats – who dubbed his thinking 'formalistic,' and his internationalism as 'cosmopolitanism.'[17] And another problem was the limited education of his students, who were mainly workers and peasants, with nothing but an elementary school education plus evening classes, and that included me! At that stage, the children of the middle or upper classes were almost rigidly excluded from Soviet institutions, which to those who fought for the proletarian revolution seemed only justice. And it seemed so to me – I too, in England, had been rigidly excluded, as a poor working-class lad, from ever getting into a college, let alone to Eton or Cambridge. But, though we were apparently parallel, in fact it soon became clear that Eisenstein's pupils did not have even a fraction of the necessary background to benefit from his erudite teachings. I, at least, had some! Eisenstein became aware of that fact. In the middle of giving some brilliant analogy, quoting examples from world art, he would suddenly say to me (in English) 'Thank goodness you at least have heard of the Sistine Chapel or of Sigmund Freud!' In one of his articles about the GIK in 1934, he said:[18]

A primary trouble encountered with almost the entire student body was the low cultural level of the admitted students. Nor has this defect been remedied. It is such a general culture and a cultural basis in the arts that is perhaps, of all fields of art, most required in film direction. Its many facets require a many-sided background. And this is one of the most serious problems that face our young people. . . . Second-year students, for example, had read neither Gogol's *Dead Souls* nor Balzac's *Père Goriot*. One listens to a student rattling off, in faultless phrases, a history of literature with Marxist appraisals of this or that literary-social phenomenon – only to find out later that he had never actually read – or even seen – the works he talked so fluently about! Such cases are also too familiar to us at the Institute. . . . Instead of an all-permeating happy science, boring asceticists, pettifogging pedants and casuists come to the institutes; in their hands the living spirit of the sorceress – dialectics, disappears, and all that remains is an indigestible skeleton of paragraphs, abstract propositions and the perpetual motion of the vicious circle of once-for-all chosen quotations.

Their activity (of course, of course – not always, not everywhere and anywhere!!) is similar to that on the threshold of Buddhist temples . . . where a similar process is rationalized in the system of 'prayer-wheels'. . . .

Incidentally – it is also a certain foreknowledge of the way these *dobrozrakovs* of dialectics will pounce on my insufficiently orthodox formulations, or maybe on my too independent attempts to investigate questions of the methods of art, outside the usually accepted norm.

A more accurate or brilliant analysis of the Communist Party propagandists could not be written. It is with these that Eisenstein had to battle for his life, but alas they had the power – absolute power.

By and large, Eisenstein suppressed his feelings about this 'agit-prop' attitude of the Party. But at times he let off steam in his class. I remember one day he came into the classroom, very tired and worn out. We knew he had had another rough time with the Party leadership at the Moscow Film Studios, over his film *Bezhin Meadow*, which was eventually banned and destroyed.

He usually greeted us, but this time said nothing. We kept silent and waited. He went up to the blackboard and started drawing in his usual swift, Picasso-like fashion. He drew a tree, then a dachs-hund, sniffing at the base of the tree, then he extended the sausage-like body of the dog, winding it at least twice round the trunk, until its nose was peering right into its own behind!

He still said nothing, but wrote underneath a subtitle, as in a silent film: 'Twenty years I've worked at Mosfilm Studios, but it's the first time I've seen *that* director.'

Apart from open attacks by the Stalinist Party leadership, it is now obvious how much Eisenstein and us foreigners were under constant surveillance by the Secret Police, the GPU as it then was.

In this regard, I remember a story I was once told by one of my fellow students, who, alas, is now dead. On returning from a Central Asian republic this fellow student told me that, when he set forth, S. M. Eisenstein had said to him (and I quote my verbatim notes), 'Now mind, you bring me back some souvenir of your province. Something unlike anything I have now.'

'OK.'

This is his story:

The time came to return and I still hadn't found that unusual souvenir for S. M. Eisenstein. I knew that Eisenstein never forgot a thing, I had to find something! I went into the photo library and started to delve into their negatives. I came across something unusual. One was a close-up of the face of a leper, the right side of whose face was eaten away. He was drinking some pale tea, some of the liquid he swallowed, but part trickled out of the missing side of his mouth! Then I found another negative of a man suffering with a goiter in his neck. But this goiter was larger than his own head! Then I came across a photo of a tray on which, surrounded by roses, was the severed head of a Basmach.[19] It seemed this present was being presented by someone to the local Commander of the Red Army.

I took these three negatives and managed to get hold of some large-grain photo paper called Chat Noire and made three enlargements and mounted them like a triptych on green paper.

At the very first lecture after my return, sure enough, S. M. Eisenstein came over and said, 'Well, bring it along to me at home,' So I went. He was dining with Maxim Maximovich Straukh and Judith Glizer.[20] 'Well show us,' he said. So I opened up the package and placed it on the table. Glizer took one look, stood up and left the table, unable to eat another thing! Straukh couldn't eat either, but remained at the table. But S. M. Eisenstein was very pleased, hugged me and said, 'Now, that's the best present you could conceive of.'

The student went on with his story:

However, the secretary of the Party Committee at GIK called me and said, 'Someone from the Radio wants you on the phone.' I went and picked up the receiver. A voice said, 'NKVD[21] is interested in you.' I replied, 'Is that good or bad?' The voice said 'We shall see. Do you think you could find some spare time to come and visit us at 11 p.m. this evening?' 'Certainly,' I naturally said. I went. Luckily for me the man I had to see was a clever chap. He had a grey moustache and tired but very clever eyes. We sat down and chatted. He asked how I was studying, who my teachers were, etc. and then asked me whether I studied photography. I said no, I was studying in the Director's Course. He went on to ask where I had been, what I was doing, and once again put the question, 'Did I take up photography.' I said, 'No.' Then he said, 'When we are told the truth, that's better. But when we are lied to, then to the sentence you are already getting, we add three years.' So I said, 'Well what do I have to do, *not* to get three years added?' Already assuming that I had copped a sentence! I then said vehemently, 'But I *don't* study the art of photography!' Well, it seemed that he believed me and said, 'OK. Now, did you bring anything back with you from Central Asia?' And then at once I understood. 'Yes,' I said, 'I brought back three photographs for my teacher, Sergei Mikhailovich Eisenstein.' He got up from the desk and said, 'I'll let you go this time, and when you meet your teacher next, tell him not to show such photographs to foreigners.'

At the next lecture S. M. Eisenstein noticed I looked somewhat downcast and finally came up and said, 'What's up?' I said, 'Sergei Mikhailovich, why do you show my present to foreigners?' 'Oy,' he said, 'It's those Mexicans! We were arguing about my film [*Que Viva Mexico*] and I showed them your photographs!'

Another time he got into trouble through an interview in the *Literaturnaya Gazeta* in which he was asked to name the outstanding art events of the year for 1935; I translate:

My most powerful impression for the outgoing year? However
sad it may be – they are imported. In the first, second and third
places – is above everything Mei Lan Fang.[22] In the second
sphere (cinema) is my unswerving favorite and friend Walt
Disney for his *Three Little Pigs*. . . .

Incidentally, one production, equally as perfected as the
craftsmanship of Mei Lan Fang, has been witnessed by the
passing year. And it by chance was dedicated specifically to Dr
Mei Lan Fang. That is *Wit Works Woe* produced by Meyerhold.
He deserves, I think, the first place for quality.

Such honesty got him again into trouble. Here he is praising two
foreign artists, and one from 'that dreadful land of world imperialism,' the USA, and the only Soviet artist he praises is Meyerhold,
the one being most attacked by the Party hacks, which led eventually to the closing of his theater and his own official murder.

I have pointed out that Eisenstein's films, like his theories, were
first welcomed and appreciated abroad. And one of the reasons he
was so anxious to go abroad was to find support for his 'intellectual
cinema' theory. Eisenstein writes:[23]

I am off on a trip through Europe and America carrying in my
suitcase the sensational discovery of the principles of 'intellectual
cinema'. The idea is a resounding success and provokes
comment.

While certain domestic critics and supporters of naturalism
tear Perspectives[24] to shreds, because of my attack on a number
of semi-official (RAPP)[25] tendentious slogans of the day (the
'Theory of the Real Man') other writers and Western journals
could not but welcome a 'trend' which offers the most immediate
means for converting abstract philosophical formulas into a
dynamic, rich, emotional expressive art form.

He was continuously attacked by Party critics on his theory of
montage and intellectual cinema. The first major onslaught on his
return from the USA was by the leading Stalinist critic, Anisimov,
in *International Literature*, no. 3, Moscow 1931, which ironically was
translated by me, and my first publication in the Soviet Press!
Anisimov said:

As is known Eisenstein made a series of attempts to prove
theoretically his views on art. In his remarks, eccentric and

fractional in character, there is one very interesting assertion. Theory is always a generalization of practice. However thinking is clearly seen in them. Before us is the philosophy of objective limitation so logically expressed in his films. Of particular interest is the theory of the 'intellectual cinema' which Eisenstein advances as the basis of his method as a 'perspective' for the development of all revolutionary cinematography. This theory is an expression of organizational technical fetishism. It is simplicity in the extreme, this theory of new rationalism. It is reduced to fetishizing the primacy of reason as against the psychological 'elementals'. It is well to remember here how Eisenstein denying bourgeois individualism, attempted to do away with personality. This very same limitation is manifested also in preaching intellectualism. Eisenstein thinks within the limits of mechanical stagnancy, and this brings him to very poor illusions.

For the creative development of Eisenstein, his theoretical reasoning has a negative significance. It not only proves that the artist has moved very little in the direction of re-education but also shows militancy and obstinacy in his defense of these limitations, which serve as a stumbling-block in his revolutionary growth. The theory of the 'intellectual cinema' represents for him a peculiar defensive device justifying his limitations. This theory will disappear when he overcomes that inertness in thinking which hinders this great artist from rising to his full height.

In an article on 'The Theory of Montage of S. M. Eisenstein' by G. Avenarius in 1937, he again was castigated:[26]

All this abstruse philosophy of montage, constructed by Eisenstein, represents nothing but an eclectic mixture of various Mach-type[27] idealistic theories.

The theory was used by him as the basis of the work on Rzheshevsky's scenario, *Bezhin Meadow*. Guided by this theory Eisenstein distorted the images of the people of our motherland, deriving colours for their representation not from contemporary actuality but from mythology (Pan, Baba-Yaga[28]) and the Bible (Samson, adolescence).

Ten years later another cinema historian (and at one time Director of the GIK over both Eisenstein and myself!), A. Lebedev, upheld these earlier attacks:[29]

> [Eisenstein's] critics were right. As an artist Eisenstein was ruined by his theories – the theory of 'montage of attractions', intellectual cinema, and as a consequence of these – the theory of the negating of the actor, dramatic plot, etc. . . . But original in form and false in content the theory of Eisenstein did not move art forward, but the opposite, to a great degree it was a hindrance to its movement.

Yet Eisenstein's co-worker, Yutkevich, in 1964, still insists that 'Soviet cinema art created a new kind of artist. Working in conditions of genuine creative freedom, not bound by any obligations, except one – to be useful to his people. . . . And our art – is genuine *INTELLECTUAL CINEMA* . . .' three years later, when re-Staliniz-ation sets in, Yutkevich goes on:

> And how contemporary sound those pages where Eisenstein as today, polemicizes with our opponents from the bourgeois camp and turncoats of the revisionist sect, pitifully prattling about the impossibility of expressing creative individuality in the so-called 'rigid' frame-work of socialist art!

Here is what Eisenstein himself said about the 'rigidity' that ruined his film, *The Old and the New*:[30]

> In passing it might be worthwhile to recall the sad fact that the epic pathos of, say, the 'rural theme' in the cinema, in its direct initial 'premise', was catastrophically smashed to pieces on the iron grill of prescribed demands of former scenario departments and former Chief Repertory Committee for the cinema:[31] 'Co-operatives not shown', 'weeding campaign not shown', 'the work of the Village Soviet is missing', etc. And the noble attempts to embody the pathos of the theme of socialism, which had alighted upon the face of the art, withered away on their roots, to use agriculturally 'poetic' terminology.

And Ivor Montagu wrote recently about Eisenstein's other film, '*October* was slashed to ribbons in response to political changes.'[32] And confirmation is given by the following:[33]

> Grigory V. Alexandrov, co-director with Mr. Eisenstein . . . who

said Stalin had ordered 3,000 feet to be cut out of *October* just
before the film's première on the 10th anniversary of the
Bolshevik Revolution in 1927, on the ground that the scenes
gave too much prominence to Lenin's role in the revolution. Mr
Alexandrov described the incident, when a few hours before the
film was to be shown, Stalin and a few other persons
unexpectedly went into the cutting room. . . . Stalin said he
wanted to see the virtually completed film and during the
showing, to our surprise, asked for cuts of several important
scenes totalling more than 900 meters (approximately 3,000 feet).

He continued:

When Eisenstein and I asked why the cuts had to be made,
Stalin said evasively: 'You don't know what is going on. This
is not the right time for Lenin's liberalism.'

As to 'intellectual freedom of film-makers', Yutkevich's own film
Miners consumed three years in adjusting to changing requirements
of Party censors. His film *Light over Russia* was totally banned,
though it was based on the Stalin-approved play by Pogodin,
Kremlin Chimes, and his film of Mayakovsky's *The Bath-House* was
withdrawn.

And this is not all. Yutkevich too was condemned as a 'cosmopolite,' which was the Party's polite word for a 'Yid' – for indeed
Yutkevich was Jewish. He was expelled from teaching at the GIK
and some of his students arrested.

But when the 23rd Party Congress in 1966 reversed de-Stalinization and instructed its members that there would be no more
washing of dirty linen in public, the 'honest, sincere, truthful,
passionate' Comrade Yutkevich slavishly obeys the Party line, and
among other things swallows its anti-semitism.

That is his 'genuine creative freedom.'

And as to this 'cosmopolitanism,' his Jewish fellow-director,
Mikhail Romm, did not keep quiet, he went on protesting re-
Stalinization right up to his death. For he was a 'cosmopolite' too.
Here is what he wrote:[34]

But to play this Overture has become a tradition. After the
October Revolution, this Overture was played the first time
during those years when the expression 'cosmopolite without a

fatherland' was invented to replace that other expression, 'dirty Yid'.

Among other things, and in certain instances, the latter expression was even printed. On the cover of the (satirical) magazine *Crocodile* a cartoon appeared during those years presenting a 'cosmopolite without a fatherland' clearly a Jewish type, holding a book in his hands on which one could read in big characters the word 'ZHID'. Not 'André Gide' but simply 'ZHID'.*

Neither the cartoonist nor any of those responsible for this scoundrel's joke had been condemned by us. We have preferred to keep quiet, to forget all this, as one could forget that dozens of our best theatre and movie people were declared 'cosmopolites without a fatherland'; for instance, comrades Yutkevich,** Leonid Trauberg,*** Sutyrin,† Kovarsky,‡ Bleiman,§ and others present here. They have been authorized to work again, some in the Party, some in their particular Union. But is it really possible to heal the wounds, to forget what one has suffered for so many years, when you were trampled on and covered with mud?

But all the Soviet Jewish film directors had to keep silent in order to survive and this included all the leading directors; Roshal, Kozintsev and Leonid Trauberg, Ilya Trauberg, Zarkhi and Heifitz, Vertov, and Romm and Room.

Another instance of Yutkevich's 'genuine creative freedom' is in the Party suppressing a series of film books that Eisenstein and he started to publish during the grand wartime alliance, when Stalin temporarily suspended some of his Cold War tactics.

---

* In Russian the words 'Gide' and 'Zhid', i.e. Yid, are pronounced almost alike. (Original footnote)
** Sergei Yutkevich, born 1904, originally a painter, became one of a group of experimental artistic designers and directors of films in the 1920s. Until the late 1940s, he had achieved enormous success with a long series of films. (Original footnote)
*** Born 1902, another of that galaxy of silent screen experimenters of the 1920s and an established director in subsequent decades. Like Romm, Yutkevich, and all the others to be mentioned below – except for Kalatozov – he is a Jew, and came under vicious attack in the late 40s. (Original footnote)
† Vladimir A. Sutyrin, born 1902, a distinguished film critic and theoretician of the cinema. (Original footnote)
‡ Nikolai Kovarsky. Also a distinguished film critic. (Original footnote)
§ Mikhail Bleiman. Born 1904. Highly successful screen writer until the late 40s and again after Stalin's death. (Original footnote)

There were two volumes, issued under the title, *Materials on the History of the World Cinema Art*, edited by Professor S. M. Eisenstein, Doctor of Fine Arts. Volume I was *American Cinematography* by D. W. Griffith, compiled by P. Attasheva and S. Ahushkov. It contained M. Bleiman on 'Griffith and the Drama'; S. Eisenstein on 'Dickens, Griffith and We'; S. Yutkevich on 'Griffith and his Actors'; plus documentations on D. W. Griffith, Lillian Gish, G. Seldes, L. Jacobs and others (Goskinoizdat, Moscow, 1944). Volume II; *Charles Spencer Chaplin*, included articles by M. Bleiman on 'The Image of the Little Man'; G. Kozintsev on 'Popular Roots of Chaplin's Art'; S. Yutkevich on 'Sir John Falstaff and Mr Charles Chaplin'; S. Eisenstein on 'Charlie the Kid'.[35]

And my dear old friend Pera Attasheva excitedly sent me a volume just as the war ended, expecting there to be many volumes to follow, of which she was the compiler. But they were all attacked by the Party, Eisenstein and Yutkevich in particular, along with Leonid Trauberg, for having contributed 'favorable' articles to volumes in honor of D. W. Griffith and Charlie Chaplin and 'spreading and elaborating the false and un-Soviet myth that the American film director D. W. Griffith was the father of world film art.'

All those named in Romm's article were Jews and all were attacked at the time (the Zhdanov period) as[36]

[a] group of aestheticizing cosmopolitans in the film industry . . . miserable tramps of humanity . . . homeless and nameless cosmopolitans of the cinema . . . base spokesmen of reactionary aestheticism . . . who organized and conducted a slander campaign against its (the Soviet's film's) lofty ideology, its truthfulness and patriotic content.

So much for Yutkevich's 'genuine creative freedom.'

And to sum up all that this self-abasement signifies, Eisenstein, in the last pages of his autobiography, quotes a Persian folk legend:[37]

[A] future epic hero . . . in order to preserve his strength for the future, obediently spread himself out in the dust beneath the feet of his mockers. Later he succeeded in accomplishing all the unprecedented deeds required of him.

This episode . . . the unprecedented self-control and sacrifice of everything, even his self-respect, to further the achievement

and realization of what had been prescribed and ordered from
the beginning, completely captivated me . . . accepting
humiliation in the name of our most passionate aspirations.

In my own personal, too personal history, I too often
perpetrated this heroic deed of self-abasement. And in my
personal, too personal, innermost life, perhaps somewhat too
often, too hurriedly, even most too willingly and also . . . as
unsuccessfully.

Unlike the Persian folk hero, Eisenstein, under Communist
Partyism, did not succeed. Even Ivor Montagu has to admit he was
like Galileo versus the Inquisition. He writes:[38]

The frustrations he met, the rows in which he became involved,
were legion. The most famous of these was the week-long
argument with his assembled colleagues and the bureaucrats of
the industry over *Bezhin Meadow*, at the end of which he
capitulated and renounced his theories, like Galileo, and then –
still more like Galileo – *E pur si muove* – bounced back with an
article in which he extended them by expla˙.ning that his fault
had been hypertrophy of only one aspect of montage, whereas
it was to all aspects of film creation – not only editing, but story
construction, dialogue, intra-frame composition, etc., everything
– that his aesthetic principles of 'conflict' and montage should
apply.

*Cold War crocodile tears at his difficulties and anguish founder on the
facts.* [My italics. HM.] The artist will always meet anguish in
creation everywhere, as well as joys, and the greater his
innovatory passion the greater the obstacles and the pain.

The only tragedy in Eisenstein's life, according to Yutkevich, was
Mexico. And the cause of the tragedy was that very capitalist
society. 'By his own creative fate Eisenstein learned of the cruel,
wolfish law of capitalist film production, forcing the artist to relive
a genuine tragedy of incompleted conception.'[39]

What was the truth about Mexico and the reason it was lost to
Sergei Eisenstein? *It was because of the CPSU and Stalin, in the last
resort!* [My italics.]

Montagu says:[40]

Then Eisenstein had a choice of a film in Japan or a film in

Mexico with Upton Sinclàir's help. I will not re-open old sores. Suffice it that in my view neither Sergei Eisenstein nor Sinclair – though each blamed the other – was really at fault in what happened. The disaster was inevitable. But what must have been a masterpiece was, taken away to be finished by other hands.

Eisenstein's widow, Pera Atasheva, in a meeting on 4 July 1961, in Moscow, told me about the Mexican film. I recorded verbatim what she said:

Shumyatsky[41] said that Upton Sinclair's demand for royalties for his film in dollars was only asked for in order to have money for Eisenstein to spend on further film production. It was a criminal waste of Government funds and it was due to Eisenstein. So Stalin sent a telegram to Upton Sinclair that the Soviet Union had no further interest in the Mexican film or its Director.

A telegram was sent personally to Eisenstein, to convince him this was no kindergarten this time and that he had to apologize.

He was considered as a deserter – and would have to ask for permission to return.

But Bogdanov (the Soviet Film Representative in New York) gave him permission to continue filming there. Later Eisenstein was censured by the Central Committee of CPSU.

So instead of $25,000 from Moscow to get half share of the film, Sergei M. Eisenstein got nothing. Finally, Upton Sinclair broke off relations.

Already in 1939, the famous Soviet author, Vsevolod Vyshnevsky, knew the truth; he wrote the following:[42]

The wreckers in charge of the [Soviet] film industry played Eisenstein a spiteful joke. He was removed from the work [*Que Viva Mexico*] just before beginning its montage. The film was lost to the USSR.

And in 1957 Mikhail Romm said:[43]

Eisenstein was not allowed to finish this picture. Who was guilty here? Shumyatsky, who would not buy the material for editing? Upton Sinclair, who did not hand it over to Eisenstein? Well the over-riding truth is that it was what we call the cult of the personality.

But, finally the true story was revealed through the publication of the correspondence of Sergei Eisenstein and Upton Sinclair by my good friends, Professors M. Geduld and R. Gottesman, for which I also acted as one of their consultants.[44]

After researching all the archives of Upton Sinclair now available they came to the conclusion that at the tragic finale of the whole matter, 'Sinclair at this point courageously and magnanimously supported Eisenstein . . . beyond question.'

And against whom was Sinclair defending Eisenstein? No longer against the 'fascist elements' in the USA, but against Joseph Stalin and the Communist Party of the Soviet Union!

Here is conclusive proof that should have once and for all put a stop to the lies and slander against Sinclair and the USA, continuously and consistently spread by the Communist Party of the Soviet Union and its fraternal Parties throughout the world.

Yutkevich still tries to 'cover up' the truth, and so does his Party counterpart in England, Ivor Montagu. For Ivor still in 1970, in his contribution to the *Eisenstein* film made by the BBC,[45] still harps on Upton Sinclair and says not a word about the really guilty Party!

Just as in the 1969 Soviet publication *The Mexican Drawings* by S. M. Eisenstein,[46] the introduction by Inga Karetnikova merely quotes Eisenstein's own attack on the 'stupid vandals, the short-witted American film-merchants' whose 'dirty hands' edited various versions. But, though in Stalin's time, Eisenstein could obviously not tell the truth, Karetnikova could in 1969, but did not.

Even as late as 1973, I found in another Soviet critic's book, the same slander and falsification.[47]

> When the American businessmen refused to send to the USSR for montage the film *Que Viva Mexico* . . . they had before them but one aim – to humiliate, insult, by their distrust of the artist and the country which he represented.

However, let us give due credit to the more honest Soviet critics who, though unable to criticize Stalin any longer in the era of re-Stalinization, nevertheless do not continue the 'impermissible, immoral and unlawful'[48] slander of the Party hard-liner. I have in mind one of the leading experts on Eisenstein, R. Yurenev, in an article 'S. Eisenstein, Letters from Mexico.'

He writes:[49]

There was no time and ńo possibility to finalize the sound track
and distribution of the film in USA. But there was a hope that
Sovkino [the official Soviet Film Organization. HM.] would buy
the material from Sinclair. 'Final montage in Moscow' – that is
what Eisenstein and Tisse declared in their first interview with
a correspondent of *Vechern'aya Moskva* [the Moscow evening
newspaper. HM.] But even these hopes failed to materialize. This
film, conceived and shot by a genius, was never completed by
him. (This tragic blow Eisenstein never forgot to his very death.)

'By irony we strive to overcome even this accident of death –
the death of one's own child, in whom was so much love, labor
and inspiration,' so wrote the mortally ill Eisenstein fifteen years
later.

Eisenstein's overriding passion was books. Every one of his friends
brought in, even smuggled in, books for him. I did my share. Marie
Seton (author of the biography, *Sergei Eisenstein*)[50] brought in as
many books as he wanted. Pera told my wife and I that Eisenstein
would say to Marie Seton, 'You are my great love and I shall love
you forever, only bring me such and such books.' Eisenstein would
shower all sorts of flattery on people only in order to get them to
bring him books from abroad. This most erudite man could not get
the books through his government, either they were censored or
foreign currency not allowed him.

Eisenstein quotes a letter to him from the famous theater designer
Edward Gordon Craig who wrote, ' "Drop everything. Come to
Paris for a month. It's spring now. We'll rummage through the
books along the Seine. . . ."[51] So Gordon Craig, another book and
bookshop fanatic, wrote to me from Italy many years later.'

How should Gordon Craig have known that one of the greatest
artists in the world would not be allowed to go abroad?

Eisenstein was perfectly aware that the Party censorship
prevented thousands of foreign works from being translated or
published; as well as being unable to buy second-hand copies in
bookshops, or from abroad. He writes, 'In the pre-war years all
buying and selling of foreign books (in Moscow) was concentrated
in this shop.'[52] In the capital city of eight million people – only one
shop was buying and selling foreign books! And the only chance

came when foreigners were leaving Russia, because Hitler had attacked.

He has written how he loved to browse through second-hand bookshops all over Europe; but he doesn't overtly point out that they practically disappeared inside the Soviet Union! From then on the few left were subject to permanent censorship by the KGB.

I remember, too, in the 1930s in Moscow, when we were secretly warned to get rid of any books by 'enemies of the people', we burned in our own apartment furnaces works by Trotsky, Bukharin, Preobrazhenskaya, etc.

Such burnings took place over the whole of the Soviet Union, both by private citizens and by the State. As the list of 'enemies of the people' grew, more and more books were burned, until they reached millions.

It is ironic that the very geniuses Eisenstein was so enamored of, such as Sigmund Freud or James Joyce, were forbidden in the Soviet Union! Among the books he studied was *A Memory of his Childhood – Leonardo da Vinci*, by Sigmund Freud. Zorkaya adds, 'and how like Leonardo is Eisenstein himself.' That was the role he chose.[53]

In his first film, *Strike*, he stated that he tried to combine Marxian philosophy, Freudian psychoanalysis, and Pavlovian physio-psychology. There is no doubt of his use of Freudian symbolism throughout his film, and he gives a psychoanalysis of himself in his autobiography, particularly in relation to the father-complex.[54]

Eisenstein, with all his problems with the Party, had more scope for reading forbidden books than the average Soviet citizen, for whom such works were completely unobtainable, unless he was a high-ranking Communist Party student or *apparatchik*.

Ironically, Eisenstein never mentions that his own works were banned, and he never expected his autobiographical fragments to be published till long after his death. The book I have compiled on *Potemkin*[55] was planned by Eisenstein and Pera in 1935. His *Montage*,[56] which I have just edited and co-translated, was written in 1937. Neither book had been published during his lifetime.

Paul Robeson arrived in Moscow in 1934 and Eisenstein asked me to go with him to meet him, being the only member of the English-speaking world in the cinema institute. We went, together with

Edward Tisse, Shura Afinogenov, the dramatist – and his wife, Jeanya, an American girl I'd originally introduced to Afinogenov.

For the first time, we met Paul Robeson. A photograph of that meeting is still extant – however, in two versions, one in the first theoretical book of Eisenstein's works (other than film scripts) ever published in the Soviet Union. It was 'Selected Essays'.[57] Facing page 193 is a photograph of two figures, Eisenstein meeting Robeson. On page 80 of Marie Seton's biography of Paul Robeson,[58] the *same* photograph is published. However, in this are *three* figures; the third is *my own*, which had been wiped out in the Soviet publication!

However, we knew nothing, then, of the tragedies to come, and Eisenstein proposed to make, with Paul, a film version of *Black Majesty* by Vandercook. A wonderful story of the black revolt in Haiti that defeated Napoleon. The story of those great negro leaders: Toussaint L'Ouverture, Christophe and Dessalines. But, again, like his other projects, this, too, was shelved.

He planned a comedy about Moscow called *MMM* (Maxim Maximovich Maximov). This was the sign over the Moscow Metro, that we were all helping to build. For in those fervent years, all of us, students, teachers, even foreigners, went to do some spare-time voluntary labor and worked underground to build this first Moscow subway. In this comedy, I had been cast by Eisenstein for a leading part, together with his boyhood friend, Maxim Straukh, one of the great actors of Russia, who is now People's Artist of the Republic at the Mayakovsky Theater, Moscow.

Eisenstein tested all the various actors he was going to use, and I remember that he had a symbol or an image for each character, and in his book he put me down as *Tsimmis*, the sweet and sour carrot dish typical of the Yiddish menu for the Sabbath, because I was then Ginger – and Sergei Eisenstein had a partiality for Gingers![59] Eisenstein was of Jewish origin, but his family, apparently his grandfather, had become Russian Orthodox at some stage or other because as Jews, advancement was severely restricted and impossible in government spheres. But, I noticed as I got to know him more, that he particularly liked to use Yiddish slang, and Yiddish humor. He was a master of other languages, of course, but he certainly loved to use Yiddish and he quite often threw off phrases that would only be understood by those who knew Yiddish.

I remember one Jewish fellow-student at the GIK after an English class had an elementary grammar book in which were illustrations to the text. There was a page of *Kitchen Utensils* and Eisenstein had ringed in ink the word 'pots' with the note, 'That's what I think he is!' Only this student understood this private Yiddish joke and so did I – [60] but never knew who Eisenstein referred to!

Well, *MMM*, like other plans, was not fulfilled. One more Eisenstein project was aborted.

Bezhin Meadow he was preparing and working on while still the head of our group. I had the privilege of seeing a sequence of the edited material, which still remains in my memory as an unforgettable work, or fragment of a work of art. This was the sequence I call 'Samson in the Temple.'[61]

The other relationship was through my wife, Fredda Brilliant, the sculptress, who was commissioned to make a statue of the boy hero of Eisenstein's film *Pavel Morozov*. And, for this purpose, Eisenstein kindly loaned his youthful actor to pose for the sculpture my wife made. This sculpture was for the Moscow Children's Cinema, which was then in the great government building, *Dom Pravitelstva*, just across the Moscow River. It was cast in hundreds of copies and presented to the children's cinemas of the USSR. But alas, just as the film was banned and physically destroyed, so my wife's sculpture of the hero also disappeared from that children's cinema; and, indeed, from all the children's cinemas in the Soviet Union.

The Party and the GPU did everything they could to make sure that not a foot remained of that aborted Eisenstein film *Bezhin Meadow*. Pera, his widow, told me that an assistant had always kept separately a 'Lavender' print of the first chosen takes, as a security measure in case of accident. And when the film *Bezhin Meadow* was stopped, and the whole negative and prints and rushes taken by the GPU (now the KGB), the Party ferreted out that someone, somewhere, had kept a duplicate. Eventually they got to her, she then told them she had destroyed it. But they didn't believe her. She was then threatened with expulsion from the Party, finally with arrest and prison camp. So at last she gave them the remaining dupe of Eisenstein's abortive masterpiece, and the Communist Party destroyed it to the last shot.

And now, thirty years later, faithful disciples have managed to find a few frames or cuts from the film and have pieced these static pieces together so that one can see, as through a glass darkly, a glimpse of what might have been a masterpiece. And I can remember to this day that most amazing sequence, and now realize, of course, that it was impossible for the philistines of the Party to understand, let alone accept, what Eisenstein was doing.

Shklovsky, the outstanding critic of that period, writes:[62]

> For later failures in their work I won't blame our regisseurs alone. They were all commissioned to do one and the same thing: to make films which should speak directly about the glory of the times, but incarnated in the glory of one man. This deprived them of the possibility of evolving as very powerful creators.

For Eisenstein was showing in *Bezhin Meadow* a true reflection of what happened in the village, in which the son informed on his uncle, and thereby became a national hero, and then the uncle kills the boy. It was a period of the 'liquidation of the Kulaks as a class,' and the liquidation of the Church as an institution, which was also attempted.

One of the sequences shows how the Party organized the desecration of a church, how the building is stripped bare of all its icons and decorations and left as a shell.

Well, this, of course, is perfectly true. It happened, and I myself witnessed it when I was working on a State farm at Yurev Polsky in 1930. I remember helping to dump sacks of potatoes and sulphur phosphate in the recently stripped marred church, that had been commandeered for use by the Party. Other churches we used as clubs and dormitories. Years later I learned that these at Yurev Polsky were among the finest treasures of church architecture in all Russia.

The Party secretary and the local GPU chief lead a procession to strip the church and start to take off the icons, the decorations, everything that had covered the walls, removing what wooden furnishings there were, curtains, etc., until nothing is left but the pillars of the altar space.

One of the peasants, a grey-bearded, hefty giant of a man, stands between the pillars, puts his hands outstreched on either side against the pillars and begins to heave.

And then, one realized that the whole of the ceremony has been created by Eisenstein, as if in the form of religious myth, just as the cream separator in *The General Line* was the Holy Grail. So here, suddenly, you realize this is Samson destroying the Temple!

The great muscles of the peasant bunch and strain as he pushes the pillars apart and the whole wooden structure, carved by previous Russian craftsmen, crashes to the ground. The final scene, as I remember, consists of a completely denuded empty church, and as the last peasant leaves the doors, a dove flies up from below, up through the pinnacles of the cupola. And I again realized that here was another religious symbol, the Holy Ghost was leaving the church!

I remember one of the leading Party men saying that we must overcome the attitude of looking upon Eisenstein as a kind of second Leonardo da Vinci, which many of his disciples and students had. And it's true we did. The Party man said that he was not a venerable genius with a beard, he was still a young man of 34 years of age! And, indeed, we had a shock. In our eyes, he was a man of venerable age and incredible experience and great erudition, but the Party did all it could to deprive him of his aura of intellect and artistry.

In a booklet on *Bezhin Meadow*, the chief theoretical critic attacking Eisenstein, for the Party, was Yuri Weissfeld. It will be seen years later in an introduction to Volume II of Sergei Mikhailo-vich's collected works, that he now writes a panegyric of praise!

The same fate awaited A. Rzheshevsky, the hapless author of the film script of *Bezhin Meadow*. Rzheshevsky and Okhlopkov I first met in Moscow in 1930, and stayed with them for some weeks in their little apartment. It was a joyous time and full of hope. But, clouds were already gathering. Okhlopkov had just finished his third and last film, *The Way of the Enthusiast*, a work of genius. I was the only foreign correspondent to write about it.[63] But it was banned and Okhlopkov never made another film. In those days, Rzhesh-evsky became fashionable as the author of the 'emotional scenario,' i.e. one not written in full technical detail, shot for shot, known then as the cast-iron scenario, but poetically; a form which Eisen-stein later used in writing the scripts of *Alexander Nevsky* and *Ivan the Terrible*.

Rzheshevsky was damned for writing like an 'American literary decadent, especially Hemingway!' He, like so many other intellec-tuals, landed up in a prison camp, emerging sick, and died prematurely.

Now, in the 1960s, Zorkaya writes of him,[64]

No matter how bitterly he was upbraided, A. Rzheshevsky was

a talented fellow, experiencing a great deal of unpleasantness
and injustice for his 'emotional scenario' which in general was
quite harmless – his *Bezhin Meadow* turns out to be in the stream
of straight forward treatment of the tragedy being played out
then in the North Urals..

In fact, it is now seen that Rzheshevsky bent over backwards to
placate the Party line and write in the typical stereotypes of those
years:[65]

the talkative humoristic old men, the religious old witches,
pioneer children, and the militant women, the president of the
Collective Farm and Chief of the Motor Tractor Station and the
exceptionally good-natured-looking, bald-headed chief of the
GPU.

The text of his script is scattered with the naivety of that period:[66]

And the peasants chattered . . . 'Raise another loan – we'll give
you as much money as you want. Give us machines, or the
harvest will fail, like water they're needed.'
     'We'll sow,' said the assistant director, smiling calmly.
     And the peasants squealed happily; 'Let's go to Ivan
Ivanovich . . . to the GPU . . . to the NKVD with pleasure.'

The only copy of the film disappeared during the war, when the
Mosfilm Studios were evacuated. According to the Mosfilm legend,
the celluloid was placed in a container and buried somewhere on
the territory of the studio. It was never found!
     But Zorkaya goes on to say:[67]

about the film *Bezhin Meadow*: This history should be investigated
because the official version – apparently about formalism and the
complex language of the film, which was the reason for its
suppression – does not correspond to reality. That is now clear.

But, as with the whole Stalin period, there is no further investiga-
tion and the official versions of its disappearance still hold sway.
For the second version of *Bezhin Meadow* that Eisenstein was forced
to make, he brought in his friend, the famous writer Isaac Babel,
and nothing much was left of poor Rzheshevsky, but it still didn't
help him. The film was finally banned and Eisenstein was forced,
again, to make a 'confession' entitled 'The Mistakes of *Bezhin
Meadow*,' in which (as Zorkaya notes):[68]

Eisenstein, this Leonardo without his *Mona Lisa*, this Le
Corbusier without his House of the Sun, wrote:

In my stylistic strivings and make-up, I have a great tendency
to the general, the generalization, to generalizing. But, is this
the generalization, the general, which Marxism teaches us about
realism? No . . . and such generalization pushes into the
background the basic task – to show the struggles of the Kulaks
against the collective farm. . . .

Even in this 'confession,' what irony!

Zorkaya continues:[69]

Eisenstein knew himself, and his auto-characteristic is correct –
he knows his strength and his weakness. But with analogous
success, Blok* could confess that alas, he wrote poetry; Chaplin
could confess, that he was comic on the screen. Eisenstein asked
pardon for the fact that he was Eisenstein!

I remember being told of an evening in the 1930s when everyone
who had been decorated by the government gathered together to
celebrate; from the Ministry, administrators, civil servants, directors, cameramen, assistants, scriptwriters; among those present only
one person was missing, Sergei Mikhailovich Eisenstein; though
everyone present had invited him for that very evening. He had
been insultingly presented with a medal of the lowest class.

All were seated according to the rank of decoration, those with
orders at the head of the table (i.e., Order of Lenin, Stalin Prize-
winners, Order of Red Banner, etc.); those with lower-class medals
and orders nearer the ends of the table.

The chairman, of course, was Boris Shumyatsky, the Minister of
Cinematography, the direct confidant of Stalin and, accordingly the
direct enemy of Eisenstein – the same man, who, as Stalin's envoy,
had frustrated his work, from *Que Viva Mexico* until the last moment.
Then, as we were all seated, Sergei Mikhailovich entered.

Shumyatsky rose to greet him, as a seeming mark of respect,
came up to him and said, 'Sergei Mikhailovich, let us kiss.'

They embraced and kissed, in the traditional Russian manner,
i.e., three times. Then, Shumyatsky said, 'Sergei Mikhailovich, I
hope that this was not the kiss of Judas.'

* Alexander Blok (1880–1921), one of Russia's greatest poets.

Eisenstein replied, 'Not at all. It was the kiss of two Judases.'

The irony, of course, lies in the fact that both were of Jewish extraction, though not in any way orthodox, and, also, from the love of Eisenstein for puns. For in old Russian the proper word for Jew is 'Iudei' from the Tribe of Judah, and for Judas it would be 'Iuda', which is also a synonym for 'traitor'.

The postscript to this history is that Boris Shumyatsky, who did everything conceivable to please Stalin, to tame and frustrate Eisenstein, was also finally arrested and executed. Pera Attasheva told me that Sergei Mikhailovich, on hearing the news, could not refrain from commenting that he never expected to outlive Shumyatsky, but there was *some* satisfaction in that.

Eisenstein's aborted film projects

Following his return from Mexico, in disgrace with the Party and Stalin in particular, Eisenstein was not able to complete a film for over *seven years*, yet he had put forward many projects and script ideas to his superiors in the Ministry of Cinematography.

First was *MMM* (Maxim Maximovich Maximov) which was to be a grotesque satire on contemporary philistines in Soviet society – along the lines of Mayakovsky's attacks in his plays *The Bedbug* and *The Bathhouse*, and poems such as 'Trash.'[70] It was based on a theme of the 'Russian boyars projected into the conditions of contemporary Moscow, giving rise to various possibilities of comic *quid pro quo!*' It intended to satirize the realities of Soviet everyday life and the work of Intourist[71] with foreign tourists, by alternating them in a grotesque way with the fantasies of his hero. Eisenstein prepared a scenario and shooting script and made some screen tests. I know, for I was to be one of his actors, alongside his oldest friend Maxim Straukh and his wife Judith Glizer, outstanding Moscow actor and actress. This was also linked with the lectures he was giving us in the GIK, particularly on comedy. However, Eisenstein, like many other Soviet artists and writers, such as Zoshchenko and Ilf and Petrov, directors like Medvedkin, etc., found that satire was not welcomed. Their works were banned, as was Eisenstein's *MMM*.

The next proposal was a film called *Moscow*, an epic project covering four centuries, and obviously influenced by his *Que Viva Mexico* script and Griffith's parallel stories in *Intolerance*, that Eisen-

stein had hoped his *Mexico* film would equal, if not surpass. It
would start with the Moscow of *Ivan the Terrible*, through Napoleon's
invasion, then the 1905 revolution and finally 1917. The heart of
the film was to be a Moscow proletarian family, whose successive
generations over these four centuries would be linked with the
history of Moscow, unfolded in parallel with their personal history.
Eisenstein wrote of his worker hero:[72]

> His face changing from age to age, he must move through the
> film both as a personal descendant of one generation to the next,
> and as a unique character, whose own life story unfolds beyond
> its normal limits, beyond those of the family history, of the
> generation, of class. . . . Compositionally, he must represent a
> new, original aspect of the wandering Jew, of the figure who,
> straddling time and space, has so often captured our fantasy and
> imagination.

Maybe the parallel with the 'wandering Jew' was not to the liking
of his bosses, for that film subject also was not approved.

Other unrealized projects included one titled *Daughter of France*,
of which I can find no information. Then, in reply to Shumyatsky's
challenge to make a contemporary film, Sergei Eisenstein proposed
the *Chelyushkin Expedition*, about the rescue of a Soviet icebreaker
trapped in the Arctic floes. As it happens, I almost became an
assistant director on the film crew that went with the expedition;
at that time it was highly publicized and approved by the Party.
But that, too, came to nothing. Then Eisenstein took up his old
project of doing a film about revolutionary China – its civilization,
older than Mexico, held great fascination for him. Then, in 1934,
André Malraux came to Moscow and to the GIK, and Eisenstein
set to work to make a film adaptation of his world famous novel
Man's Fate (*La Condition Humaine*). I was involved in making an
English version of this, which with a Russian text is in my archives
at my Center at Southern Illinois University. It may be this is the
only surviving version, for Jay Leyda says there is nothing left.[73] But
that, too, came to nothing. Then Maxim Gorky wanted Eisenstein to
direct a script he had written, but Eisenstein didn't like it and
turned it down. That didn't help him with Stalin or the Party, for
Gorky was then their sacred cow, and a cover-up for the terror that
soon followed. In which, according to the Communist Party of the

Soviet Union, Gorky was allegedly poisoned by the head of the GPU, Yagoda!

In Hollywood, Eisenstein had toyed with the idea of a film about the successful revolt of the black slaves in Haiti against Napoleon. That, too, as I have noted, came to nothing.

However, at our classes in the GIK, Eisenstein spent a whole session explicating episodes from the book, which were fascinating. Some of this has been published in Nizhny's *Lessons with Eisenstein*.[74]

Then came the tragic *Bezhin Meadow*, which was finally vetoed by Shumyatsky (for Stalin of course) in March 1937, and the film destroyed.

He proposed a joint project called *We the Russian People*, but even though it was accepted by Mosfilm Studios for production, it also was stopped, which Vyshnevsky said was 'yet another of those films which Eisenstein's enemies obstructed.'[75]

During the visit of the German novelist, Feuchtwanger, to Moscow, came the possibility of filming Feuchtwanger's historical novel *The Ugly Duchess*. Feuchtwanger also proposed his other novel *The False Nero*, for which Eisenstein made some sketches and designs; but, again no productions. A film script by V. V. Distler, on gold prospectors in Siberia, was also discussed; but still no production. Meanwhile, Eisenstein assuaged his soul by throwing himself into teaching us at the Institute, and also putting all his ideas on paper. Finally, in 1937, the Party proposed he make a film about the great Russian hero, Prince Alexander Nevsky, who by now was a saint!

Eisenstein, at first, was not interested in the subject, and was ironic about a Marxist now making a hero out of a saint, who had been until then, castigated by the Party's own historians as a faithful vassal of the Mogul Khan, which of course he was. This fact is touched on by Eisenstein in the beginning of the film and then cut out of the script by Stalin.

Not only that, this time he was to have two political commissars, Piotr Pavlenko to work with him on the script, and Dmitri Vasiliev on the direction of the film, to make sure he stuck to the 'cast-iron scenario' that had been approved by the Party and the All-High. Inevitably, Eisenstein had to accept the project, and clearly decided that even with the obvious restrictions, political and artistic, he would use it for his own ends, in audio-visual compositions; he succeeded in doing this. He wrote:[76]

The most difficult situation in our work, for a creative imagination. To 'invent' for the screen a character that would strictly conform to thematic 'demands', theoretically expressed with a mathematical exactitude in a formula! This was the formula – to create the images to accord with it! . . . But there are situations when you have no choice. And this was precisely the case as far as we are concerned.

The final result brought new dimensions to the art of sound cinema. Its style, now the diametrical opposite of the apparently documentary *Potemkin* and *Ten Days*, was almost an opera with its simplistic characters, Nevsky himself, Buslai the brave and Gavrilo the wise, their melodramatic gestures and psychological lack of depth. He even made fun of what should have been a bitter bloody battle. It is interspersed with comic episodes like Buslai knocking over heavily armoured knights with a bash of an iron pail and wooden shaft!

In fact, Eisenstein was carrying on his researches in the middle of this melodrama, as he said in *Notes*, 'abandoning creative work for scientific analysis is often what I am guilty of.'[77] As he says in his autobiography, 'a dose of philistinism ensures peace and stability.'[78]

For *Nevsky* he at last received the long withheld Order of Lenin on 1 February 1939, and finally, was given the title of Doctor of Scientific Art Studies, while only just before Shumyatsky had been arrested as 'a tool of political enemies' and never heard of again.

Once more, Eisenstein set to preparing another film script – this time based on the Civil War and the final victory over the Whites at Perekop in the Crimea. He was writing the script with Fadeyev, about the victorious campaign of the Red Commander, Frunze. He wanted to make it his answer to the Party ideal film *Chapayev*, which he really considered demeaned the Civil War. However, this project was 'temporarily' shelved for a project suggested by Pavlenko and the Committee for Cinema Affairs. This was the Ferghana Canal in Uzbekistan. He grew so enthusiastic (it obviously had some parallels with Mexico), that he travelled thousands of miles in Central Asia, studied the classic cities of Bukhara and Samarkand, and their legendary histories and heroes like Tamerlane. It was to be the life and death struggle for water in that desert area. It would have three parallel strands, from antiquity to the present, ending with the building of the great Ferghana Canal.

Once more, Eisenstein was inspired, the script was finished, costumes designed, all his research completed, sets completed and the film unit went on location, but then just as he was about to start casting and production, the film was halted. Only some documentary footage had been shot. An official Party order came cancelling the whole production – Stalin again! Again, Eisenstein was reduced to despair, even to thoughts of suicide, from which, I learned, only Pera and his students rescued him.

Now came another ironic moment, the Hitler-Stalin pact, the banning of *Nevsky* and all anti-fascist works. It was proposed he produce Hilter's favorite composer and *The Valkyries* at the Bolshoi Opera. In retrospect, it was but a step towards *Ivan*. In his own comments on the production he wrote, 'that the Twilight of the Gods symbolized the death of the whole world of murder and plunder, legalized by falsehood, deceit and hypocrisy,'[79] which, as Barna pointed out also, 'could be interpreted as his comment on the contemporary Soviet scene.'[80] Whatever the Party's intentions politically, Eisenstein again used its prescribed framework for his own artistic research.

Again came more projects, a film on the great scholar Lomonosov, a color film on *Giordano Bruno*, which Mosfilm Studios actually proposed. However, that clearly had dangerous overtones and came to nought. Then, *Tommaso Campanella* came along as another colorful subject. Then again, most strangely, a film about the Beilis case and Russian anti-semitism called *The Prestige of an Empire*, based on a play by Lev Sheinin. This was obviously not to the taste of the All-High, and was rejected again. Finally, his project on the biography of a poet – Alexander Pushkin, *A Poet's Love*, where at last Eisenstein would deal with 'a great, lasting and wonderful love.' However this project, which was above all a color film that would demonstrate his theory of color in cinematography, had to be abandoned because of the poor and backward quality of Soviet color film and processing.

In Volume I of Eisenstein's *Collected Works*, we have all that remains of his autobiography.[81] The bulk of this was written just for himself and for posterity, when he realized that he was near death. Knowing this, he wrote with perhaps a little greater freedom than he would have done otherwise. And yet, one fact emerges – that never once is there an obvious overt negative criticism of the Soviet State, or the Communist Party. And from what I learned from his nearest and dearest, they, too, never heard such emerge from his lips *directly*, it was always ricochet. Yet it is clear that Eisenstein, like the other Soviet men of genius and intellect, began to apprehend what was really happening. But they could not admit it even to themselves and hardly to others. And I think it is true to say that of the four great geniuses of Soviet cinematography – Pudovkin, Dovzhenko, Vertov, and Eisenstein – all died of *broken hearts*. All of them were equally frustrated in their artistic work by the Party dictatorship of philistines. They all had fear. This had been most clearly and succinctly expressed by the poet Yevtushenko in his poem 'Fear'.[82]

> People were very quietly tamed
> and on everything a seal was set.
> When they should have been silent –
> to shout they were trained.
> When they should have shouted –
> silent they were kept.

Many have written of this inherent 'dualism' as one called it, or 'double-think' as Orwell so brilliantly named it. Zorkaya, a leading contemporary Soviet cinema critic, wrote of Eisenstein's work:[83]

> The varying expressions of the author, articles, notes, certain pages of his diary, now published, unfortunately even now cannot serve as irrefutable evidence of the true intentions and views of their author . . . the discord between what was in reality . . . becomes completely stabilized in Eisenstein's public statements. Here the point is not, of course, in something double-faced in him personally, but in the misfortune of a permanent moral compromise, which under the phraseological narcoticism was no longer felt and became the normal condition of a man. Alongside of confessional notes of a deadly tired heart, alongside of observations of genius – are elementary-stupid, bureaucratically banal expressions, as if reckoning on someone's continuous interference and prejudiced reading.

(That 'someone,' of course, being the Communist Party under

Stalin.) And that sums up the tragic condition of man in Communist society.

When Eisenstein finally left America, his parting words were published in the *Los Angeles Times*; part of it is so prophetic of his generation:

> People are told on all sides how hard it is to crash through, how almost impossible it is to make the grade. That is the mistake. Encourage them, bring them on. What's the difference whether the result is a lot of broken hearts or not. It's broken hearts that make up a great art. It is the broken hearts that have failed as painters, or writers, or sculptors that have made those three arts alive and vital, while and when they were.

Stalinist party assault on Eisenstein and his colleagues

Imagine the state of mind and feelings of men of culture and talent, in some amounting to genius, who almost *en bloc* were told by the Party what illiterate distorting ignoramuses they were!

Here is an extended quotation from a Soviet Bulletin of the Society for Cultural Relations with Foreign Countries, published in 1946:

> Parallel with this grand success of Chiurelli's *The Oath* throughout the world [sic!], was carried the news that the Central Committee of the Communist Party of the Soviet Union in their decree of 4th of September 1949 subjected to a ruthless criticism of films: *The Great Life*, 2nd part director Leonid Zhukov; *Ivan the Terrible*, 2nd part, director Sergei Eisenstein; *Admiral Nakhimov*, director Vsevolod Pudovkin and; *The Simple People*, directors Gregory Kozintsev and Leonid Trauberg.
>
> Why does the Central Committee criticize such famous directors? For the same reason as they criticized the film, *The Great Life*, i.e., for their ignorance, and for their untrue representation of events which they are portraying in productions. The outstanding shortcomings of the films, in *Admiral Nakhimov* and 2nd part of *Ivan the Terrible* are (1) the distortion of historical truth in the first form, where the main theme is history, the theme of the great hero and patriot Nakhimov is substituted by insignificant details; (2) Carelessness in the representation of historical facts which reflected in

showing the progressive [sic] warriors of *Ivan the Terrible*'s
bodyguard in the form of a band of degenerates, something like
the American Ku Klux Klan, and *Ivan the Terrible* as a man of
powerful will and character is shown as weak, nervous, will-
less, something in the nature of Hamlet.

S. M. Eisenstein eclectically combined the theme of *Ivan the
Terrible* — the mighty leader, diplomat and statesman, creator
of a multi-national Russian state, the forerunner of Peter the
Great, with the theme of Hamlet-style despot, of an historical
bloodthirsty tyrant with a shattered conscience and sick will.

What film-maker was held up as the paragon? Mikhail Chiurelli,
who made *The Vow* and *The Fall of Berlin*. Those inflated epics were
devoted to glorifying Stalin.

However, the point I started with was to show how these great
artists died of broken hearts, because the works that they created
were no longer their works and they were no longer able to create
them. They had to make them according to the instructions of Stalin
and the Party. The greatest tragedy of all was that none of these
tragic victims were able to express, hardly even to themselves, the
nature of the tragedy they were involved in. They were not allowed
to admit it, as Yevtushenko could only write in his poem, 'Fear',
after Stalin's death and *before* Khrushchev's overthrow. They were
forced to write statements and letters, such as Eisenstein wrote,
abasing themselves before the tyrant.

Every now and then, it emerges in the autobiography of Eisenstein. To begin with, he shows how the image of his father – his
tyrant Papa – had crushed and distorted his own personality and
what a great battle he had to get away from the Papa tyrant. He
says:[84]

No doubt remembering them I broke into pieces, with such
delicate excitement, the giant figure of Alexander III in the first
episode of *October*. And if I add, that the dismantled and
overturned naked figure of the Tsar served as a symbol of the
February overthrow of Tsarism, then it is clear that the beginning
of the film, reminding me of the downfall of Papa's creation
through the image of the Tsar, also spoke to me personally of my
liberation from Papa's authority. . . . Tyrannical papas were
typical of the XIXth century. But mine grew over into the XXth!
And do not these pages cry out against the moral oppression

that ruled in our family?! How many times the exemplary boy Seryozha, like a learned parrot, replied to Papa's questions: 'Aren't my creations wonderful?!', with studied formulas of delight – profoundly against his own ideas and convictions. Let me cry out in protest at least now, at least here.

Here one can feel that his crying out in protest is against that other father-tyrant Stalin, to whom he has to reply 'like a learned parrot – with studied formulas of delight'. And now on his deathbed, Eisenstein cries, 'Let me cry out in protest at least now, at least here!'

Zorkaya, in her surprisingly frank portrait of S. M. Eisenstein, writes:[85]

It was then, in childhood, on Nikolayevskaya Street, that one of the most powerful, permanent, clinging motives of Eisenstein's creative work was born – the motive of stupid inhumanity, irreversible ruin, senseless and evil carnage on the weak and defenseless.

Eisenstein would have been the last to even dream that this leitmotif would become just as valid under his own Soviet Russia as it was under Tsarist Russia, finding its expression in *Bezhin Meadow* and *Ivan the Terrible.*

And I think of the dearest friends and professional colleagues of Eisenstein: Vsevolod Meyerhold, Isaac Babel and Sergei Tretyakov, all falsely accused, all arrested, all executed without trial. No one could protest, their names were never mentioned. Yet in his autobiographical notes, Eisenstein writes of his spiritual father,[86] Meyerhold:

Apart from one's physical father, one always finds on the highways and byways a spiritual father . . . and I must say, of course, that I never loved, idolized, worshipped anyone as much as I did my teacher.

Will one of my lads say that about me one day?

No. And the matter lies not in my students and me, but in me and my teacher.

For I am not worthy to unloose the straps of his sandals[87] though he wore felt boots in the unheated theater workshops of Novinsky Boulevard.

And to extreme old age I shall consider myself unworthy to

kiss the dust from his feet, although his errors as a person have evidently swept away forever the footprints of the greatest master of our theater from the pages of our theatrical history.

Eisenstein is writing this in 1948, just before the second Stalinist terror, when anti-semitism becomes an emergent factor in Party propaganda, when the cream of the Jewish intelligentsia of the Soviet Union were arrested, imprisoned, tortured, murdered, and the whole of Jewish culture suppressed: schools, synagogues, theaters, newspapers, organizations, people. Eisenstein was of Jewish descent; Meyerhold's wife, Zinaida Reich, was Jewish.

I had the unique privilege, because of Eisenstein, to work as a student-assistant to Meyerhold during his production of *La Dame Aux Camelias*, in which his wife, the beautiful Zinaida Reich, played the leading role, and I can but echo Eisenstein's words.

What pain and what irony is the sub-text of this last paragraph in Eisenstein's autobiography. Only in the sub-text (to use the Stanislavsky terminology) can one read what Eisenstein dare not say in the text. His 'spiritual father,' the one he loved, idolized, worshipped, was murdered by the same Party they both served, Meyerhold as an active Communist since the very first day of the Revolution. And as with Babel and Tretyakov, Eisenstein could not bemoan his dying, let alone try to prevent it. This applied to the whole of the artistic intelligentsia.

I remember being with the talented young film director, Ilya Trauberg, in 1930 (and have a photo of that meeting). What enthusiasm, what hopes! After the purges he too disappeared and his name was never mentioned again.

My other friend and inspirer was Dziga Vertov,[88] the documentary genius of the Russian Revolution, who influenced the whole world of documentary film, and *cinéma vérité*. He made masterpieces like *The Three Songs of Lenin* and the first brilliant sound film *Enthusiasm* (or *The Donbas Symphony*), highly praised by so many including Charles Chaplin; yet, after these, though he lived until 1955, he was *never allowed to make another film!*

The film director Boris Barnet recruited me to act an English officer in his film *Okraina* (The Outskirts). The actress Kuzmina (later the wife of the film director Mikhail Romm) played the leading role. Boris Barnet survived the terror only to commit suicide eventually in 1965, because the last three films were considered 'failures' – by the Party, of course.

Eisenstein adored Isaac Babel's work. He had been friends with Babel since their futurist days. During his lectures, he would constantly refer to them.[89] While working on the '1905' (*Potemkin*) script with Agadzhanova, he worked parallel with Babel on a script of Babel's play *Benya Krik*.[90] This was first translated into English by Ivor Montagu and Sergei Nolbandov in 1929.

Then at the famous 1935 Union of Soviet Writers' Congress, that same Babel courageously spoke up for the freedom of the writer and his right to be silent if he chooses. But, the Communist Party cannot let any of its artists even remain silent,[91] and if they did, usually they silenced the silent with imprisonment and execution, without trial, as with Isaac Babel.

It is this peculiar cruelty of the Party that is seen in the behavior of 99 per cent of Soviet artists and intelligentsia. They have to speak out in favor of the Party line, quite irrespective of truth or their own convictions or feelings.

In the case of Eisenstein, this is particularly brought out by what he was forced to do when the Hitler-Stalin Pact was announced. Zorkaya says:[92]

His [Sergei Mikhailovich Eisenstein's] diary at the time of the pact of non-aggression [Hitler–Stalin] is filled with horror and alarm at the rapprochement with fascist Germany.
Nevertheless, he produced *Die Walküre* in conditions utterly alien to his spirit.

His self-abasement also included performing for the Party a broadcast to Germany to celebrate the Hitler–Stalin pact! In his speech on the Comintern Radio, 18 February 1940, he said, 'The pact of August 1939 forms a solid base, for it increases cultural co-operation between the two Great Peoples.'[93]

During this period, anti-fascist works of art in the Soviet Union were at once banned, including plays, books, and films such as the anti-Nazi *Professor Mamlock* and Eisenstein's own *Alexander Nevsky*.

It must be remembered that Eisenstein's descent was Jewish, a fact which was brought out only when Hitler attacked Russia. For *then*, Eisenstein joined in with other Soviet Jews and broadcast now the opposite to the Jews of the world, thus declaring he was Jewish and asking for support of his Jewish brethren in the world anti-fascist struggle!

In his autobiographical notes, Eisenstein expresses vividly the 'implacable image of relentless fate' in his films which also followed him in real life:[94]

> How many times during my hours of wandering along the tracks, have night monsters of trains sneaked upon me so treacherously, alongside me, scarcely clanking, out of the darkness!
>
> I think that they, their implacable, blind, pitiless movement, have migrated into my films, now dressed as soldier's boots on the Odessa Steps, and now directing their blunt snouts into knight's helmets, sliding over the stone slabs of the Cathedral, in the wake of the candle shaking in the hands of the stumbling Vladimir Staritsky.
>
> This image of a night train has wandered from film to film, becoming a symbol of fate.
>
> In *An American Tragedy*, this image is first the inertia of the crime, then, the source of the soulless automation of justice and law. . . .
>
> *Later, I myself fell into the tenacious clutches of the Image, NOW COME ALIVE.* [My italics. HM.]
>
> My intention, formed in the Autumn of 1943, collapses. The beginning of 1946 reaps the fruit.[95] This is probably the most dreadful Autumn of my life. If one does not count two catastrophes: the ruin of *Mexico* and the tragedy of *Bezhin Meadow*.
>
> This implacable image of relentless fate . . . in the black forms of the 'oprichniki'[96] of Ivan the Terrible . . . come alive in the soulless automations of the 'apparatchiki' of Stalin the Terrible . . . and the victim in the film, Vladimir Staritsky, is an image of Sergei Eisenstein, the victim in real life.

Writing in the Penguin Film Review of September 1948, to commemorate Eisenstein's death, Ivor Montagu says:

> Back in USSR Sergei Mikhailovich Eisenstein was heartbroken and for long confined himself to lecturing in the film college. A Soviet Film Jubilee, with top honors for almost everyone else, and a reported dictum of Stalin ('I'm damned if the old rascal gets anything until he wakes up and does some creative work

again') shook him into activity. There followed the abortive *Bezhin Meadow*, twice started and twice stopped, *culminating in the grand assault of the Central Committee of the CPSU on Eisenstein as a formalist, egotist and what have you, and every word of it just*, as spoken of Sergei Mikhailovich Eisenstein in his mood of that time.

Let Eisenstein answer his 'comrade' Ivor himself:[97]

Formalist was another academic expression which has always met with approval, particularly during the years of persecution against formalism: it's a mistake to call a man interested in form, a formalist. There's as much justification for this as there is in calling a man studying syphilis, a syphilitic.

Ivor Montagu writes of Eisenstein's film treatment of *Ivan the Terrible*, saying, 'No one, seeing the film, could conceive of it as a white-washing operation.'[98]
Ehrenberg, in his final chapters of *Men, Years, and Life*, said:[99]

Sergei Eisenstein told me of his meetings with Stalin who spoke of the necessity to extol Ivan the Terrible and added that Peter the Great didn't cut off enough heads.

Here is what the Soviet film critic, Zorkaya, says of the general treatment of *Ivan the Terrible* during the Stalinist period:[100]

Gradually an historical analysis was substituted by idealization. The unbridled tyrant (on which earlier every single interpreter agreed, including even those who considered *Ivan the Terrible* objectively progressive) was transformed into a wise Tsar, a defender of the people. The wars of *Ivan the Terrible*, including the fratricidal Novgorod campaign and the ruinous, lost Livonsky War, were pronounced masterpieces of strategy, and acts of far-sight-state politics.

Ivor Montagu, echoing the Stalinist general line,[101] says, 'the oprichniks are clearly the men of the people!'
Zorkaya says:[102]

The body guards, 'oprichniki' – that extreme expression of barbarism and despotism, were considered to be a progressive power, and their lawless terror and debauchery, that left behind in Russian history, a bloody memory of horror, rape and evil, was treated as a necessary and just measure in the struggle with boyar and feudal dismemberment.

Eisenstein, from the beginning of his artistic biography, accepted the interrelationship of the society-client and the artist-master. However, in this case, the principal, natural social command bore the imprint of the individual taste of one man. [i.e., *Stalin*, HM.] Eisenstein either did not see that, or it didn't disturb him, for he gave birth to the concept that was prompted as if it were his own. . . .

The undoubted dualism [*double think*. HM.] inherent in the very art of Eisenstein, and in the author's observations about his themes, have called forth in our day contradictory and opposite points of view.

Sergei Mikhailovich Eisenstein's treatment of the political theme directly corresponded to the official version of Ivan IV's reign – it was a hymn to autocracy. Eisenstein it seems had a difficult task to convince himself, trained in the democratic slogans of October, to believe in the historic necessity and justice of absolute power and tyranny.

The script tries 'to motivate the irrefutable villainy and base-lessness by that same end, which, according to the classic formula of Machiavellism, justifies every means. Eisenstein preferred this motive.'[103]

The blinkers of the time, all kinds of hypnosis, which even the mighty mind of Eisenstein could not withstand with sufficient firmness, were revealed in the conviction that the victims and terror of the tsar were justified and necessary.

So, Eisenstein produced the *official version* of *Ivan* in Part I, *and the tragic truth of the epoch in Part II.*[104]
The Soviet critic continues:[105]

It is suffocation and painful to breathe in the film. Painful above all that incompatibility of the brilliantly restored material environment and the crude inventions in the sphere of ideas. Most painful, the spiritual poverty in the midst of lavish pictorial surroundings and painstaking and finished reproductions.
And so beginning with the glorification of autocracy, the film ends with judgment on tyrannical power, and exposure of despotism and curses on all despotic rule. [My italics. HM.]

But Ivor Montagu goes on:[106]

The explanation so often given, that Eisenstein introduced in 'Tale Two' topical allusions about ruthlessness that the authorities found too near the mark has no warrant in fact. This is a cock that will not fight. The theory is facile, but it just will not work.

What he says was absolutely contradicted by the widow of Eisenstein, Pera Attasheva, who stated to me:

We tried to persuade Eisenstein *not* to try and produce Part 2 as per the script he had prepared. He was firm, though he had a sick heart. He was told it would be the end of him. But he would not retreat. Later certain scenes were cut from the film.

Pera further told me:

Sergei Mikhailovich was so angry when she tried to get him to alter the Part II of *Ivan*. She said that now Stalin was victorious, he would not tolerate that treatment of *Ivan* in Part II, with degeneracy and murder and cutting off heads right and left. She said Eisenstein should jump over these terrible episodes and go straight to Ivan conquering and arriving as victor on the shores of the Baltic. But, Sergei Mikhailovich turned white with anger and clenched his lips tight and said: 'When you make a film about Ivan you can do what you like with Ivan, but I do what *I* do. And now no more car to Barvikha!'[107] [the Sanatorium of the Central Committee of the CPSU where Eisenstein received medical treatment. HM.] He was angry with me for a very long time. Even later when he had to come to see me he would not even take his overcoat off and stay as a guest. [And she was then his wife! HM.]
   He had received the approval of Stalin for Part I, because he was the only artist who had put into words what Stalin could not say to any man: 'Oh God, am I right in what I do?' And in Part I of *Ivan*, God seemed to answer that he *was* right![108]
   But in Part II with its parallels, Sergei Mikhailovich was sure to be arrested, maybe shot. He had to save his life and it wasn't worth the risk. Better to live and perhaps later things would change. But no, Sergei Mikhailovich didn't swerve an iota from the course he had deliberately chosen.

This was confirmed in the memoirs of Mikhail Romm, a witness to the first showing of Part II of *Ivan*:[109]

> When the film was completed, a group of directors was summoned to the Ministry [of Cinematography]. We were told: Just look at Eisenstein's film! There will be trouble. Help us decide what to do. . . .'
> We saw it and felt the same alarm and the same disturbed feelings as those in the Ministry. But Eisenstein conducted himself with daring gaiety. He asked us: 'What's the matter? What's wrong? What have you got in mind? Tell me straight.'
> But no one dared to tell him straight, that in Ivan the Terrible was sensed a pointed allusion to Stalin, in Malyut Skuratov an allusion to Beria, and in the *oprichniki* – an allusion to his myrmidons. And there was a lot more we sensed but dared not say.
> But in the boldness of Eisenstein, the flash of his eyes, in his challenging skeptical smile, we felt that he acted consciously, that he had decided to go the whole hog.
> It was terrifying.

So, this Soviet evidence refutes every word of Ivor Montagu's foreword to the scenario of *Ivan the Terrible*,[110] although, I, at the time, sent him a detailed refutation myself, as co-author of the translation. But Ivor Montagu basically never altered his Stalinist position, which, alas, he has only recently reaffirmed, in his book *With Eisenstein in Hollywood*. He says:[111]

> Others, guessing post facto, have supposed that in this film he had modern and contemporary parallels with the latter days of Stalin in mind. This is absolutely incorrect. . . . This is confirmed by those who were close to him when he conceived and was making the picture – *he intended no criticism* and was solely intent on fathoming and vividly representing the true essence of a past patriotic glory, spots and all.

But then Ivor adds a footnote, that a Soviet professor, Veselovsky, in a recent study quite disagrees with this interpretation of the historical *Ivan*. Then, finally:[112]

> To one intimate who then warned him that the final sections of the picture were liable to run into trouble, he replied inflexibly,

with the savage obstinacy of his integrity as an artist, . . . 'This will be the first time in history a man has committed suicide by cinema!' (In the event, the fate he foresaw did not befall him, it partly befell him, it partly befell the picture.)

Incidentally, Ivan the Terrible was a vicious anti-semite; of this Eisenstein could show nothing and Montagu, as a Jew who is free to, says nothing!

Ivan the Terrible's holy Russia forbade the Jews to live in its territory or even to enter it on pain of death. These are facts.

Ivor Montagu insists there is no parallel whatsoever with Stalin on page 116 of his book, and, on page 138, he says about *Ivan*, 'Part I was a success. Parts II and III – of which latter several reels were completed – *struck too near the knuckle for Stalin* and were stopped.'[113] And, 'Ivan . . . turned out to be topical to a perilous degree.'[114] Thus Montagu keeps contradicting himself throughout.

As Eisenstein was forced to attempt to whitewash Ivan, so Montagu is whitewashing both Ivan and Stalin, taking advantage of 'bourgeois' democracy without the terrible threat and danger that his Soviet comrade was working under.

A leading Soviet film critic, Freilich, wrote recently of the film:[115]

> The historical conception of *Ivan* is contradictory. It isn't accidental that to one person it seemed that *Ivan* was almost a justification of the cult of the personality. To others, that *Ivan* indirectly protested against the repressions of the period of the cult of the personality, for which reason the Second Part was not shown on the screen during the life of Stalin.

So here is confirmation from yet another modern Soviet critic as to the true intentions of Eisenstein.

However, the strange quirks of so-called 'Marxist thinking' are shown, when Freilich too tries not to label the one-time bitterly attacked formalistic poetic school of Eisenstein as socialist realism! He says, 'The method of Eisenstein helps one to perceive yet another unity – the unity of art and contemporary actuality, embodied in the principles of social realism.'[116]

So the trap the would-be Marxist in contemporary Russia falls into is to state that Eisenstein's protest against Stalin's terror is shown by his film *Ivan* being united with contemporary actuality, and becoming socialist realism!

History, of course, is always the final judge of all men and all
art. Eisenstein, on the one hand, is beginning to receive some of his
proper due in his own country, and yet, at the same time, is
subjected to criticism, from both orthodox and progressive Soviet
critics.

In Solzhenitsyn's latest work *Bodalsya Telenok S Dubom* (translated
into English as *The Oak and the Calf*), I came across a reference to
Eisenstein's classic film. It seems that the Chief Censor of the Soviet
journal *Novy Mir*, a certain Alexander G. Dementiev, wanted to
correct *One Day in the Life of Ivan Denisovich* before its publication in
that journal. Among other things Solzhenitsyn writes, and I quote,
'He accused me of disgracing the banner and symbol of Soviet art
– *Battleship Potemkin*, and the whole conversation about it must be
cut out.'[117]

And here is what Solzhenitsyn wrote – I have myself re-translated
from the original:

> Caesar is persuading the Captain: 'For example, those pince-nez
> dangling on the ship's rigging, remember?'
> 'Mm – yes'. . . . The captain went on smoking. 'Or the baby
> carriage down the steps . . . bumpiti-bump, bumpiti-bump. . . .'
> 'Yes. . . . But the life at sea there was somewhat puppet-like.'
> 'Well you see, we're spoiled by the modern technique of
> shooting films. . . .'
> 'And those maggots of the meat crawled as big as earthworms.
> Were they really like that?'
> 'But you can't show that sort of thing on the screen on a
> smaller scale!'
> 'I'm thinking, if they brought that meat to us in the camp
> now instead of our fish, even without washing it, or scraping,
> and plomped it in the cauldron, how we'd have. . . .'

Here is indeed supreme irony – that the rotten meat that was the
final spark that set off the mutiny on the battleship would have been
relished in the Communist prison camps of the Gulag Archipelago.

A further and even more stern criticism of Eisenstein is found
later in the same book; again I quote my own translation. The
prisoners are discussing *Ivan the Terrible*:[118]

> 'No little father,' says Caesar gently, 'objectivity compels us to
> recognize the genius of Eisenstein. Isn't *Ivan the Terrible* a work

of genius. That dance of Ivan's bodyguard and that Cathedral scene?'

'It's a farce,' No. H 123 grows angry, 'pepper and opium in the eyes and then this infamous ideal of justifying personal tyranny. It's an insult to three generations of Russian intellectuals.'

The old man eats his soup without even noting it. 'But what other interpretation could have been acceptable then?'

'There you are . . . "Acceptable" . . . exactly. So don't come running to me shouting that Eisenstein is a genius. What you should say is that he is a grovelling boot-licker . . . geniuses don't suit their work to the whims of a tyrant.'

Well, it is easy for those to criticize who *have not* lived under such a terror – but those who *have* lived and suffered under it do have the right.

The evidence is overwhelming that Eisenstein deliberately, consciously risked his life and freedom to show the degeneration of Stalin and his *apparatchiki*, in *Ivan*, and his *oprichniki*. The reaction of the authorities was not unexpected when they condemned and banned Part II of *Ivan*.

So in reply to the author of *One Day in the Life of Ivan Denisovich* and all others, one can say, 'Yes, Eisenstein did have his say about the tyrant in Part II.' No other Soviet film director got away with such a challenge. All other artists were reduced to impotence and silence.

Notes

Introduction

1 The *Listener*, 22 and 29 March, 5 April 1973.
2 Sergei Yutkevich, 'Great Expectations are being lost', *Literaturnaya Gazetta*, no. 135, 18 November 1972.
3 See S. M. Eisenstein, *Autobiography* (trans. Herbert Marshall), Boston, Houghton Mifflin, 1983.
4 See fuller translation in Bulletin no. 8 of the Center for Soviet and East European Studies, Southern Illinois University, Winter 1972.
5 H. Marshall (ed.), *Battleship Potemkin*, New York, Avon Books, 1978.

Vsevolod Pudovkin

1 The Russian initials *V*sesoyuzni *O*bshestvo *K*ulturni *S*vyaz SSSR Zagranitsei, stand for the All Union Society for Cultural Relations of the USSR with Foreign Countries.
2 The Russian acronym for *Gosudarstvennyi Institute Kinematografii*, The State Institute of Cinematography, Moscow, USSR, subsequently referred to as the GIK.
3 This paradox Bertolt Brecht eventually put into a poem which I translated for my anthology *Battleship Potemkin*, New York, Avon Books, 1978, pp. 361–2.
4 Quote from the speech to the Film Society, London, 1929. Translated by Herbert Marshall from *Naturschik vmesto aktera* (A type instead of an actor) from *Vsevolod Pudovkin, 'Sobranniye Sochinenii.'* vol. I, Moscow, Izd. Isk., 1974, p. 1982.
5 The secret police has been known by various names since 1917: CHEKA (*Chrezvychainaya Kommissia*, All Russian Extraordinary Commission for Fighting Counter-Revolution and Sabotage); GPU (*Gosudarstvennoye Politicheske Upravleniye*, State Political Administration); OGPU (*Obedinennoye Gosudarstvennoye Politicheskoe Upravleniye*, United State Political Administration); MVD (*Ministersvo Vnutrennykh Del*, Ministry of Internal Affairs); NKVD (*Narodny Komitet Vnutrennikh Del*, People's Commissariat of Internal Affairs); KGB (*Komitet Gosudarstvdnnoi Bezopasnosti*, Committee of State Security).

6 See V. Pudovkin, *Film Technique and Film Acting*, trans. I. Montagu, London, Newnes, 1935, p. 14.

7 A. V. Karaganov, *V. Pudovkin*, Moscow, Izd. Isk., 1973, p. 232.

8 See V. Pudovkin, *Film Technique and Film Acting*, trans. I. Montagu, New York, Grove Press, 1970, p. 18.

9 Montagu, op. cit., p. 18.

10 A. Groshev, in *Kino Segodnya* (Cinema Today), ed. V. N. Zhdan, Moscow, Izd. Isk., 1971, p. 150.

11 L. Kuleshov, 'The First Film School through the Eyes of a Pedagogue', in *Kuleshov on Film*, trans. R. Levaco, Berkeley, University of California Press, 1975, pp. 203–4.

12 L. Kuleshov, 'Our First Experiences' (1934), in Levaco, op. cit., p. 173.

13 Former film producers in the Tsarist period.

14 L. Kuleshov, 'Our First Experiences' (1934), in Levaco, op. cit., p. 174.

15 ibid., p. 174.

16 Herbert Marshall (ed.), *Battleship Potemkin*, op. cit., p. 15 *et al.*

17 The French term *mise-en-scène* is now used in most European languages including Russian. The term in the American theater is 'blocking'. But I retain the European usage as more suitable, particularly as Eisenstein coined a neologism from this, which has no equivalent. That is '*mise-en-cadre.*' *Mise-en-scène* means, literally, the placing on the stage, i.e., the composition of the actors in the set. *Mise-en-cadre* means the composition of the actors and objects in the shot.

18 A. V. Karaganov, *V. Pudovkin*, Moscow, Izd. Isk., 1973. Translated here by Herbert Marshall.

19 Russian acronym for the Revolutionary Association of Proletarian Writers.

20 Karaganov, op. cit., p. 101.

21 ibid., p. 102, from *Preussische Zeitung.*

22 *Kino* Moscow newspaper, 5 March 1929.

23 Karaganov, op. cit., p. 103 (trans. HM).

24 Montagu, op. cit., p. 318.

25 H. Marshall, *Mayakovsky*, London, Dobson, 1965, p. 364.

26 Alexander G. Rzheshevsky (1903–67), Soviet film-writer.

27 *Istoriya Sovietskovo Kino*, vol. I, Moscow, Izd. Isk., p. 308.

28 J. Leyda, *Kino*, London, Allen & Unwin, 1960, p. 294.

29 V. Pudovkin, *Izbrannye Stat'i* (Selected Essays) ed. A. Groshev, Moscow, Izd. Isk., 1955, p. 24. Translated here by HM.

30 *Istoriya Sovietskovo Kino*, vol. 1, Moscow, Izd. Isk., 1969, p. 308.

31 *Iskusstvo Kino*, 1970, p. 26.

32 *Experimental Cinema*, journal, ed. Seymour Stern, 1930, USA, p. 17.

33 *Experimental Film*, no. 19, in French (trans. H. J. Salemson), 1931.

34 ibid., no. 20.

35 Livanov later became the artistic director of the Moscow Art Theater. His story will appear in the projected second volume of 'Crippled Biographies'. *Masters of Soviet Theatre.*

36 V. Pudovkin, *Film Technique and Film Acting*, New York, Grove Press, 1970, p. 194.
37 E. W. and M. M. Robson, *The Film Answers Back*, London, Bodley Head, 1947.
38 From V. Pudovkin, *Izbrannye Stat'i*, op. cit., p. 316.
39 Karaganov, op. cit., p. 19.
40 *Sovietskoye Kino*, Moscow, 1927, nos. 8 and 9.
41 See Karaganov, op. cit., p. 30.
42 An Old Bolshevik leader who was also tried in the fake trails, accused of being an enemy of the people and executed. After Stalin's death he was rehabilitated.
43 Karaganov, op. cit., p. 18.
44 ibid.
45 M. Bleiman, *O Kino* (About Kino – A Witness), Moscow, 1973.
46 Karaganov, op. cit., p. 114.
47 ibid. (HM's italics).
48 ibid., p. 114.
49 ibid., p. 115.
50 See *Sight and Sound*, film journal, London, Winter 1975.
51 Y. Annenkov *People and Portraits*, vol. II, New York, Inter-Language Literary Association, 1966, p. 107.
52 S. M. Eisenstein, *Ivan the Terrible* (trans. I. Montagu and Herbert Marshall), New York, Simon & Schuster, 1963, p. 201.
53 V. Pudovkin, 'How I Became a Film Director', in *Izbrannye Stat'i*, op. cit., p. 47.
54 ibid.
55 Karaganov, op. cit., p. 182.
56 ibid.
57 ibid., p. 183.
58 Hertzen's publication from exile.
59 Karaganov, op. cit., p. 189.
60 V. I. Lenin, Collected Works (in Russian), vol. XXI, p. 216 (trans. HM).
61 Karaganov, op. cit., p. 189.
62 Original title *Fürcht und Elend des Dritten Reich*.
63 Karaganov, op. cit., p. 193.
64 English translations of these two poems (by Herbert Marshall) are published in his Bulletin of the Center for Soviet and East European Studies, Southern Illinois University, Winter 1972, no. 8.
65 K. Simonov, *Razgovor s tovarishchami*, p. 34.
66 Pudovkin, *Izbrannye Stat'i*, op. cit., vol. I, p. 434.
67 Karaganov, op. cit., p. 202.
68 ibid.
69 Pudovkin, *Izbrannye Stat'i*, op. cit., pp. 349–50.
70 ibid.
71 Pudovkin, *Izbrannye Stat'i*, op. cit., p. 322.
72 Karaganov, op. cit., p. 207.
73 *Iskusstvo Kino*, 1955.

74 See essay on Dovzhenko, pp. 163–4.
75 Karaganov op. cit., p. 210 (trans. HM).
76 ibid., p. 210.
77 ibid., p. 211.
78 ibid., p. 217.
79 ibid., p. 221.
80 ibid., p. 222.
81 See essay on Eisenstein, p. 199.
82 Alexander Werth, *Russia – The Postwar Years*, New York, Taflinger Publications, 1971, p. 99.
83 Freilich, *Filmy i Godi*, Moscow, Izd. Isk., 1964, p. 0.
84 *Voprosy Kino Iskusstva* (Questions of Cinema Art), cinema journal, no. 2, 1968, p. 131.
85 Extra money is only earned when they are in actual production of a feature film; if no film, they are reduced to a low minimum salary.
86 Montagu, op. cit., p. 17.

Dziga Vertov

1 Seth R. Feldman, in his otherwise very thorough work *Dziga Vertov: A Guide to References and Resources*, Boston, G. K. Hall, 1979, says however that Samuel 'Brody also translated the Paris lecture into the first English language presentation of Vertov's ideas.' However this was in 1935; Britton's article and translation was published in 1930.
2 A neologism Vertov invented for his Men with a Movie Camera, from the Old Slavonic and Ukrainian 'oko' which means 'eye,' i.e. Kino-Eyemen, film director-cameramen trained in his method.
3 See *Shedevry Sovietskovo Kino* (Masterpieces of Soviet Cinema), *The Three Songs of Lenin*, Dziga Vertov, compiled by E. I. Vertova-Svilova, Moscow, Izd. Isk., 1971.
4 I notice that, like the Soviet editors, Feldman (op. cit.) also doesn't state that he is Jewish, or the real reason he went to the Psychoneurological Institute or what lay behind his changing his name, just as Koltsov did. People only changed their names in Russia because they were Jewish or as revolutionaries adopting pseudonyms. Feldman writes (p. 19): 'Also of interest is the discrepancy between Vertov's patronymic ("Arkadevich") and that of his brother ("Abramovich"). Maria Enzensburger has suggested in conversation that Vertov may have Russified his patronymic early in life, a common practice of non-Russian people working in Tsarist Russia.' I am surprised that the author (who I conjecture from her name is herself Jewish) doesn't realize that Vertov is avoiding giving away that his father is Jewish (Abram), and takes on a Russian name as his surname. For Kaufman is a Jewish name and Bialystok was of course a Jewish cultural center like Vilna and famous for its pogroms.
5 V. Shklovsky, *Abram M. Room, Life and Work*, Moscow, Teakinopechat, 1929, p. 6.
6 Mikhail Koltsov, *Ispanskii Dnevnik*, Moscow, 1957.

7 *Istoriya Kino, Materialy Dokumenty*, Moscow, 1959, p. 59.
8 From *LEF* magazine no. 4, 1924. LEF (the Russian acronym stands for 'The Left Front of Art') was the organ of the Futurists, headed by the Russian poet Vladimir Mayakovsky. See *Mayakovsky*, trans. H. Marshall, London, Dennis Dobson, 1965.
9 V. I. Lenin, *The Party and Cinema*, Moscow, 1939. pp. 31–2.
10 S. M. Eisenstein, *Izbrannye Stat'i* (Selected Works), Izd. Isk., Moscow, 1956, p. 116–17 (trans. HM).
11 N. P. Abramov, *Dziga Vertov*, Moscow, Izd. Akademii Nauk., 1962, p. 55 (trans. HM).
12 As I write the wheel has turned full circle. Now the Soviet cinema produces its own soap operas, detective, psychological and theatrical films, and shows many foreign films, still carefully censored of course.
13 Abramov, op. cit., p. 17.
14 Drobashenko (ed.), *Dziga Vertov: Articles, Diaries, Notes*, Moscow, Izd. Isk., 1966, p. 97.
15 ibid., p. 87.
16 Eisenstein's first two films, clearly influenced by Vertov.
17 Drobashenko, op. cit., pp. 87–9.
18 The Leningrad Cinema Studio of the Eccentric Actor, headed by Yutkevich.
19 Alluding to Eisenstein's first formulation of his theory of The Montage of Attractions, while he was still working in the Prolet-Cult Theatre (*LEF*, no. 3, Moscow, 1923).
20 Alluding to the then popular box-office films, mainly imported. One called *The Minaret of Death*, another Soviet film called *The Bay of Death* directed by A. Room.
21 Eisenstein later adopted this slogan.
22 A neologism made up by Vertov.
23 Herbert Marshall (ed.), *Battleship Potemkin*, Avon Books, New York, 1978.
24 *Istoriya Sovietskovo Kino*, vol. 1, Moscow, Izd. Isk., 1969, p. 318.
25 V. Shklovsky, *From the Current*, Moscow-Leningrad, 1927, pp. 64–5. Symbolism was the stylistic trend attacked by the Communist Party as a 'bourgeois hangover'.
26 Abramov, op. cit., pp. 107–9.
27 Abramov, op. cit., p. 112, quoting Affedorov Davydov, 'Towards a Realistic Art', *Kino Gazeta*, 30 March 1936.
28 Vertov, 'About Life for the Living Man,' *Iskusstvo Kino*, no. 6, 1958, pp. 98–9. 'Michurin garden' is a reference to the Soviet Luther Burbank who pioneered developing new hybrids in plants and fruits, about which Dovzhenko made a film; see p. 159.
29 Abramov, op. cit., p. 98.
30 Ippolit Sokolov, 'On the Possibilities of Sound Cinema', *Kino*, no. 45, Moscow, 1929.
31 D. Vertov, 'The First Steps,' *Kino*, no. 21, Moscow, 1930.
32 Abramov, op. cit., p. 123.
33 ibid., p. 124.

34 Abramov, op. cit., p. 124.
35 ibid.
36 See my article 'Sergo Paradjanov' in *Sight and Sound*, journal of the British Film Institute, London, Winter 1975.
37 Compare with the finale of Mayakovsky's epic poem 'Lenin', Mayakovsky, op. cit., pp. 325–30.
38 From *Shedevry Sovietskovo Kino* (Masterpieces of Soviet Cinema), op. cit.
39 Compare titles in *Lenin Kino Pravda*, no. 13 and Tretyakov's titles in *Potemkin*.
40 We must be grateful to Vertov's faithful assistant, disciple and wife, Elizabeth Svilova (a wonderful parallel to Eisenstein's widow, Pera Attasheva, and Dovzhenko's widow, Yulia Solntseva), for preserving and getting published some of his diaries. HM.
41 Abramov, op. cit., p. 165.
42 Drobashenko, op. cit., p. 168.
43 Drobashenko, op. cit., p. 175.
44 ibid., p. 177.
45 *Mayakovsky*, op. cit., p. 404.
46 Mezhrabpom Film Studios produced *The Three Songs of Lenin*.
47 See *Sight and Sound*, London, December 1975.
48 ibid., April 1976.
49 Russian acronym for the Revolutionary Association of Proletarian Writers.
50 Drobashenko, op. cit., p. 37.
51 As for instance with the great Soviet actor-director Solomon Mikhoels. While Stalin gave his prize to Mikhoels and his Moscow State Yiddish Theater he was planning the assassination of Mikhoels and the liquidation not only of this world famous theater but the bulk of the Soviet Jewish intelligentsia. My next book is about Mikhoels.
52 Drobashenko, op. cit., p. 38.
53 See E. Yevtushenko, *Poems* (trans. Herbert Marshall), New York, Dutton, 1966. Introduction to 'Bratski Ges', p. 143.
54 Drobashenko, op. cit., p. 40.
55 Yevtushenko, op. cit.
56 Drobashenko, op. cit., p. 41.
57 ibid.

Alexander Dovzhenko

1 R. Yurenev in *Soviet Film*, Moscow, no. 9, 1974.
2 Alexander Dovzhenko, *The Poet as Film-maker*, Selected Writings, edited and translated by Marco Carynnyk, Cambridge, Mass., MIT Press, p. 127 (afterwards referred to as Carynnyk, op. cit.).
3 A. Maryamov, *Iskusstvo Kino*, 'Dovzhenko', 'Art of the Cinema', 9, 1964, p. 9.
4 Carynnyk, op. cit., p. 12.
5 Maryamov, op. cit., p. 23.

6 A. Dovzhenko, *Sobrannye Sochinenii*, vol. 4. Moscow, Izd. Isk., 1969, p. 81.
7 V. Shklovsky, 'Happiness' in *Lenin Prize Winners*, Moscow, Progress Publishing House, 1969, p. 87.
8 *Za Bolshoye Kino Iskusstvo*, Kinofotoizdat, Moscow, 1935, p. 68.
9 ibid., p. 65.
10 i.e. Stalin.
11 Carynnyk, op. cit., pp. 251–2.
12 *Za Bolshoye Kino Iskusstvo*, op. cit., p. 59.
13 See essay on Pudovkin, p. 9.
14 *Za Bolshoye Kino Iskusstvo*, op. cit., p. 59.
15 ibid., p. 60.
16 ibid., p. 61.
17 Directed by Kozintsev and Trauberg, Lenfilm, 1935.
18 I. Metter, *Vashe Slovo T.A.*, Moscow, 1967, p. 98.
19 *Za Bolshoye Kino Iskusstvo*, op. cit., p. 72.
20 Carynnyk, op. cit., p. 64.
21 Carynnyk, op. cit., p. 251.
22 See my essay on Okhlopkov in the projected second volume of 'Crippled Biographies'.
23 *Za Bolshoye Kino Iskusstvo*, op. cit., p. 63.
24 Carynnyk, op. cit., p. 14.
25 I. Andronnikov, *Poeziya Dovzhenko*, Moscow, Izd. Sov. Pisatel, 1965, p. 386.
26 ibid.
27 ibid.
28 Andronnikov, op. cit., p. 381.
29 I. Montagu, 'Dovzhenko – Poet of Life Eternal', *Sight and Sound*, Summer 1957, p. 47.
30 ibid.
31 ibid.
32 Montagu, in *Sight and Sound*, op. cit., p. 46.
33 S. M. Eisenstein, *Izbrannye Sochineniya* (Collected Works), vol. V, Moscow, Izd. Isk., 1964, p. 438, 'The Birth of a Master'.
34 See ibid., 441.
35 A. Piotrovsky, *Zhizn Iskusstvo*, no. 16, 14 April 1929, p. 7.
36 *Kino-Gazetta*, no. 19, 23 April 1934.
37 Often the Party attacks anonymously, which gives it a more terrifying impact – who knows who prompted it, maybe the Central Committee or Stalin himself?
38 See the book by A. Piotrovsky, *Artistic Trends in Soviet Cinema*, Moscow, Izd. Teakinopechat, 1929.
39 *Kino-Gazetta*, op. cit.
40 The term biologism is used to indicate a certain tarnishing of mysticism and pantheism.
41 *Zhizn Iskusstvo*, no. 15, 2 April 1929.
42 *Kino-Gazetta*, no. 19, 22 April 1934.
43 Carynnyk, op. cit., p. 15.

44 ibid.
45 Herbert Marshall, *Close-Up*, September 1930.
46 From *Izvestia*, Moscow, 4 April 1930. I have made a complete translation, the first ever made in English. It is now of course 'forgotten' in the Soviet Union! A copy is in my archives. HM.
47 By Alexander Pushkin, Russia's classic poet. (My translation, HM.)
48 *Diary of Dovzhenko: Literaturnaya Gazetta*, 10 November 1962.
49 N. Khrushchev, *Khrushchev Remembers*, ed. Strobe Talbott, London, Andre Deutsch, 1971.
50 ibid., pp. 79–80.
51 I. Andronnikov, in *Lenin Prize Winners, Soviet Stars, Masters of Stage and Screen*, Moscow, Progress Publishing House, 1969, p. 71.
52 Andronnikov, *Poeziya Dovzhenko*, op. cit., p. 382.
53 ibid.
54 ibid.
55 ibid.
56 ibid.
57 Montagu, in *Sight and Sound*, op. cit., p. 48.
58 George Bernard Shaw, *Man and Superman*, Epistle Dedicatory: p. xxxvii, London, Penguin Books, 1946.
59 S. Tsimbal, *Rabochi i Teatr.*, 19, 6 April 1930, p. 10.
60 *Kino-Gazetta*, 19, 22 April 1934.
61 Carynnyk, op. cit., p. 157.
62 *Istoriya Sovietskovo Kino Iskusstvo*, Moscow, 1973, vol. 2, p. 368.
63 Carynnyk, op. cit., p. 16.
64 Carynnyk, op. cit., pp. 17–18.
65 The chief Bolshevik theoretical organ.
66 Fedir Taran, the official Party critic, sharply attacked *Ivan* for 'distorting Ukrainian reality' (*Kino*, 19–20, 1932, in Ukrainian; *Kommunist*, September 1932, in Russian).
67 Mykola Skrypnyk (1872–1933): prominent Ukrainian old Bolshevik and associate of Lenin; charged with 'national deviations', he committed suicide in 1933.
68 Carynnyk, op. cit., p. 64.
69 Carynnyk, op. cit.
70 Carynnyk, op. cit., p. 170.
71 ibid., p. 178. Diary of 13 July 1952.
72 ibid., p. 105.
73 *N. Gogol*, Collected Works (Russian edition in 6 volumes), vol. VI, Moscow 1953, p. 34.
74 See ibid., pp. 103–4.
75 Carynnyk, op. cit., p. 20.
76 A sect of the Russian Orthodox Church which is very conservative and anti-Western.
77 *Istoriya Sovietskovo Kino*, op. cit., p. 371.
78 Ilya Ehrenburg, *Men, Years, Life*, vol. IV, 1933–41, London, 1963, p. 53.
79 L. Idenbom, *Kino-Gazetta*, 22 April 1934.

80 J. Leyda, *Kino*, London, Allen & Unwin, 1960, p. 353.
81 ibid., p. 354.
82 Khrushchev, op. cit., pp. 340–1.
83 I. N. Dubovoy, another army commander, was shot in July 1938.
84 *Istoriya Sovietskovo Kino*, op. cit., vol. II, p. 361.
85 Leyda, op. cit., p. 354.
86 ibid.
87 A. Dovzhenko, *Shchors*, Gosizdat Iskusstvo, Moscow 1957, p. 94.
88 Sbornik, *Voprosy Kinodramaturgii*, vol. I, Moscow 1954, p. 18.
89 Leyda, op. cit., p. 355.
90 Carynnyk, op. cit., pp. 112–13.
91 Paul Rotha, *The Film Till Now*, Feltham, Middx, Spring Books, 1957, p. 575.
92 Otherwise known as *Aerograd*; see p. 142.
93 Dovzhenko; *Izbranniye Sochineniye* (Selected Works), ed. M. Vlasov, vol. II, Moscow, Iskusstvo, 1966, p. 509.
94 ibid., Introduction, p. xxviii.
95 Ivan Bolshakov (b. 1902): Chairman of the All-Union Cinema Committee, 1939–946, then Minister of Cinema.
96 Dovzhenko, Selected Works, op. cit., vol. II, pp. 93–4.
97 Dovzhenko, Selected Works, op. cit., vol. II, p. 544.
98 ibid., vol. II, pp. 98–9.
99 ibid., p. 544.
100 Khrushchev, op. cit., pp. 172–3.
101 Carynnyk, op. cit., p. 107.
102 *Literaturnaya Gazetta*, no. 134, 10 November 1962.
103 Leyda, op. cit., p. 377.
104 ibid., p. 375–6.
105 Carynnyk, op. cit., p. 104.
106 ibid., p. 79.
107 ibid., p. 155.
108 This is the date of the attack by Stalin and Beria.
109 Carynnyk, op. cit., p. 155.
110 *Encyclopedicheskii Slovar*, in two volumes, Moscow 1964, p. 38.
111 V. Shklovsky, 'Happiness', in *Lenin Prize Winners*, op. cit., pp. 83–4.
112 Dovzhenko, Selected Works, op. cit., vol. III, p. 741.
113 ibid.
114 *Za Bolshoye Kino Iskusstvo*, Isk., op. cit., p. 78.
115 Carynnyk, op. cit., p. 139.
116 Montagu, in *Sight and Sound*, op. cit., p. 47.
117 Carynnyk, op. cit., p. 158.
118 Montagu, in *Sight and Sound*, op. cit., p. 48.
119 Carynnyk, op. cit., p. 136.
120 Carynnyk, op. cit., p. 141.
121 Carynnyk, op. cit., p. 253.
122 Ivanova, op. cit., p. 67.
123 *Literaturnaya Gazetta*, Moscow, 1949.
124 Dovzhenko, Selected Works, op. cit., vol. III, Introduction.

125 Dovzhenko, Selected Works, op. cit., vol. III, Introduction.
126 *Soviet Short Stories*, Pilot Press, London, 1944, p. 101.
127 *Literatura i Iskusstvo*, no. 32, Moscow, 1943, pp. 66–8.
128 It's the same today – they 'try to fit in' everything in the Moscow *Literaturnaya Gazetta*.
129 *Literatura i Iskusstvo*, no. 32, Moscow, 1943, pp. 66–8.
130 Carynnyk, op. cit., p. 134.
131 Nikolai Rozhkov, Reminiscences, recorded by HM, Moscow, August 1973.
132 Probably a play on 'Blue Blouses,' the original agit-prop theater groups.
133 Dovzhenko, *Selected Works*, op. cit., vol. II, p. 508.
134 Carynnyk, op. cit., p. 54.
135 Author of the play and film, *The Deputy of the Baltic*, based on the life of Professor Timaryazev. The book was *Wonder Hero* by J. B. Priestley.
136 It was not until 1964 that I translated three-quarters of *Kobzar*, which was published in Moscow by the Shevchenko Centenary Committee in *Taras Shevchenko*, Selected Works, Progress Publishing House, Moscow, 1964.
137 *Za Bolshoye Kino Iskusstvo*, op. cit., p. 80.
138 Montagu, in *Sight and Sound*, op. cit., pp. 46–7.
139 ibid.
140 Carynnyk, op. cit., pp. 160–1.
141 *Sobrannye Sochineniye*, Moscow, Izd. Isk., 1966–9.
142 W. and A. Durant, *Life of Greece* (Story of Civilization), London, Angus & Robertson, 1939.

Sergei Eisenstein

1 Sergei Eisenstein, Autobiography (trans. Herbert Marshall), Boston, Houghton Mifflin, 1983.
2 ibid.
3 Guido Aristarko, *Iskusstvo Kino*, 1956, no. 12 in *Istoriya Teorii Kino*, (trans. from the Italian by G. Bogemsky), Moscow, Iz. Isk., 1966, p. 125.
4 New York, Avon Books, 1978.
5 N. Zorkaya, 'Portraits', for *Iskusstvo*, Moscow, 1965, pp. 70–1.
6 Acronym for The Left Front of Art, Mayakovsky's society of futurists.
7 See essay on Dovzhenko, pp. 130–1.
8 *Battleship Potemkin*, op. cit., p. 4.
9 Eisenstein, Autobiography, op. cit.
10 ibid.
11 Eisenstein, Autobiography, op. cit.
12 ibid.
13 Y. Yevtushenko, *Poems* (trans. Herbert Marshall), New York, Dutton, 1966.
14 See essay on Pudovkin, pp. 11–14.

15 Ivor Montagu, *With Eisenstein in Hollywood*, East Berlin, Seven Seas Books, 1968, p. 31.
16 An acronym from the Russian title of the Higher State Institute of Cinematography, *Gosurdarstvennyi Institute Kinomatografii*.
17 A Soviet anti-semitic euphemism. Eisenstein, being of Jewish origin, could be accused of being subject to 'Zionist' influences.
18 S. M. Eisenstein, *Izbrannye Sochineniya* (Collected Works), vol. I, Moscow, Izd. Isk., 1964, p. 474.
19 A national revolutionary in Turkestan and Bukhara who fought against the Soviets.
20 Famous Soviet actor and actress, man and wife, and People's Artists of the USSR at the Mayakovsky Theater. Maxim was a boyhood friend of Eisenstein. See his *Memoirs*.
21 The People's Commissariat of Internal Affairs, i.e. the Secret Police.
22 The famous Chinese actor of female roles in visiting Peking opera.
23 Eisenstein, Autobiography, op. cit.
24 A film essay, to be found in S. M. Eisenstein, *Film Essays* (trans. Jay Leyda), New York, Praeger, 1970.
25 The Revolutionary Association of Proletarian Writers.
26 *Iskusstvo Kino*, no. 7, Moscow, Iz. Isk., 1937.
27 The Austrian psychologist and philosopher, attacked by Lenin and by other Marxists for his idealistic and solipsistic conceptions.
28 A witch in Russian folk tales.
29 N. A. Lebedev, *Essay on the History of Cinema in USSR*, Moscow, Gozkinoizdat, 1947, pp. 161, 163.
30 Eisenstein, Collected Works, op. cit., vol. I, p. 474.
31 *Glav Repertkom*: The chief censoring organ over all the performing arts.
32 I. Montagu, op. cit., p. 143.
33 New York Times, 10 October 1963.
34 Mikhail Romm, *A Film Director Speaks Out*, Moscow, Gos. Izdat, 1964, p. 97.
35 Which I translated and published in *Sight and Sound*, Spring 1946.
36 Romm, op. cit., p. 97.
37 Eisenstein, Autobiography, op. cit.
38 Montagu, op. cit., pp. 144–5.
39 From the *Literaturnaya Gazetta*.
40 Ivor Montagu, 'Sergei Eisenstein' (1891–1948), *Sight and Sound*, London, no. 7, September 1947.
41 The Stalin-appointed chief of the Soviet film industry.
42 Jay Leyda, *Kino*, London, Allen & Unwin, 1960, p. 360.
43 *Besyedy o Kino*, Moscow, Issk., 1964, p. 87.
44 M. Geduld and R. Gottesman, *The Making and Unmaking of Que Viva Mexico*, Bloomington, Indiana University Press, 1970.
45 *Eisenstein*, on 'Omnibus', BBC 1, made in conjunction with the Novosti Press Agency by Norman Swallow and Grisha Alexandrov. First broadcast by the BBC, London, 6 December 1970. I also contributed as a consultant and in a filmed interview included in the full feature.

46 S. M. Eisenstein, *The Mexican Drawings*, Moscow, Sovietsky Khudozhnik, 1969.
47 Alexei V. Romanov, *Nemerknuschii Ekran (The Unfading Screen)*, Moscow, Iskusstvo, 1973, pp. 151–2.
48 ibid., p. 152.
49 R. Yurenev, *Prometheus. An Historical Biographical Almanac*, Molodaya Gvardiya, 1972, pp. 185–99.
50 Published by Grove Press, New York, 1960.
51 Eisenstein, Autobiography, op. cit.
52 Eisenstein, Autobiography, op. cit.
53 Zorkaya, op. cit., p. 73.
54 Zorkaya, op. cit., pp. 46, 47 and 50.
55 *Battleship Potemkin – Best Film of All Time*, op. cit.
56 Translated by Herbert Marshall and R. Reader.
57 Eisenstein, *Selected Essays*, ed. R. N. Yurenev, Moscow, Izd. Isk., 1956, p. 193.
58 Published by Dobson, London, 1958.
59 Eisenstein, Autobiography, op. cit.
60 'Pots' means 'prick'.
61 See page 210.
62 *Znamya*, 12, 1962, p. 180.
63 See *Close-up*, November 1930.
64 Zorkaya, op. cit., p. 98.
65 ibid.
66 ibid., p. 99.
67 ibid., p. 102.
68 ibid., p. 107.
69 ibid., p. 107.
70 See H. Marshall, *Mayakovsky*, London, Dobson, 1965, p. 138.
71 The official Soviet tourist organization.
72 Y. Barna, *Eisenstein*, Bloomington, Indiana University Press, 1973, p. 188.
73 S. M. Eisenstein, *Film Essays* (trans. J. Leyda), op. cit., p. 124.
74 V. Nizhny, *Lessons with Eisenstein* (trans. Ivor Montagu and Jay Leyda), New York, Hill & Wang, 1975.
75 Marie Seton, *Sergei M. Eisenstein*, New York, Grove Press, 1960, p. 379.
76 Barna, op. cit., p. 206.
77 ibid., p. 199.
78 ibid., p. 190.
79 Barna, op. cit., p. 199.
80 ibid., p. 199.
81 op. cit.
82 Translation HM; see also Yevtushenko, *Poems* (trans. Herbert Marshall), New York, Dutton, 1965.
83 Zorkaya, op. cit., p. 118.
84 Eisenstein, Autobiography, op. cit.
85 Zorkaya, op. cit., p. 66.
86 Eisenstein, Collected Works, op. cit., vol. I, pp. 305–6.

87 An almost exact quotation of the famous words of St John the Baptist heralding the Messiah: St John, 1:27.
88 See pp. 61–97.
89 See *Battleship Potemkin*, op. cit., pp. 55–9.
90 Eisenstein, Collected Works, op. cit., p. 420.
91 Stalin stated clearly he regarded silence as protest.
92 Zorkaya, op. cit., p. 111.
93 Seton, op. cit., p. 398.
94 Seton, op. cit., pp. 436–7.
95 When he was attacked by Stalin and Zhdanov over Part II of *Ivan the Terrible*. (See page 220.)
96 The bodyguard of Ivan, his KGB. Eisenstein liked puns and he equates
the *opprichniki* of Ivan with the *apparatchiki* of Stalin, members of the Party apparatus, *his* KGB. [HM]
97 Eisenstein, Autobiography, op. cit.
98 Ivor Montagu, Preface to *Ivan the Terrible* (trans. Ivor Montagu and Herbert Marshall), New York, Simon & Schuster, 1963, p. 12.
99 Ilya Ehrenburg, *Men, Years, and Life*, vol. III, Macgibbon & Kee, 1963.
100 Zorkaya, op. cit., p. 121.
101 Montagu, Preface to *Ivan the Terrible*, op. cit., p. 16.
102 Zorkaya, op. cit., pp. 116–17.
103 ibid., p. 128.
104 ibid., p. 131.
105 Zorkaya, op. cit., p. 138.
106 Montagu, Preface to *Ivan the Terrible*, op. cit., p. 15.
107 He would not send her his car to visit him in the Soviet elite hospital where he was getting treatment.
108 See Solzhenitsyn's treatment of Stalin in *The First Circle*, New York, Harper & Row, 1968, pp. 112–16.
109 M. Romm, *Besyedi O Kino*, Izd. Isk., 1964, p. 91, translated here by HM.
110 Montagu, Preface to *Ivan the Terrible*, pp. 7–17.
111 Montagu, *With Eisenstein in Hollywood*, op. cit., p. 116.
112 ibid.
113 ibid.
114 Montagu, *With Eisenstein in Hollywood*, op. cit., p. 143.
115 Freilich, *Filmy i Godi*, Moscow, Izd. Isk., 1964, p. 343.
116 ibid., p. 342.
117 See A. Solzhenitsyn, *One Day in the Life of Ivan Denisovich*, New York, Bantam Books, p. 89.
118 A. Solzhenitsyn, *One Day in the Life of Ivan Denisovich*, Moscow, Posev, 1966, p. 89. Translated by Herbert Marshall from the original.

Index